LAW AND STRUCTURES OF SOCIAL ACTION

LAW AND STRUCTURES OF SOCIAL ACTION

By KENNETH S. CARLSTON

LONDON: STEVENS AND SONS LIMITED
NEW YORK: COLUMBIA UNIVERSITY PRESS
1956

'The combination of causes is beyond the grasp of the human intellect. But the impulse to seek causes is innate in the soul of man. And the human intellect, with no inkling of the immense variety and complexity of circumstances conditioning a phenomenon, any one of which may be separately conceived as the cause of it, snatches at the first and most easily understood approximation, and says here is the cause.' Tolstoy, *War and Peace* (Garnett Translation, London, 1904), Vol. 3, Pt. XIII, Chap. 1, p. 208.

'To be master of any branch of knowledge you must master those which lie next to it. And thus to know anything you must know all.' O. W. Holmes, Jr., 'The Law as a Profession,' *American Law Review,* 1886, Vol. 20, p. 742.

ACKNOWLEDGMENTS

Some of the material included in this volume has previously appeared in the pages of the *Journal of Public Law, Law and Contemporary Problems, Northwestern University Law Review* and the *Yale Law Journal,* as well as *Lectures on Federal Antitrust Laws* (Ann Arbor, 1953). Permission to print the same is gratefully acknowledged.

CONTENTS

CASES

TREATY REFERENCES

Chapter I

THE BASES OF LAW

Law as Social Behaviour

The scene is the Trobriand Archipelago, a group of coral islands surrounding a wide lagoon. A formless pattern of canoes moving across the face of the lagoon, of groups of individuals upon the land, is seen. To the tourist or casual observer the pattern of activity is disordered or even anarchic. To the trained observer, Bronislaw Malinowski, 'definite technical systems of catching fish and complex economic arrangements' emerge. The natives are found to have 'a close organisation in their working teams, and a fixed division of social functions.' Small groups function together to achieve common goals. Within the canoe, each man is seen to have a specialised role. One is the leader or 'master.' He is the head of the team and the fishing magician. He finances the building of a new canoe when the old is worn. He maintains it in repair, with the help of the rest of the team. He has custody of the canoe. But his control of the canoe is functional. When a communal fishing takes place, he cannot refuse his canoe. Each crew member has his specialised role or function, 'steersman,' 'watcher for fish,' 'keeper of the nets.' Each canoe has its place in the fleet and its part to play in the joint fishing activity.[1]

Thus, out of apparent disorder common patterns of conduct are seen to emerge. Some are repeated but unpredictable in their occurrence, as, for example, joking and by-play. Others, such as paddling, steering, throwing the net, are more predictable in a given situation. Each member of the canoe team, in the performance of his task, must carry out its requirements as understood and accepted by the other members of the group. Such performance is expected of him; meeting such expectancies in a satisfactory way becomes essential to effective co-operation. The throwing of the net, the handling of the canoe in an emergency, must not be interfered with by inappropriate behaviour such as

[1] B. Malinowski, *Crime and Custom in Savage Society*, 1926, pp. 17–20.

horseplay. Each member feels that he has a duty to the others to appear at his post, to carry out his task or role in the established way. Each member feels that he has a right to such behaviour on the part of those with whom he interacts as will be in conformity with his expectancies of their role performance, and thereby enable the performance of his role to mesh successfully with that of the complementary role. In the words of Malinowski:

> 'There is in every act a sociological dualism: two parties who exchange services and functions, each watching over the measure of fulfilment and the fairness of conduct of the other. The master of the canoe, whose interests and ambitions are bound up with his craft, looks after order in the internal transactions between the members of the crew and represents the latter externally. To him each member of the crew is bound at the time of construction and ever after, when co-operation is necessary. Reciprocally, the master has to give each man the ceremonial payment at the feast of construction; the master cannot refuse any one his place in the boat; and he has to see that each man receives his fair share of the catch. In this and in all the manifold activities of economic order, the social behaviour of the natives is based on a well-assessed give-and-take, always mentally ticked off and in the long run balanced.'[2]

The scene now changes to a modern industrial plant, the Western Electric Company's Hawthorne Works in Chicago. The spotlight falls upon a relatively isolated small group in that plant, a group of fourteen workers responsible for wiring banks of terminals used in central office telephone equipment. The group was placed in a separate room. A trained investigator was seated inconspicuously at a desk to observe and record group behaviour. The primary contacts of the group with the external life of the factory were through supervisors and workers who brought in materials and removed completed work. Within the room certain sequences of behaviour repeatedly took place: these may for convenience be called wiring, soldering, inspection, trucking and supervision. Each of these functions or tasks was allocated to a separate individual or sub-group. When a wireman completed his task, the solderman stepped in. When the

[2] *ibid.*, pp. 19–20.

soldering was completed, the inspector stepped in. If a serious breakdown in the system occurred, the supervisor or group chief stepped in. A standard for the performance of the respective roles emerged and became accepted by the group, approximately 6,000 to 6,600 connections per day. Output should not materially fall below this rate, otherwise the worker was viewed as a 'ratebuster.' When one worker exceeded 7,000 connections a day, 'The rest of the fellows kick because I do that.'[3]

This last remark is enormously significant. It points to two different kinds of conduct. On the one hand, it points to conduct which in the eyes of the members of the group, must be performed if the group is to reach its goals effectively. On the other hand, it points to conduct which deviates markedly from the expected or usual conduct and thereby interferes with the attainment of the desired goals. This latter type of conduct in turn leads to still other conduct within the group designed to control and repress the deviation. 'The rest of the fellows kick because I do that.'

Thus we have two different types of norms for conduct, one of which *must* be performed and, when performed, leads to no reaction by the group, other than approval, and the second of which *must not* be performed and, if performed, leads to the application of group sanctions. The latter is a product of the former in that the *must* conduct is the standard used to determine the *must not* conduct. The sanctions applied are designed to eliminate the *must not* conduct so that the *must* conduct will take its place. The stimulus to the application of such conduct lies in the 'expectancies' of conduct of others which become imbedded or 'internalised' in the consciousness of each member of the group. It became expected that each member of the group would perform his role in the established or expected way. Each member felt that he owed the rest such a performance and each felt that he had a right to it from the rest.

The elements, meaning and structure of behaviour are the same in each of these two examples of group life, but the cultural

[3] F. J. Roethlisberger and W. J. Dickson, *Management and the Worker*, 1939, p. 417. See also E. Mayo, *Human Problems of Industrial Civilisation*, 1933; T. N. Whitehead, *The Industrial Worker*, 1938; G. C. Homans, *The Human Group*, 1950, Ch. 3–6. For a later study see E. Mayo and G. Lombard, *Teamwork and Labour Turnover in the Aircraft Industry of Southern California* (Graduate School of Business Administration Research Study No. 32, Harvard University), 1944.

anthropologist terms certain aspects of this behaviour 'primitive law' in the first case, while the social scientist may term them 'social norms' or 'sanction patterns' in the second case. The cultural anthropologist dealing with essentially the same kind of data in a primitive society *not* characterised by the separate legal institutions of modern society feels free to distinguish certain ways of life from others and to call them rules of law:

> 'The rules of law stand out from the rest in that they are felt and regarded as the obligations of one person and the rightful claims of another. . . . "Civil law," the positive law governing all the phases of tribal life, consists then of a body of binding obligations, regarded as a right by one party and acknowledged as a duty by the other, kept in force by a specific mechanism of reciprocity and publicity inherent in the structure of their society. . . . Law dwells not in a special system of decrees, which foresee and define possible forms of non-fulfilment and provide appropriate barriers and remedies. Law is the specific result of the configuration of obligations.'[4] 'Personally, I would not quarrel on terminology. Whether we call a certain rule of conduct law or custom, the really important thing about it is to study whether this rule is actually obeyed, what are the conditions of its validity, and what are the social mechanisms by which it is enforced.'[5]

We may find it helpful to distinguish this kind of law, that is, norms for conduct which are regarded as obligatory because of the requirements of the situation and the performance of effective social action therein, as Living Law.[6] It is conduct which ought to be performed if the goal of the particular group is to be attained in the accustomed or accepted manner. It is conduct which the performer of a role feels that he has a right to expect from the performer of the complementary role. For example, a worker in a steel rolling mill making white hot rails feels that he has a right that his co-worker shall co-operate in the usual manner in directing the rail in place. Any society, primitive or

[4] B. Malinowski. *op. cit.*, pp. 55, 58, 29.

[5] B. Malinowski, Introduction H. I. Hogbin, *Law and Order in Polynesia*, 1934, p. xxiv.

[6] E. Ehrlich, *Fundamental Principles of the Sociology of Law*, 1936; E. Ehrlich, 'Sociology of Law,' 37 *Harvard Law Review* (1922), p. 130; B. Malinowski, 'A New Instrument for the Interpretation of Law—Especially Primitive,' 51 *Yale Law Journal* (1942), p. 1236.

modern, will exhibit this kind of law, though this is not to say that we ought to engage in the prodigious task of determining the content of all such norms, as urged by Ehrlich.[7] In any society individuals must in the performance of their social roles reasonably conform to what is expected of them. Each role has its ideal or approved norms for performance, yet actual behaviour does not always conform to them. When deviational behaviour leads to inter-personal conflict, we see another kind of law emerge. The ideal norm remains a point of reference for the deviant behaviour, but in the case of the legal norm it becomes a *corrective* point of reference.[8] When the performer of the role markedly departs from the approved norm for behaviour, creating inter-personal conflict, that is to say, when the steel mill worker looks not at the twisting and turning white hot rail but at a passing girl in a red sweater, with resultant injury to his co-worker, we then see some form of law come into play as an instrument of social control.

Law as a Means for Social Control

Always present in any group is the problem of the spread between the ideal and the actual, between standards and practice, between what ought to be or is expected to be done and what is in fact done. Group standards and values are not invariably the determinants of individual conduct. Theft, adultery, failure to pay debts, wounding, killing and sacrilege, are forms of deviant behaviour which create 'trouble' within the primitive group. In such situations the group is faced with the problem of keeping order if it is to endure. The function of law in the group is one of applying such mechanisms as will clean up 'social messes when they have been made.'[9] Law then has a maintenance function.

[7] For a recent suggestion to the effect that each of the members of a new world organisation should state 'the specification of its specific ideology and living law norms,' see F. S. C. Northrop, *The Taming of the Nations*, 1952, p. 272. Commenting on the scope of Ehrlich's proposal that the fact-norms of all phases of social life be determined so that the legal propositions can be brought in harmony therewith, Sir Courtenay Allen states: 'I mean no disrespect to the labours of a very learned, sincere, and original jurist if I call this kind of product Megaiomaniac Jurisprudence,' C. K. Allen, *Law in the Making*, 1946, p. 35.

[8] J. Fried, 'The Relation of Ideal Norms to Actual Behaviour in Tarahumara Society,' 9 *Southwestern Journal of Anthropology* (1953), p. 286.

[9] K. Llewellyn and E. A. Hoebel, *The Cheyenne Way: Conflict and Case Law in Primitive Jurisprudence*, 1941, p. 20.

'The members of the group, working within its order, then either manage so to handle divergent claims as to keep the group still 'the group,' or else the law jobs fail to get done, and the group explodes or dribbles apart or dies.'[10]

Law thus has a dual aspect. It may, on the one hand, be conduct which has become so institutionalised (*i.e.,* established) within the group and so clearly related to and necessary for reaching group goals that the group regards it as obligatory. It may, on the other hand, be conduct which is the group response to deviant behaviour and which is designed to control such behaviour. Law in this latter sense consists of those patterns of behaviour which are utilised by the group to control conduct which markedly interferes with the attainment of group goals and which departs from institutionalised ways of behaviour directed toward reaching such goals. Law as such is an *instrument* of social control. As Malinowski says:

> 'Every element of primitive law, every claim, is determined by the need to maintain the identity of the group. This, however, is not merely a formal principle. A group like the family has a definite purpose to achieve. The same is true of a team of buffalo hunters, of a military society, of people who combine for any pursuit, economic, religious, or administrative. Hence, in the above quotation I would like to make one correction. "The group explodes or dribbles apart, or dies" not merely because the law-jobs fail to be done. The law-jobs have to be done, because this is an indispensable condition for the achievement of the real tasks of each group. Law is not an end in itself, but an indispensable instrumentality for the achievement of the real, ultimately biological ends of human activities.'[11]

Malinowski refers to 'the need to maintain the identity of the group' and finds the basis of its identity in the fact that it 'has a definite purpose to achieve.' The deviant behaviour with which law must deal is behaviour which interferes with 'the achievement of the real tasks of the group.' Instead of the concept of the identity of the group, we may use the concept of group equilibrium and say that deviant behaviour disturbs the equilibrium of the elements which go to make up the group, namely,

[10] *ibid.* at p. 274.
[11] B. Malinowski, *op. cit.*, note 1 above, p. 1245.

the institutionalised or repeated sequences of human behaviour which characterise the group action. Deviant behaviour is behaviour which interferes with or frustrates effective role performance, reduces the efficiency of the group in performing its common task and reaching its common goal, or markedly disturbs the equilibrium of the group. When such behaviour occurs a certain amount of the energy of the group must be diverted to its control in order to restore the original equilibrium.

Social control in the primitive group is brought about through 'reciprocity, systematic incidence, publicity and ambition,'[12] as well as by fixed ways of group punishment. The modern industrial group adopts such measures of informal control as complaint, ridicule and limited physical sanctions (*e.g.*, 'binging,' striking a blow on the upper arm).[13]

But such diffuse group pressures are not enough. Some deviant behaviour strikes at deeply felt group sentiments. Sorcery by one person against another, sacrilege, incest and repeated breaches of tribal custom demand the application of ceremonies of ritual purification and punishment. The general assembly of the group or a body of its elders now becomes the *institution* through which the retributive and restitutive functions of law are channelled. Instead of norms for behaviour, we have norms for decision by certain persons designated by their office. Law becomes institutionalised, a fact of enormous importance in the growth of society. In modern society, the fact of the institutionalisation of law has become such an accepted part of our perception of the world in which we live that we no longer think of law as Living Law but only as 'social control through the systematic application of the force of politically organised society,' to use Pound's oft-quoted definition.

Our attitudes and our concepts travel with us as we go backward in time to the investigation of primitve societies still surviving in the backwaters of the modern world. Thus for Hoebel: 'A social norm is legal if its neglect or infraction is regularly met, in threat or in fact, by the application of physical force by an individual or group possessing the socially recognised privilege of so acting.'[14] In other words, if certain conduct is likely to

[12] B. Malinowski, *op. cit.*, note 1 above, p. 68.
[13] F. J. Roethlisberger and W. J. Dickson, *Management and the Worker*, 1938, pp. 422–423.
[14] E. A. Hoebel, *The Law of Primitive Man*, 1954, p. 28.

result in the application of social force to the performer in an established manner by an authorised body, then we have a law. Certainly we have here an analogy to law in modern society. Certainly we may, if we wish, term this analogy law. We may, with Radcliffe-Brown, make even nicer distinctions between 'public delicts' and 'private delicts,' according to whether the sanction is 'penal' or merely 'retaliatory.'[15] The terms we apply, the concepts we create, are our intellectual offspring and we may fashion their shape as we will. But in so doing we must meet the tests: Do they furnish insight into our data? Do they describe all our data? Are they useful in other contexts? Above all, we must be careful that our preoccupation with the concepts and ways of behaviour of our own society do not close our eyes to relevant data. Provinse remarks, with reference to anthropological investigations in the field of law, that: 'It would seem that our investigators' mental images of twelve men in a jury box have obscured a real ethnological problem and precluded the recording of some worthwhile observations.'[16]

Yet control of deviant behaviour could become institutionalised otherwise than in a separate social unit or body. The injured party and his relatives might engage in the warfare of the blood feud. Or the injured man or his kin may, through the mediatorial functioning of the Anglo-Saxon court, suspend hostilities in a prescribed manner and agree not to renew the dispute, following payment of prescribed sums such as the *wergild* or the *bot*. Or he may pursue that curious procedure known as the appeal, in which the wrongdoer is apprehended by the neighbours through the hue and cry and the court regulates the ensuing duel between the parties.

The sanction may take the form of the forfeiture of a cow or a pig, as among the Nabaloi of Luzon. But such a sanction may become inappropriate under changed conditions. In the Nabaloi, cows and pigs were becoming few and precious. Could the community afford a depletion of its stock to carry out the ancient rule? Would it seek refuge in a fiction, say a token drawing of blood, or would it instead seek to adjust the rule to

15 A. R. Radcliffe-Brown, 'Primitive Law,' 9 *Encyclopedia of the Social Sciences*, 1933, p. 202.

16 J. H. Provinse, 'The Underlying Sanctions of Plains Indian Culture,' in F. Eggan (Ed.), *Social Anthropology of North American Tribes*, 1932, pp. 341, 368.

the new circumstances? The council of wise men met and, in accordance with the prescribed ritual, decreed a change in the rule itself which was then, also in accordance with established forms, submitted to and approved by a majority of the people.[17] The council could not only declare the law, it could change or make the law, that is, lay down new rules for conduct.

While among the Cheyenne material goods were private property to be generously shared with others, this rule of behaviour was pushed to the breaking point when horses were freely borrowed from their owners without previous request. When complaint of such a borrowing was made by a warrior before his society, the Elk Soldiers, the offender made restitution and the chiefs of the society laid down a new rule for conduct, namely, that there should 'be no more borrowing of horses without asking.'[18] In this episode law is revealed both as an instrument of control for deviant behaviour and as a means for legislating new norms for behaviour. It is this latter aspect of law which we will take up in the next section.

Law and Authority

Leadership and authority

We began our examination of law in society with the small group. It is the molecule of social life. Within it individuals as atoms find their place and their role. Given a fixed group-goal in a stable environment, we find a high degree of repetition in the behaviour and interactions of its members. The pattern of interaction between one role and its complementary role becomes highly predictable. The requirements of each role and the expectations implicit in its performance become fixed.

But any group is highly ephemeral. It moves out upon the stage of life, gives its performance, retires to the wings, and thence dissipates into the streets, where new and different groups are formed out of its members. Yet, given the cue, it will again emerge and give its performance for as long as satisfactions brought about through the performance do not fall below the margin of indifference as against competing satisfactions. The group forms because it is a necessary instrument to the satisfac-

[17] E. S. Hartland, *Primitive Law,* 1924, pp. 206–207.
[18] K. N. Llewellyn and E. A. Hoebel, *Conflict and Case Law in Primitive Jurisprudence,* p. 128; *op. cit.,* p. 128; E. A. Hoebel, *op. cit.,* p. 143.

tion of the felt needs of its members. Its existence against the background of society is found in the high degree of interaction among its members. Its instrumental character is found in the interdependency of the specialised functions of its members necessary to the attainment of its goal.

We start with the fact that the individual is a mobile unit in continuing interaction with others, first in his family and then as a member of other social groups. Through his participation in group life, the group becomes an instrument for the satisfaction of his needs. The group itself may be the object of his need or it may be the means for satisfying a need outside the group. The source of his gratification may be the group activity itself or it may be found in the manner in which the group affects or modifies the environment in which it functions. If the latter result is the purpose of his participation in the group, then he is using it to satisfy a need outside the group and the group activity becomes an instrument rather than an object of action. The members of the group interact with one another with a common perception of their unity, a common perception of their goal, and with common expectations of the conduct required of one another in the performance of their respective roles necessary to reach their common goal. This is not to say that the group *goal* necessarily coincides with the individual *need*. It may be a matter of indifference to the workman in the Western Electric Company plant that the plant is making electrical equipment. It will be a critical matter with him if he is not paid and if certain satisfactions are not provided in his working conditions.

Within each group the individual finds his place or status, acts the role which determines his status, and thereby responds to the demands and expectations of the other members in the performance of their roles. His performance in its turn becomes the stimulus to the institutionalised responses of the others. Institutionalisation of conduct exists 'when each actor in the situation does, and believes he should do, what the other actors whom he confronts believes he should do.'[19] An institution 'is made up of a plurality of interdependent role-patterns or components of them.'[20]

[19] T. Parsons and E. A. Shils, *Toward a General Theory of Action*, 1952, p. 194.

[20] T. Parsons, *The Social System*, 1951, p. 39.

Behaviour is not always situationally appropriate in the light of the demands and expectations of the members of the group.[1] It may depart from established group norms as variant but still permissive behaviour or as deviant and prohibited behaviour. The latter becomes subject to the imposition of sanctions by the group. When the deviant behaviour is a departure from obligatory behaviour, we have behaviour upon which organised group pressures come to act as a means of restoring the group to its original equilibrium.[2] The deviant behaviour interferes with group locomotion,[3] that is, throws it off its track to its goal. The group responds by the imposition of sanctions, such as ridicule or even physical violence, upon the performer of the deviant behaviour. Energy is thus used towards returning the deviant member to the accustomed path.

The kind of group behaviour we have been describing is the kind typically found in task-oriented groups engaged in performing rather simple physical routines. However, as men multiply and settle the earth the structure of social action becomes more complex and the linkages of systems of action ramify. The atom-individual associates in the molecule-group and the molecule-group associates in the compound-organisation. The environment in which these new and larger groups function is complex, refractory and rapidly changing. New relationships between men emerge. No longer will relatively simple sequences of behaviour enable effective group performance in the attainment of group goals. Planning, co-ordination, the allocation of functions or specific tasks, decisions as to conduct necessary to meet new problems or obstacles faced, the determination of the kind

1 S. S. Sargent, 'Conceptions of Role and Ego in Contemporary Psychology,' in J. H. Rohrer and M. Sherif (Eds.), *Social Psychology at the Crossroads,* 1951, p. 355 at p. 360.

2 'The social situation, like a psychological situation, is a dynamic whole. It means that a change of one of its parts implies a change of the other parts,' K. Lewin, *Resolving Social Conflicts,* 1948, p. 17. 'A social system is in equilibrium and control is effective when the state of the elements that enter the system and of the mutual relationships between them is such that any small change in one of the elements will be followed by changes in the other elements tending to remove the amount of the change,' G. C. Homans, *op. cit.*, note 3 above at pp. 303–304. See also 4 V. Pareto, *The Mind and Society,* 1935, Sec. 2067 *et seq.*; L. J. Henderson, *Pareto's General Sociology,* 1935, p. 112 (Cambridge, 1935).

3 'By movements, we have to understand not only bodily locomotions but, above all, social and mental "locomotions." These three kinds of locomotions are somewhat different, but all three are to be recognised in psychology and sociology as real events,' K. Lewin, *op. cit.*, p. 5.

of behaviour which will be appropriate to a complex and fluctuating environment, the maintenance of the organisation and the imposition of pressures and sanctions necessary to bring about desired conduct, the resolution of conflict, the allocation of the energy and resources of the organisation in such a manner that it will efficiently attain its goals and preserve a surplus of satisfactions for those engaged in the common enterprise—these are some of the new requirements or functions of organisational life which become the task of 'leadership.'

Any actor in a situation may be said to possess his 'space of free movement'[4] or 'area of freedom.'[5] The individual or organism is always in a situational context, but the situation is not limited to the immediate environment:

> 'If one approaches the description of a situation from the dynamic point of view (that is, from a point of view which should finally allow prediction), one has to understand the situation as a totality of possible events or actions. Every change in its social position . . . means that certain things, persons, or activities are made available or cease to be available. One may speak here of the *space of free movement* and its boundaries. By movements, we have to understand not only bodily locomotions but, above all, social and mental "locomotions." . . . The space of free movement of a person or a social group can be represented as a topographical region encircled by other regions that are not accessible. Mainly two factors prohibit the accessibility of regions. One is the *lack of ability,* for instance, lack of skill or intelligence. The other is social *prohibition* or any kind of taboo which stands as a dynamic "barrier" between the person and his goal.'[6]

Each member of a small group has his area of freedom determined by the consensus of the group upon its goal and the common acceptance of patterns of conduct appropriate for reaching that goal. Within these limits he may select those activities which will, in his view of the requirements of the situation, be appropriate to the performance of his role.

A small group is characterised by consensus, consensus upon

[4] *ibid.*
[5] N. R. F. Maier, *Principles of Human Relations,* 1952, pp. 24 *et seq.*
[6] K. Lewin, *op. cit.,* pp. 5–6.

goals and means for reaching these goals. An organisation, however, is characterised by co-ordination through leadership, authority and responsibility. When the requirements of a situation can be met by fixed, simple and relatively narrow sequences of behaviour, a group may be large in number and may function with little or no leadership. When, however, the ways to group goals are many and choice must be exercised as to which way shall be followed, when decision as to the way to be followed must in turn be shaped by the need of efficiency, so as to minimise the expenditure of group energy, and of lessening friction, so as to avoid the expenditure of group energy in maintenance functions, leadership emerges. That is to say the group will now accept the proposition that one or more of its members may and must select or decide upon those procedures which will most likely reach the group goal with a minimum expenditure of energy and creation of friction.[7] The group will also accept the fact that some of its members will have a greater degree of access to its physical facilities and control over the performance of its members than others.[8]

The concept of the area of freedom is a universal concept applicable to the activity of each member of an organisation but in the case of a member said to possess authority we introduce an additional and relational concept. The person in authority is not seen alone but in relation to others of whom he is their 'superior' while they are his 'subordinates.' He must communicate to them his decision and bring about their behaviour in conformity with it. If the repeated communication of his decisions made within his area of freedom is repeatedly or usually followed by the desired behaviour of the group members with whom he is in relation and who are under his supervision, he

[7] 'The task of decision involves three steps: (1) the listing of all the alternative strategies; (2) the determination of all the consequences that follow upon each of these strategies; (3) the comparative evaluation of these sets of consequences. . . . The criterion of efficiency dictates that choice of alternatives which produced the largest result for the given application of resources,' H. A. Simon, *Administrative Behaviour*, 1951, pp. 67, 179.

[8] 'The most general or universal kinds of differentiation which exist or develop between persons as units in small groups' include 'Differential degree of access to resources' and 'Differential degree of control over persons,' R. F. Bales, 'A Theoretical Framework for Interaction Process Analysis,' in J. H. Rohrer and M. Sherif (Eds.), *op. cit.*, note 1, above, pp. 29, 33–34.

possesses *authority*. 'Authority is exercised over an individual whenever that individual, relaxing his own critical faculties, permits the communicated decision of another to guide his own choice.'[9]

Authority from the standpoint of human behaviour is not a matter of legitimacy, though acknowledgment of legitimacy of specific persons asserting authority will in part determine whether they possess authority. Authority is a product of leadership. A leader must have followers. A leader determines the conduct which shall be carried out by the members of his group. Such a decision is meaningless, however, unless it becomes a social fact through the acceptance of his decision by the members of his group. Thus a person in authority has his particular area of freedom in the sense of determining conduct for reaching a goal and, in addition, the bringing about of such co-ordinated conduct by virtue of his power, in his office, to influence others in the performance of their roles within the organisation.

Authority, in the sense in which we use the term, cannot be delegated. In the formal sense of the term, authority may be delegated. From the standpoint of legitimacy, one vested with authority may relinquish part of that authority to another, if he follows the approved ritual. From the standpoint of human behaviour, the delegation of authority implies the communication by a leader to another of his decision that such other shall be responsible for reaching a particular segment of the broad goal with which the leader is concerned. In this sense, the delegation of authority involves a recognition by a leader that his leadership cannot be effective as an authoritative relationship unless he defines his broad goal in terms of narrower and more precise goals and creates a new set of leaders who will be charged with reaching these lesser goals.

Each member of an organisation, whether leader or follower, is said to be responsible or accountable for the manner in which he carries out his task or area of freedom. If his behaviour within his particular segment of group life becomes grossly variant or deviant, he then becomes subject to group sanctions, including decisions as to their application by his superior or others. In this sense an organisation may be defined as 'a social group in which

[9] H. A. Simon, *op. cit.*, p. 151.

members are differentiated as to responsibility in relation to the accomplishment of a common task or goal.'[10]

'Authority' thus becomes a complex concept characterised by purpose, by the selection by the person possessing authority of the desired behaviour to accomplish purpose, by the communication from the person possessing authority to those under him of the nature of the desired behaviour, and the habitual performance by the latter of the desired behaviour.

Types of authority

The product of the exercise of authority is power. Out of the co-ordinated performance of the specialised roles of each member of the organisation stems its energy. This energy-potential or power of any group is limited because its resources, human and physical, in a world of scarcity are limited. It is true that certain procedures and situations will strengthen the intensity and efficiency with which the members of the group perform their respective roles and hence increase the power of the group. The degree to which the individual accepts the requirements of the role, is loyal to and identifies himself with the group, will influence the manner of performance of his role. If procedures be adopted towards strengthening the willing acceptance of commands by subordinates, the total energy-potential of the group will tend to increase. If obedience be brought about through force, then not only is part of the available power of the group diverted to the creation of such force itself but the remaining available power is not as much as it might otherwise be. All of this has been said in much simpler terms in the familiar phrase that the strength of democracy lies in the consent of the governed. In other words, if the governed participate in decision-making by those in authority, we have democracy. If the participation or consent of all is necessary to decision, we have pure democracy. If the participation or consent of a majority is necessary, we have majority-rule democracy. If the participation or consent of none is required, we have autocracy. Democracy, in other words, increases to the extent that decision-making is decentralised from

[10] R. M. Stogdill, 'Leadership, Membership and Organisation,' 47 *Psychological Bulletin* 1 (1950), reprinted in D. Cartwright and A. Zander, *Group Dynamics: Research and Theory*, 1953, p. 535; see N. R. F. Maier, *op. cit.*, note 5 above; H. A. Simon, D. W. Smithburg and V. A. Thompson, *Public Administration*, 1950.

the person in authority to all those involved in the authority relation.

Law and authority

Superimposed upon the area of freedom of each member of the organisation is, first, the commonly accepted rule that the commands of his superior within the latter's sphere of authority must be obeyed. Indeed, it is the high frequency of individual response to this rule which creates the organisation and distinguishes it from the rest of society. In addition, there are norms of behaviour which each member *must* perform as a part of his role (*e.g.*, in the case of the workers in the bank wiring room, presence of the worker in the room during certain hours of the day and the accomplishment of a certain standard of production),[11] norms of behaviour which he *may* perform (*e.g.*, a certain amount of relaxation and informal play), and certain norms of behaviour which he may *not* perform (*e.g.*, habitual lateness to work, habitual failure to meet work standards). Those which he *must* perform represent the Living Law of the organisation. Those which he must not perform will be subject to the imposition of sanctions and will constitute another, and more familiar, type of law within the organisation. Decision as to the imposition of sanctions may lie in the members of the group generally (*e.g.*, 'binging') or it may become institutionalised in the sense that the making and enforcement of such decisions are allocated to specific personnel.

Authority becomes legal or lawful authority when it rests 'on a belief in the "legality" of patterns of normative rules and the right of those elevated to authority under such rules to issue commands.'[12] The concept of 'legality' or 'legitimacy' is a product of the institutionalisation of law in society, about which we shall speak at some length in the next chapter. It is desirable, however, briefly to touch upon the concepts of 'society' and the 'state.'

Society and the State

A society is usually considered to be a self-sustaining social

[11] See p. 3 above.
[12] M. Weber, *The Theory of Social and Economic Organisation*, p. 300 (Translation by A. R. Henderson and T. Parsons), 1947, p. 300.

system which contains 'all the structural and functional fundamentals of an independently subsisting system.'[13] It 'involves a plurality of interacting individuals,' is 'self-sufficient for the actions of this plurality,' and is 'capable of existing longer than the life span of an individual of the type (or types) involved.'[14]

The primitive society, the Greek and Roman society, or the feudal society may well have been largely 'self-sustaining' and 'self-sufficient,' though even some primitive societies and certainly the Greek and Roman societies were supported by external trade. The *territorial* society of the modern State, however, can no longer exist in isolation within its boundaries. The State is by definition limited to a defined territory within which is found a permanent population under an independent established government.[15] This territorial society within the boundaries of the modern State constantly strives for a self-sufficiency which ever recedes as raw materials become exhausted and overseas markets more critical to national wellbeing.

The net work of corporate and organisational life in each State is part of a world-wide system of relationships which ignores State boundaries. It is transnational while the systems of law under which it functions are national. The western world, at least, is a unity of corporate life devoted to the satisfaction of the various and insatiable wants of man. A unity of trade, intercourse and communication cuts into a jigsaw pattern of national States. Man's existence is dependent not only upon the particular network of corporate and organisational activity comprised in his national society but upon all the ties, direct and indirect, of each such network with the corresponding patterns of trade and intercourse of the rest of the world. For raw materials and products and art and ideas are found and used in a world-pattern, not exclusively in national compartments.

We shall have occasion to consider further the nature of world society in Chapter IV while in Chapter III we will explore further the concept of the State and seek to redefine it in a

[13] T. Parsons, *op. cit.*, p. 19.
[14] M. J. Levy, Jr., *The Structure of Society*, 1952, p. 112.
[15] 'The State as a person of international law should possess the following qualifications: (a) a permanent population; (b) a defined territory; (c) government; and (d) capacity to enter into relations with the other States.' Convention on the Rights and Duties of States of December 26, 1933. *U.S. Treaty Series*, No. 881; 6 M. O. Hudson, *International Legislation*, 1937, pp. 620, 622. See, however, Chap. 3 below.

manner which will take cognizance of the fact that part of the modern national society extends beyond the territorial limits of the State, and that the force and authority of the government of the State is made manifest beyond its borders.

Law and Values

The Cornell Value Study Group said that: 'Values are not the concrete goals of behaviour, but rather are aspects of these goals. Values appear as the *criteria* against which goals are chosen, and as the implications which these goals have in the situation.'[16] A value, accordingly, 'is a conception, explicit, or implicit, distinctive of an individual or characteristic of a group, of the desirable which influences the selection from the available modes, means and ends of actions.'[17] Value as thus defined is a universal concept: it applies to all forms of conduct in so far as the element of choice is present.

A somewhat more generalised conception of the meaning of value lies in the familiar view that statements of value are normative as distinguished from existential—'X is good' or 'X is bad' as distinguished from 'X is.' In other words, value statements lie in the phrases 'X ought to be' or 'X ought not to be.' Under this conception of value, it is necessary to analyse the elements of 'oughtness' and 'ought-notness' involved in X and determine why X is to be regarded as desirable or undesirable. This conception of value is often applied to data in the field of the natural sciences. In this usage, the statement 'This is a chemical compound known as sulphuric acid' is said to be factual and verifiable while the statement 'This is good' is said to be emotive and unverifiable.[18]

Is it possible, in behaviourist terms, to work out a conception of value in which law, which implies public instead of private values, will have a place?

Let us begin with the second conception of value as above summarised. The statement 'This is sulphuric acid' implies evaluation in the sense of classifying certain elements of the

16 Quoted from an unpublished memorandum 'Summary of Discussions of the Cornell Value Study Group (June 11, 1949)' in T. Parsons and E. A. Shils, *op. cit.*, p. 429.

17 C. Kluckhohn and others, 'Values and Value-Orientations in the Theory of Action,' *ibid.*, p. 388 at p. 395.

18 See D. W. Gotshalk, 'Value Science,' 19 *Philosophy of Science* (1952), p. 183.

immediate situation into relevant cognitive categories. Basically, the statement implies that if certain accepted procedures and standards were followed *this* substance in hand could be verified to be *that* substance known as sulphuric acid. Here, evaluation implies the determination of the validity of the statement. But that very process stems from the fact that our social system includes certain established organisations or institutions of a scientific character whose function it is to develop and use such information. For actors in such an environment the statement that 'This is sulphuric acid' is *good* because it is useful, because it aids in accomplishing the purpose of their activity. Inasmuch as knowledge of the properties of sulphuric acid may be useful, directly or indirectly, to any person whatever who may come into contact with it, the statement 'This is sulphuric acid' implies also the concept 'This is bad,' because it is part of our common knowledge that personal contact with sulphuric acid will injure.[19]

Let us now move to the normative concept of value and the dichotomy of normative-existential. The statement 'We have a war in Indo China' is a statement describing certain kinds of human behaviour as distinguished from statements describing physical phenomena. We move from 'nature' to 'action,' but in both cases we have a statement involving a cognitive classification. When we say 'We ought not to have a third world war,' we are expressing a normative evaluation. We are saying that of the courses of action available to the States of the world, war should not be chosen because of its undesirable consequences. We are evaluating the conduct in question, war, from the standpoint of an actor who is not an individual but who is a vast collection of individuals and groups—the State.

Yet the statement 'We ought not to have a third world war' can be both a statement of value of the individual as well as of the State. From the point of view of the individual the statement expresses the undesirable individual consequences of rationing, conscription, aerial bombardment and atomic warfare. From the standpoint of the *actor* in the situation, the State, it involves a question of policy but still of evaluation, namely, of the available alternative courses of action, what are the desirable and the undesirable consequences of war? The decision upon that question

[19] *ibid.*

is a decision entrusted to certain political institutions known as the executive and the legislature. They must answer that question from the standpoint of survival and other similar values as they affect the national society. From the standpoint of the economic organisation, the question must be answered by evaluating the consequences of war as they affect the organisation in question. A munitions plant may benefit from war while a luxury industry using critical materials may not. Thus the same existential concept, 'war,' may involve individual values, group values and social values, depending on the identity of the actor whose interest is involved. Talcott Parsons states that:

> 'Existence and value are intimately related, interdependent, and yet—at least at the analytical level—conceptually distinct. It is a fact both of introspection and of observation that there are three fundamental types of experiencing: what is or is believed to be (existential); what I and/or others want (desire); what I and/or others ought to want (the desirable). Values are manifested in ideas, expressional symbols, and in the moral and aesthetic norms evident in behavioural regularities. Whether the cognitive or the cathectic factors have primacy, in the manifestation of a value at a particular time, both are always present. Values synthesise cognitive and cathectic elements in orientations to an object world, most specifically a social object world—that is, a social relationship system. Values define the limits of permissible cost of an expressional gratification or an instrumental achievement by invoking the consequences of such action for other parts of the system and for the system as a whole.' [20]

If we consider the problem of value from the standpoint or frame of reference of the actor involved, it becomes possible to see the relationship between value, purpose, authority, law, responsibility and power. Any individual placed in a situation has *activity needs* and *effect needs*. He may select certain behaviour or activity for its own sake, its cathectic effect. 'The satisfaction . . . contemporary with the activity itself (provided the processes are unobstructed) . . . can be distinguished from the contentment that follows some achieved effect.' [1] The effect

[20] T. Parsons and E. A. Shils, *op. cit.*, p. 394.
[1] H. A. Murray, 'Toward a Classification of Interactions,' in T. Parsons and E. A. Shils, *op. cit.*, pp. 434, 445.

of conduct primarily shapes and determines conduct when the actor is engaged in the performance of a role in a group whose activity is in turn directed towards some goal external to the group. The formula stimulus-organism-behaviour then becomes stimulus-organism-behaviour-effect, in which effect represents the result of behaviour.[2] The norms and requirements of each role are shaped by its instrumental character. Its criteria for choice of action by the performer of the role are shaped successively by the total situation faced by the group and by the segment of the total situation faced by each respective member of the group. In organisational life, values for the incumbent of each specialised role within the organisation are shaped by the area of freedom allocated to him and by the needs, both activity needs and effect needs, inherent in his role. The design or style of his performance of his role is fixed by his personality as it adjusts itself to the required, permissible and impermissible elements of behaviour inherent in his area of freedom or role. The personality of General Wood in Sears, Roebuck varies from that of Sewell Avery in Montgomery Ward, with consequent variances in the style of the performances of their respective roles and consequent impact upon the character of their organisations. A person possessing authority in whom the need for the exertion of social power is strong will permit that value to shape, within the permissible limits of his role, his behaviour in the performance of his role. Yet purpose, both of his organisation and of his specialised role within the organisation, fashions the boundaries, as well as the content, of his behaviour. The commands of authority and the sanctioned rules for behaviour of law similarly impinge upon his area of freedom. His responsibility for an effective performance of his role will cause judgment and choice to be made as to how conduct may be shaped so as to achieve power and energy.

The element of law will always relate to particular social behaviour, concrete sequences of behaviour as they affect other concrete sequences of behaviour and facilitate, impede or prevent the performance of such other sequences or facilitate, impede or prevent the attainment of the goals, both immediate and ultimate, to which such sequences are directed. Law always involves behaviour which is to be desired (commanded) or not

2 See N. R. F. Maier, *op. cit.*, p. 31.

to be desired (prohibited) or to be left alone (permitted) and in which the standard or value is essentially one of maintenance of the relevant social system. Is the behaviour essential to the group, organisational or social purpose? Does it so frustrate the attainment of such purpose that its performance must be visited with sanctions in order to maintain the desired equilibrium of power-elements?

We may view this question of value from the standpoint of the widest possible segments of behaviour. We may concern ourselves with *ultimate* values, which relate to the fundamental requisites of a society, such as health, sex and reproduction, authority, prestige, leadership, roleship, property, knowledge, beauty, ideology, and others.[3] Another analysis of the functional requisites for any society includes provision for an adequate physiological relationship to the setting and for sexual recruitment, role differentiation and role assignment, communication, shared cognitive orientations, a shared articulative set of goals, the regulation of the choice of means, the regulation of affective expression, adequate socialisation, effective control of disruptive forms of behaviour and adequate institutionalisation.[4] A further similar set of values is that of power, respect, enlightenment, wealth, well-being, rectitude, skill and affection.[5]

The foregoing are perceptions of much the same kind of data which are classified by the anthropologist under the concept of the 'universal culture pattern,' to use Wissler's highly suggestive phrase. From the behavioural point of view cultures differ. The patterns of human behaviour centring about marriage, education or religion, for example, differ enormously between societies. Yet different societies do exhibit kinds of behaviour which, though different in content, can be subjected to a uniform system of classification. The universal culture pattern is a product of 'the fundamental biological and psychological nature of man and the universal conditions of human existence.'[6]

[3] H. A. Murray, *op. cit.*, p. 463.
[4] M. J. Levy, Jr., *op. cit.*, Ch. 4.
[5] H. D. Lasswell and A. Kaplan, *Power and Society*, 1950, Ch. 5; H. D. Lasswell and M. McDougal, 'Legal Education and Public Policy: Professional Training in the Public Interest,' 52 *Yale Law Journal* (1943), p. 203; M. McDougal, 'The Role of Law in World Politics,' 20 *Mississippi Law Journal* (1949), p. 253 at p. 262; M. McDougal, 'Law and Power,' 46 *American Journal of International Law* (1952), p. 102 at p. 108.
[6] G. P. Murdock, 'The Common Denominator of Cultures,' in R. Linton (Ed.), *The Science of Man in the World Crisis*, 1945, pp. 123, 125.

When, however, we have classified behaviour into such ultimate categories or abstractions, we have almost entirely removed ourselves from the domain of law. The emphasis accorded particular values or goals at a particular time in the history of a society will determine the extent to which human conduct is channelled into particular ways of behaviour. Such problems are the problems of the leadership function. In the largest sense, they involve planning and the allocation of the available resources or power of the whole society. To state this otherwise, they involve problems of policy, of conflicting pressures and demands of interest groups, rather than individual conflicts and disputes.

Their resolution is, in the national State, entrusted to the political institutions known as the executive or legislature. Such institutions must decide whether it shall be 'guns' or 'butter,' whether a Maginot line of radar and air defences shall be set up as against the demands for reduced taxes and a balanced budget. Even the prodigious resources of a United States are limited, and a choice must be made as to the allocation of these resources among the respective values of the national society. There are, however, no rules of law for the solution of problems such as these. There is only the configuration of the demands of the culture or society at the particular time in its history. When the particular choice has been made by the political institutions authorised to make it, the commands of the legislature may establish new rules of law, new organisations or new institutions to accomplish the desired objectives. The power of the national society will be channelled into new streams by legislation.

It is true that ultimate values such as these are in the background of any *dispute* with which the judicial institutions of a State are required to deal, if for no other reason than that in last analysis all social conduct will be found to centre about such basic goals. But the solution of disputes can be reached by no simple and automatic application of such concepts or values as power, respect, enlightenment, and the like. Very concrete behaviour is here involved—negligent injury, appropriation of property, trade mark infringement and the rest. This particular behaviour must be examined in a very specific social setting of group and organisational life. It must be evaluated against desired specific norms conducing to the efficiency and maintenance of the group and organisational life and of the society of which they are a part. The problem is one of mechanics, of the conservation of energy, protection against frustration of purpose and aggression. No abstract formulas or values will solve these disputes.

When the question is whether the legislature shall authorise Snake River Dam or a T.V.A., one of the values influencing the decision is that of wealth or, in other words, the resulting increase in national power. But other values enter into the decision as well, and the final decision usually reflects an adjustment of those values to group pressures. Some of these are: Shall there be a further increase in the centralisation of government? Shall there be a further increase in governmental functions? Shall there be a greater bureaucracy? Shall there be an increase in the national budget? Are there national needs, such as for maximum electric power as well as for conservation, which only a governmental organisation can supply? When the question concerns such a concrete issue as certain recent antitrust legislation, the conflict of values in the process of legislative decision 'shows policy emerging as a by-product of group actions and interactions.'[7]

When two persons engage in an exchange of products or services, their transaction may be said to be concerned with the value of wealth. Yet from the standpoint of the individual actor, the value which influenced the selection of the particular transaction may not have been wealth. Presumably the purchaser of this volume acquired it not for wealth but for enlightenment. Out of the modes of action available to him, the selection was made of a particular transaction, the purchase of this volume. Each transaction in the stream of transactions which go to make up the process of exchange in society is a product of choice. The actual transaction is always the outcome of choice between at least two possible and potential transactions. From the standpoint of individual motivation, a transaction is not limited to the two parties by whom it is consummated but includes as well two others, namely, the next best alternative for each. There are two sellers and two buyers, the actual buyer and seller and the next best counterpart for each. The seller exercises a choice between at least two buyers and the buyer exercises a choice between at least two sellers; in each case, the best and the next best from the standpoint of the party to the transaction. The

[7] E. Latham, *The Group Basis of Politics*, 1952, p. 221.

values which determine the 'best' and the 'next best' are the values of the parties.

From the standpoint of the judge, the values which influence the parties to the transaction are of no consequence. The judge is concerned with disputes arising between parties to a transaction and these disputes arise out of deviant behaviour. The judge must ensure that the bargaining process is not abused and that contract and property are confined to their proper spheres. The area of contract must be limited and some types of conduct prohibited altogether, such as contracts of gambling or prostitution. The conditions of the bargaining process must be controlled so that there should be a workable equality of bargaining ability as between the participants. The infant, the insane, the person of little understanding, even the ignorant and inexperienced, deserve special protection in certain circumstances if bargaining is to perform a public instead of a private end. Certain modes of bargaining, including misrepresentation, fraud and duress, must be denied participants in the bargaining process, and those who, nevertheless, employ such methods must not be permitted to gain thereby; otherwise the social purpose of the bargaining process will be perverted. Mistake may occur in a transaction otherwise satisfying the requirements of a contract: shall the resulting contract be permitted to have legal effect when abuse of the contract right would be the social consequence? The conduct involved in the transaction which is being judicially weighed must be considered in the light of what the judge conceives to be the normal or socially approved or socially desirable transaction, and the question answered whether the deviant conduct must be controlled in some manner. The problem is always factual, with the question of values in the background, it is true, but with the decision to be reached dependant upon an analysis of the bargaining process in a particular transaction-setting and the basic question one of determining whether, *in the particular circumstances of this concrete and specific case,* the transaction shall be given finality or in some respect controlled and regulated.

Thus the judge comes to lay down rules of behaviour which are binding upon the parties to each transaction. He weighs the conduct in the transaction before him, out of which the dispute stemmed, against what he conceives to be expected, usual or desirable behaviour. In determining what may be desirable behaviour for the purposes of his decision, no such simple, unital value as wealth shapes his decision; rather is it an adjustment of values in a highly concrete situation. Professor Commons states:

> 'There is a fifth party to every transaction, namely, the governor, or rather, the judge who lays down the working rules of the concern under the name of rights, duties, liberties, *etc.*, involving the further social relation of command by a superior representing the power of the group, and obedience by inferiors, who are members of the group.
>
> 'A transaction, then, involving a minimum of five persons, and not an isolated individual, nor even only two individuals, is the ultimate unit of economics, ethics and law. It is the ultimate but complex relationship, the social electrolysis, that makes possible the choice of opportunities, the exercise of power and the association of men into families, clans, nations, business, unions and other going concerns. The social unit is not an individual seeking his own pleasure: it is five individuals doing something to each other within the limits of working rules laid down by those who determine how disputes shall be decided.'
>
> . . . . . .
>
> 'Thus every transaction has its physical dimensions of performance, avoidance, forbearance; its economic dimensions of opportunity, power, economy and expectations; its psychological dimensions of thinking, feeling, willing, persuading, coercing, commanding, obeying and expectation; its ethical and legal dimensions of rights, duties, liberties, and exposures, and its governmental dimensions of authority and authorisation in the use of physical power, economic or moral powers, according to common rules or working rules that set the limits and directions of conduct.'[8]

For example, two businessmen acquired jointly a lease on certain valuable city property. As this lease neared its termination, one of them acquired a long-term lease of the property in question as well as adjacent premises. In the role of a business man, his

[8] J. R. Commons, *Legal Foundations of Modern Capitalism*, 1925, pp. 67, 83.

conduct exhibited energy and foresight. In the role of his relationship with the co-holder of the expiring leasehold, his conduct exhibited a lack of loyalty. Was his conduct to be regulated or not? Was the value of preserving loyalty between co-adventurers in a business enterprise of the particular kind involved in the case to prevail over the value of freedom of competition and opportunity to enter into transactions? The rule was laid down that an interest in the new lease should be held in trust for the co-adventurer, since the parties were governed by a rule of conduct 'something stricter than the morals of the market place.'[9]

Thus a working rule was laid down governing transactions in which one of the parties occupies a certain type of fiduciary position in relation to another. That bundle of expectancies which is involved in the role of the co-adventurer was made more precise by the court and certain obligatory conduct was imposed by law upon the performer of such a role. Yet the sequences of human behaviour and the value problems involved therein were narrow. Occasionally a trend in decisions may reflect an emerging value, such as that of supporting the organic solidarity of group endeavour.[10] In the field of public law, in particular, a decision may become a landmark in recognising and preserving human values.[11] By and large, however, judicial opinion deals with highly specific problems of human behaviour and correspondingly specific and narrow value problems.

Although the judge may move interstitially in his decision-making, his decisions will nevertheless be subject to the steady and irresistible forces of the society of which he is a member. He is a product of his culture; he shares its traditions and assumptions. Unless his decisions reflect the ultimate values of his society, they will create rather than resolve conflict in the functioning of the social process. He becomes a part of the drift of the forces of society, joining in its massive pressures and yet,

[9] *Meinhard* v. *Salmon* 249 N.Y. 458, 164 N.E. 545 (1928).

[10] *Perlman* v. *Feldman* 219 F. 2d 173 (2d Cir. 1955); *Zahn* v. *Transamerica Corp.* 162 F. 2d 36 (3d Cir. 1947); *Insuranshares Corp.* v. *Northern Fiscal Corp.* 35 F. Supp. 22 (E. D. Pa. 1940).

[11] *e.g.*, *Brown* v. *Board of Education of Topeka* 347 U.S. 483 (1954); K. S. Carlston, 'Equality of Access to the Basic Social Institutions of Society as a Goal of the Democratic State,' 3 *Journal of Public Law* (1954), p. 71. See O. Lee, 'Social Values and the Philosophy of Law,' 32 *Virginia Law Review* (1946), p. 802.

because of his position as arbiter, at times exerting a restraining influence. He must rise above the partisan claims of litigants and view them in the light of the needs and demands of the society as a whole. His must be the responsibility for determining those values which are ephemeral or harmful and those which are enduring and necessary to foster or preserve.[12]

Concept of the Organisation

We have used the term 'organisation' a number of times and have defined it in a preliminary way in pages 11 to 15 above. Among other things, we took occasion to examine the concept of the 'role,' pointing out that in group action of a permanent or established character the patterns of behaviour of each member evidence certain repeatable sequences as a result of the fact that he tends to carry out a specialised function within the group, that the behaviour of each member becomes institutionalised in that he accepts in his consciousness the requirements of his role and realises that others, with whom he interacts, expect that he will perform or behave in the usual or customary way, and that such institutionalisation of conduct is essential to the successful meshing of role performances in group action. We also pointed out that the organisation involved leadership functions and the conscious co-ordination of action of the members of the group to reach a common goal.

We shall now hazard a somewhat more detailed description of the organisation. It is felt that the description will fit a considerable number of specific forms of group endeavour in modern society; indeed, it is a form of co-operative activity without which no national society could today exist. In other words, the organisational structure is not limited to the economic life of a society.

A ball team has many of the characteristics of an organisation. Each of its nine members has a highly concrete role; the behaviour of each is highly predictable. The performances of its members are directed to common ends. All are part of a system of relationships. Yet, when the team moves out upon the playing field, it is not an organisation but rather a small group. Each member of the team has his fixed role. Each knows what is

[12] C. E. Wyzanski, Jr., 'Process and Pattern: The Search for Standards in the Law,' 30 *Indiana Law Journal* (1955), p. 133.

expected of him and what he may expect of others in carrying out their respective roles. Hence the game may be played without a leader, for, from the moment the first ball is thrown by the pitcher, each member has his familiar part in carrying on the game.

When, however, a professional baseball team moves out upon the playing field, we say that it does so as a part of organised baseball. It does so not as an isolated team or small group but as part of an organisation. Others have determined that it shall play at this particular time and place. Others have determined its membership. The members of the team in turn accept the authority of its manager and are responsible to him. When they return to their showers, they are still a part of the organisation, though the team has as of that moment ceased to exist.

The organisation, then, is of a much more permanent and established character than the ephemeral small group. It is characterised by the fact that the conduct of its members is not only shaped by the institutional requirements of their respective roles but by leadership reinforced by authority. Responsibility on the part of the members for the effective performance of their roles is another distinguishing feature of the organisation. This responsibility is marked not only by the obligation to perform the role effectively but by the imposition of sanctions when it is not so performed. Deviant behaviour within the organisation may involve conduct which will lead to the intervention of the courts or it may involve conduct which merely leads to the application of measures of control within the organisation itself, for the organisation has its own internal norms of conduct and means for the control of deviant behaviour.

All groups are purposive in one way or another. They involve a type of conduct not limited to stimulus-response but embracing stimulus-response-effect. The effects designed to be brought about by the performance of the group we term its purposes. An organisation is characterised by the conscious co-ordination of human effort through leadership supported by authority to accomplish its purposes. Each of these requires further definition.

To play baseball in organised baseball requires that schedules of games be worked out, train schedules investigated, transportation and hotel accommodations purchased, baseball fields and seating facilities for spectators maintained, and the conditions for an effective performance by the team established. These involve such unknown factors that investigation, planning and conscious co-ordination are required to enable a successful co-operative performance.

Each organisation, therefore, must have one or more members whose function it is to co-ordinate and direct the activity of the rest. They are the focal point of lines of communication within the organisation. They represent the ultimate centre of its system of authority. To them information continually flows concerning present and anticipated problems of the organisation. From them flows the stream of decisions co-ordinating the action of the members. They decide the directions in which the energies of the organisation shall be used and the relative balance or proportion among the competing demands for the power of the organisation. They decide what the particular objectives of the organisation shall be and allocate the human and physical resources of the organisation to the accomplishment of such objectives. In the exercise of these functions, all the stresses, forces, claims and demands of the members of the organisation are brought to bear upon them. They must maintain an equilibrium or balance among such forces. They must ensure that there is a surplus of satisfactions for the members as against competing possibilities for satisfaction in order that the organisation may endure.

The existence of the organisation is dependent upon its significance to its members, the satisfaction of their felt needs. The values of the organisation to its members, however, may be quite different from the purposes of the organisation. A business organisation is directed to the satisfaction of certain economic wants. This determines its value and importance to society. It is the sharing in the ensuing monetary rewards, however, which in large measure, though not exclusively, determines the value of the organisation to its members. To view an organisation solely from the standpoint of its significances to its members is to create an atomistic structure of social action. It must be viewed from the standpoint of its external as well as its internal relations.

The system of relations which we call the organisation may be classified into those which may be called internal and those which may be termed external. A product of the fact that no one organisation can satisfy all the fundamental human drives of say self-maintenance, self-perpetuation, self-gratification and religion is the interdependency of organisational action. The purposes or objectives of any organisation are limited. This means that no organisation can exist in isolation. It is a part of the social system we term society. When the interactions of one of its members are limited to contacts with other members, the resulting relation is internal. When he interacts with others who are in no continuing relationship with the organisation and who do not accept its system of authority, the resulting relation is external. In an economic organisation, the pattern of interaction of members with non-members usually takes the form of the transaction. A continuing, repeated series of transactions may be called an external relation. The external relations of an economic organisation are found in the transactions of exchange whereby the goods or services of the organisation are transferred to others and the bargained benefit received from such others. In governmental organisations the services and even at times the products of such organisations are likewise extended to constantly changing members of the citizenry.

Responsibility of the part of the members for the effective performance of their roles in accordance with accepted norms is another distinguishing feature of the organisation. Responsibility implies more than a designation of a task or role to be carried out. It implies an obligation to perform that task or role in accordance with the standards and rules of the organisation. It further implies measures of control, that is, the imposition of sanctions when it is not performed in accordance with established rules. Usually sanctions against deviant role performance will be applied wholly within the organisation itself, such as the imposition of suspension from work, fines or even expulsion from the organisation. Sometimes, however, reliance upon the courts must be had.

Certain members of certain types of organisations possess a kind of authority termed legitimate. That is, certain organisations may, by following certain procedures established by the government of a state, create certain offices whose occupants may call upon the organs of the government legitimately exercising social power through force to reinforce and sanction their commands. The individual may say 'Keep off my property' and do so with the knowledge that the courts will support him.

When, however, he says 'Keep off the property of this organisation,' he may expect the support of the courts only if he possesses legitimate authority within the organisation and if this be an appropriate exercise of his organisational office or role.

Thus some types of organisations, notably the private corporation and the public agency, may rely upon the power of the government itself to support the commands of those persons possessing legitimate authority or office within the organisation.

An organisation cannot function without effective means of communication. In an organisation whose spatial dimensions have expanded to embrace considerable territory, as, for example, a foreign office and its overseas appendages, a national or an international business organisation, the difficulties of rapid and accurate communication at times result in a breakdown of the leadership function. Cables back and forth cross one another and are not received in uniform sequence. Statements are made which have no significance because they are not received in the sequence in which they were sent. At these times, if authority is to exist and co-ordination is to be accomplished, leadership at the centre must be relinquished in favour of the exercise of discretion at the periphery. If breakdowns become too frequent, authority is said to be decentralised or delegated, that is, new and legitimate foci of authority are established.

In a technological society an organisation usually cannot function without some facilities and equipment, say offices, typewriters, desks and cabinets. It must have within its control and for differential allocation to its members in the performance of their tasks physical resources and facilities.

As a consequence of the high frequency of interactions of members of the organisation with one another, the name by which it becomes known, its symbols and traditions and the satisfactions which it affords, its members come to identify themselves with the organisation. They regard themselves as belonging to the organisation. They refer to the organisation as 'we' and not as 'they.' The practices of the organisation become 'ours' and not 'theirs.' In the case of the economic organisation, some consumers have so frequently turned to an organisation for the satisfaction of the relevant want that even they identify themselves with the organisation; they refer to themselves as 'General Motors people' or 'General Electric people.'

An organisation is thus a complex system of relationships. It is characterised by the conscious co-ordination of human behaviour through leadership, supported by authority, to accomplish purpose. The behaviour of its members is in part defined by the institutionalised patterns of their roles and in part by authoritative orders. All are responsible for a performance which shall stay within their respective areas of freedom and shall not markedly deviate from expected or established norms. Any such deviant behaviour will lead to responses by other members of the organisation designed to control its further occurrence and alleviate its consequences.[13]

13 The foregoing discussion of the elements of an organisation cannot for footnoting purposes be neatly classified into the numerous studies drawn upon. Some of the sources which will be particularly helpful are C. I. Barnard, *The Functions of the Executive* 1948, H. Fayol, *General and Industrial Management* (Trans. by Constance Storrs), 1949, L. Gulick and L. Urwick, *Papers on the Science of Administration*, 1937, J. D. Mooney, *The Principles of Organisation*, Rev. ed., 1947, H. A. Simon, *Administrative Behaviour*, 1951, L. Urwick, *Notes on the Theory of Organisation*, 1952, and M. Weber, *The Theory of Social and Economic Organisation*, 1947.

CHAPTER 2

THE INSTITUTIONALISATION OF LAW

PRIMITIVE LAW

IN the preceding chapter we distinguished three types of human behaviour, all under the term 'law.' We pointed out how the type of behaviour categorised as law in the modern State shaped our classification of data in the primitive society and even at times tended to close our eyes to relevant data. Thus some peoples cannot recognise dark blue because their only term for it is black. Or orange is brown because there is no 'orange' concept. Consequently, when we use the term which began this present section, that is, 'the institutionalisation of law,' it becomes necessary to make quite clear the several meanings implicit in this phrase.

In the first place, we are not now concerned with that form of institutionalised behaviour which we called Living Law in the preceding chapter, though perhaps not using the term with the utmost historical accuracy. Institutionalised behaviour, in the sense of repeated, predictable behaviour which the performers of complementary roles feel they have a reciprocal duty of performance and right to performance, may be regarded as a form of law in that it is socially obligatory behaviour. We are here concerned however, with the emergence in society of a set of interdependent roles in which the functions of leadership and the making of decisions as to the application of sanctions against deviant behaviour become vested.

We noted in the preceding chapter that social behaviour could be classified according to whether it involved adherence to established patterns of role performance or whether it was a product of individual determination and decision. When an individual permitted the communicated decision or order of another to supplant his own determination of behaviour, we said that such behaviour was a product of authority. We further said that organised behaviour, that is, behaviour within an organisation, was a product of leadership reinforced by authority, with the leadership function being directed to the planning and co-ordination of human activity towards reaching the common goals of the organisation. We finally pointed out that the maintenance of the organisation demanded that a certain amount of human energy be used to control deviant behaviour which markedly interfered with the attainment of group goals.

The history of the institutionalisation of the functions of leadership and control of deviant behaviour is the history of the growth of law and of the modern State.

In the family or the small group, such as the fishing team mentioned in the preceding chapter, there are some situations to which there is no automatic, institutionalised response. Whether the time is propitious for planting or fishing, where fishing shall be done and for how long, are questions which demand decision rather than a set response. Even within the small group, specific persons tend to assume the role of leadership and to make decisions which will be obeyed by the members of the group. Sometimes the culture itself designates the centre of authority in a group, as in the patrilineal joint family of Bengal in which the eldest male member is the absolute head.

In the larger tribal society there may be different heads or chiefs according to the function which they serve in the group. In Polynesia and some parts of New Guinea there is a system of dual chieftainship, with one chief being vested with sacred functions and the other being the war chief. Among the Roro peoples the function of one chief was to see that the orders of the other were obeyed. In some African societies the function of the chief is primarily religious, though the tendency to monarchical and even despotic authority is probably more characteristic of African tribal societies.[1]

Even in African society the king is no absolute autocrat. The exercise of his authority is shared to a greater or lesser degree with a group of councillors. The council is a common form of institutionalisation of authority. In the French family it survives as a restraining force upon the exercise of authority by the head of the family. In Australia the council of elders is a characteristic repository of authority. In Samoa there was a nominal ruler of the several local districts but governmental authority was largely decentralized into the district assemblies. The ruler of the

[1] W. H. Rivers, *Social Organisations* (W. J. Perry. Ed.), 1924, Ch. IX: R. H. Lowie, *Primitive Society*, 1947, pp. 369–382.

Natchez tribe in North America had a very considerable centralisation of authority yet he shared his functions with two war chiefs, two temple officials and officers regulating peace treaties and the performance of festivals.[2]

It is in the North American Plains Indian culture, however, that the separation of the functions of leadership and social control into specific roles and institutions becomes particularly marked.

The organisation of the tribe into the buffalo hunt or the war party demanded both leadership and social control of deviant behaviour. In the communal hunt or war party the situation facing the group is not stable or predictable, as in the work group. Co-ordinated action will not flow as an habitual response to a commonly recognized, familiar situation. Leadership is demanded for effective group action and consequently a new norm for conduct emerges: Obey the command of your leader.

In the Comanche war party the leadership role rested in the warrior as an individual. Any Comanche was theoretically privileged to lead a war party but followers would be attracted only if he were a warrior of proved reputation. When his group was gathered together and functioning, his command was fully authoritative. There was no known instance in which his followers failed to do what he asked.[3]

The leadership function may, however, become through repetition or institutionalisation vested not in the man but in the office. In the words of Julius Stone, power, in the sense of leadership possessing authority, becomes transpersonalised.[4] The diffuse pressures of the group, ridicule, reciprocity, physical sanctions and the like, as instruments for the control of deviant behaviour, may also in time coalesce into an office.

In the Plains Tribes the leadership function was to a considerable extent centred in the so-called military societies. Particular societies might historically be vested with this function, as in the Hidatsa and Mandan, or they might be designated to assume this role in turn, as in the Crow. The society designated held office from the spring until the first snowfall in the Crow, and

[2] R. H. Lowie, *op. cit.*, Ch. XIII.

[3] E. A. Hoebel, 'The Political Organisation and Law-Ways of the Comanche Indians,' 42 *Memoirs of the American Anthropological Association*, 1940, Supplement No. 54, pp. 23–24.

[4] J. Stone, *The Province and Function of Law*, 1950, p. 711.

also held a seasonal appointment in the Blackfoot. In others, they appear to have served rather continuously, though their control of the communal buffalo hunt was of course confined to the summer months. The tribe must act as a unit in the hunt; premature and individual hunting efforts were punished by confiscation of the offender's game, physical beating and destruction of his weapons and tent. Similarly, on war parties the police restrained parties from setting out at inopportune times, kept order while the party was in movement, guarded against surprise attacks, restrained the over-zealous, and kept the members of the party within the group.

Within the camp, the police kept order and settled disputes.[5]

'In summary,' states Provinse, 'we find that this police function was involved most frequently and most rigorously for the following purposes: (1) to regulate the communal hunt; (2) to regulate tribal ceremonies; (3) to settle disputes, punish offenders, and preserve order in camp; and (4) to regulate war parties and restrain such at inopportune times.' He adds that: 'What social intervention in the affairs of individuals is found among the Plains Tribes appears to be directed toward securing a better integration, internally and externally, of the group.'[6]

Though the societies thus had social functions integrating the tribal group, they also existed to satisfy the felt needs of their members. Wissler states that 'our informants maintained that the purpose of all these organisations was to enhance social and fraternal relations among their members.'[7]

Finally, the organisational structure of the societies themselves should be noted:

> 'Usually they were composed of an indefinite number of lay members and one or more of the following officers regularly elected from the membership ranks: leaders, pipe-keepers, lance-bearers, whip-bearers, heralds, food-passers,

[5] J. H. Provinse, 'The Underlying Sanctions of the Plains Indian Culture,' in F. Eggan (Ed.), *Social Anthropology of North American Tribes*, 1937, p. 341; R. H. Lowie, 'Military Societies of the Crow Indians,' and 'Hidatsa Men's Societies,' 11 *Anthropological Papers of the American Museum of Natural History*, 1916, pp. 147, 225; K. Llewellyn and E. A. Hoebel, *The Cheyenne Way: Conflict and Case Law in Primitive Jurisprudence*, 1941, Ch. V.

[6] J. H. Provinse, *op. cit.*, p. 351.

[7] C. Wissler, 'Societies and Ceremonial Associations in the Oglala Division of the Teton-Dakota,' 11 *Anthropological Papers of the American Museum of Natural History*, 1916, pp. 7, 64.

drummers and singers. Actual direction of the society's affairs was vested in some one of these sets of officers, usually the leaders or the pipe-keepers; police functions were performed by the whip-bearers. In the control of members and officers we find well illustrated most of the control sanctions we have already discussed for the entire community. Penal sanctions were applied for various offences against the society's regulations—failure to attend meetings, failure to participate in the dances, failure to carry out the duties of one's office. These sanctions were backed up by regular machinery, consisting for the most part of duly elected officials who punished by cutting up the culprit's blankets, by whipping, or by expulsion from the association. Other sanctions operated also: the use of ridicule, the presentation of gifts, the singing of praise songs, and informal approval or disapproval in general conversation.' [8]

Roman Law

One of the earliest forms of organisation is the collection of families related by blood known as the clan. The unifying thread of gentile relationship may at times be the tenuous one of descent from a remote or even a mythical common ancestor but it is, nevertheless, the factor commonly accepted by individuals in establishing their identification with the social system and in determining the centres of authority. The symbol or myth of the gentile tie is congruent with social fact, that is, with an interdependency of individual action in work, play and worship of the clan.

Among the Romans, as among many other peoples, the unity of the society was formally expressed through the clan or *gens*. It was through the *gens* that the structure of the State was established. The *gentes* were organised into the *curia*, the *curia* into the *tribus*, and the three *tribus* formed the State. Political and legal rights flowed from the status of being a *quiris* or a member of a *curia*, for which membership in a *gens* was essential. The entire body of the members of the *gentes* was the *populus*. Through membership in the *gens* membership in the State was achieved. Without such membership an individual was not a legal person but a thing. He was outside the law and enjoyed

[8] J. H. Provinse, *op. cit.*, p. 364.

neither political rights nor rights of property. Authority lay in the *senatus,* a council consisting of the elders of the clans, and in the king as chieftain. The latter office grew out of the position of the senior member of a clan, for each member of the ancient senate could in theory act as the king. The history of Roman law is the history of the process by which these institutions and the *jus civile* or 'law for citizens' was supplanted by institutions of imperial authority and by the *jus gentium.*

The Roman society, however, spread as towns and territories were brought within Roman power by conquest. The law of the city of Rome must be made co-extensive with the individuals brought under Roman authority. The city law of Rome was a law of a peasant community; the rigid form of the *jus strictum* was a law of a society in which commerce was lethargic and limited. That law had to be expanded to become the law of a wide-flung empire and had to be transformed in character from a *jus strictum* to the free principles of a *jus aequum.* The legal status of the *gens,* which was congruent with its social position in the formation of the early Roman State, had to be supplanted by that of the *civis* as the *gens* ceased to be a structure of social action and was supplanted by the individual engaged in the rich economic life of the expanded Roman society. New institutions for governing that society had to be found. Finally, recognition of the group itself as a person in law had to be worked out.

All this had to be done, moreover, in a spirit of free inquiry. Spiritual and magical sanctions, which had been so powerful a force in supporting the law of a primitive society, became chains throttling growth when that society matured. In the early Roman State, the king was both military chief and head priest. The *senatus* not only had political authority but it had the final decision in any matter involving religion. In the growth of the Roman State, legal institutions had to be differentiated from spiritual if law was to function effectively in a changing society.

The first task was to create a system of law which would embrace the populations of the conquered territories and enable them to have legal capacity. Coupled with this was the task of supplanting the quiritary law, whereby property was recognised only through the *gens,* with a law which would recognise the principle of separate private property. Such a transformation of the legal system became necessary as the structure of social action changed from the *gens* to that of individual free association. The first task was accomplished in a succession of steps whereby the conquered populations became *clientes* or dependents of a *gens,* then, as plebeians, became increasingly enfranchised with legal rights until the plebeian and patrician ranked as equals in law. Eventually, the *populus Romanus* ceased to be composed of the *quiris* and the citizen became the *civis.* The second task was accomplished slowly but, nevertheless, by direct attack. The separate ownership first of movables and then of land became possible. Land, the most important kind of property in primitive society, became something which was held not through the *gens* but individually. It became a *res mancipii,* something that 'could be taken with the hand.'

The system of law at first remained the *jus civile,* the law for Roman citizens. It was a law which reflected the fact that the city (*urbs*) was a dominant factor in Roman history and society. Only through the eroding force of the city was it possible for the individual to supplant the *gens* as a subject of law. Yet, the *jus civile* was still essentially a static law of a peasant community. The next task in the growth of the Roman State was to create a law for the empire in the *jus gentium.* We now turn to the institutions by which that task was accomplished.

In the Republic the ancient judicial power of the king became vested in a consul. In the early days of the Republic consuls were sometimes given the honorary title of *praetor* or general. In 367 B.C. the judicial function was separated from the consular power and the *praetor urbanus* became the official in whom the ancient judicial power was vested so far as the city was concerned. He could grant or refuse an action; or grant an action subject to conditions. The old actions of the *jus civile* (*legis actione*) were inflexible rituals which had to be meticulously followed. For example, under the Twelve Tables, a *legis actio* for injury to one's vines would fail if they were referred to as trees. The *judex,* or 'lay' judge, who heard and decided the case, was as much subject to the prescriptions of the Twelve Tables as was the *praetor.* But outside the *legis actio,* by the middle of the second century B.C., a new procedure and a new law arose which were eventually to supplant the *legis actio* and even the *jus civile* itself.

We should first understand that the *praetor* appeared in what might loosely be termed pre-trial proceedings. Functionally, however, the *praetor* was vested with a judicial role in the formulary procedure. He heard the parties, analysed the case, determined the issue in dispute, and addressed a written precept to the *judex* containing an authoritative statement of the issue in the case and the principles upon which the *judex* was to decide it. In administering the *jus civile* as between *cives,* the *praetor* could utilise this procedure subject to existing law. But he could also create new law in deciding cases as between foreigners or *peregrini* when he could decide each case on its merits. Thus, in this field, the law became secularised and freed from the dead hand of the past. The *praetor* could examine the facts of the case and recommend a decision on the merits which would enable the smooth functioning of that segment of the social process involved in the case. In 242 B.C. the *praetor peregrinus* was appointed to handle cases where one or both of the parties were foreigners or *peregrini,* the *praetor urbanus* being limited to disputes between Roman citizens. The result, so far as the general system of law was concerned, was that the *praetor urbanus,* limited to the decision of disputes involving Roman citizens was free to apply the entire body of Roman law, both the *jus civile* and the *jus gentium.* The *praetor peregrinus,* on the other hand, limited to disputes between foreigners or citizens and foreigners, was free to develop and apply the *jus gentium.* The Roman citizen could avail himself of the new *jus gentium* as well as the old *jus civile* and he could resort to the new formulary procedure as well as the old narrow *legis actio.* The validity of the formulary procedure for a *judicium* for Roman citizens was settled by the *lex Aebutia* of about 130 B.C. The two systems of law and procedure accordingly existed side by side, and in the resulting competition for survival the flexibility of the formulary procedure and the vitality and equity of the *jus gentium* prevailed.

It was not solely through the role of the *praetor* that the system of Roman law developed. Though the formulary procedure emanated from his jurisdiction, the jurists also contributed strength and order to the system. The specialisation of function which the process of institutionalisation enables was an essential instrument in the growth of Roman law. The first jurists were the *pontifices,* who acted as skilled legal advisers successively to the king, the consul and the *praetor*. In the early days of the State they were also the repositories of knowledge concerning the *jus sacrum* and the science of astronomy. But their chief role eventually came to be one of consultants on the formulae of *legis actiones* and juristic acts. They were masters of both the letter and the spirit of the law, their mastery of form being subordinated to function. The growth of the science of law was at first confined to the college of *pontifices*. Their precedents or legal opinions (*responsa*) were kept in the college and became the means of instructing new members and developing law as a science. This science of the law was at first reserved to the patricians, from whom the *pontifices* were drawn, but Tiberius Coruncanias about 254 B.C. opened this knowledge to all when, as the first plebeian *pontifex maximus,* he announced his readiness to give answers on legal questions to any one. About fifty years before, Flavius had published the *legis actiones* in the form which the *pontifices* had given them. About 100 B.C. Scaevola, *pontifex maximus,* published his great treatise on the *jus civile* in eighteen books. The science of law was no longer a secret monopoly of the college of *pontifices*. The stage was now set for the entry of jurists other than the *pontifices*.

With the spread of juristic knowledge, by the end of the Republic, it became the practice for jurists other than members of the college of *pontifices* to give *responsa* or opinions on legal questions. Not being members of the college, their *responsa* were not binding on the *judex*. It became necessary to make this *de facto* practice one which was also *de jure*. Emperor Augustus ordered that all *responsa* should be given *ex auctoritate ejus* or with the sanction of the emperor. Thereafter, the *jus respondendi* was vested in certain distinguished jurists and their opinions became binding on the judge. Out of the collections of the *responsa* grew a juristic literature culminating in the writings of Salvius Julianus, who consolidated the edict law of the *praetors* in the *Edictum Hadrianum* of Emperor Hadrian and who expounded the whole body of the Roman law in his great Digest of ninety books. The *jus* of the earlier days ceased to be readily accessible and the writings of jurists became the source of law. Eventually, imperial authority codified the law from all its sources in the great Justinian Code of A.D. 529.

Authority cannot exist without obedience, law cannot exist

without subjects. It still remained necessary to bring within the Roman state those who had become subject to its *jus gentium*. The practice grew of granting the Roman *civitas* to whole communities. In A.D. 212 the Emperor Caracalla conferred the *civitas* on every community within the Empire. Rome became an empire with one emperor, one law and one citizenry; there was a unity of law and social interdependency.

The law which we have been describing was a law which grew by accretion through the developing judicial institutions of the Roman State. Legislation, similarly, eventually became a function of imperial authority. A *lex* was originally in the nature of a covenant, it was something which was 'settled' or 'laid down,' proposed by one party to another in a certain form and accepted by the latter. The *lex publica* was a statute which was proposed by the magistrate and accepted by the people, which became binding by virtue of its reciprocal declarations. In the days of the Republic the *senatus* could only interpret laws and could not originate them. With the establishment of the Empire, however, the emperor could originate a decree of the senate or *senatusconsulta* through a motion or *oratio*. With the passage of time the senate's consent to the *oratio* became a mere matter of form and authority lay in the *oratio* instead of the *senatusconsultum*. The *oratio* then became an *edictum* or *lex generalis* promulgated directly by the emperor to the State. The legislative function of the imperial office became distinguished from its judicial role. 'The principle established itself that only what had been weighed in its bearings on the national interests as a whole should have the force of law binding on the whole nation. The course of legislation was to be determined, not by the accidental requirements of single cases, but the general requirements of the empire.' [9]

The essential pattern of the modern State thus appeared. Authority became both structure and function, characterised by relation and purpose. Its exercise became not personal and arbitrary but institutionalised and predictable. The legislative process became fixed in the office of the emperor and its exercise became directed to public purpose. The judicial process became vested in a specialised personnel. Both offices became subject to

[9] R. Sohm, *The Institutes* (3d Ed.), 1907, p. 113.

constitutional norms for conduct. Authority, wherever found, was a relation between superior and subordinate characterised by public purpose. The system of authority in the State became coextensive with the society. The society, however, was not a society of atomistic individuals. The individual did not alone take the place of the *gens* in the structure of social action. It is only a half-truth to say that 'The Clan and the Household are social groups; the State is a collection of individuals.'[10] The State was also in part a collection of groups. For new forms of group action other than the *gens* developed as Roman society expanded. Somehow, the law must include within its control the activities of these groups. The step is accomplished by a legal fiction. The collectivity becomes a legal, a juristic person. It is treated as if it were a person and its exercise of authority thereby becomes the exercise of legal authority. The *collegia*, *sodalities* and *universitates* attained the capacity to acquire and hold property. The *municipium* or town community acquired a legal personality and was endowed with legal rights and duties. Finally, the Roman State itself, in the form of the *fiscus*, acquired juristic personality. 'The collective person, the organised body capable of rights and liabilities, is quite a different person, a juristic person, a third person, over and above the natural persons who are its members.'[11]

To return to the proposition that 'the State is a collection of individuals' which we questioned above, we now see the State as comprising a system of relationships not only between the government and individuals, but also embracing relationships between the government and corporate groups. By allocating rights as well as duties to the corporate group and reinforcing the latter's system of authority with the right of property, the authority system of the corporation enters into the authority structure of the State.[12]

10 E. Jenks, *Law and Politics in the Middle Ages*, 1919, p. 163.
11 R. Sohm, *op. cit.*, p. 191.
12 *ibid.*, pp. 186–203; O. Gierke, *Das Deutsche Genossenschaftsrecht*, 1881, Vol. 3, Secs. 4, 6. See generally on the history of Roman law, in addition to R. Sohm, *op. cit.*, the following: W. W. Buckland, *A Text Book of Roman Law from Augustus to Justinian*, 1932; H. F. Jolowicz, *Historical Introduction to the Study of Roman Law*, 1952, H. S. Maine, *Ancient Law*, 1907; F. R. Cowell, *Cicero and the Roman Republic*, 1948.

Feudal Law

At first in northern Europe, and then entering even into the ancient imperial territory of Rome itself, the Teutonic tribes wandered and conquered. Their very names are pregnant with meaning. The 'Frank' was a warrior, the 'Saxon' was a swordsman, the 'Alamann' was a stranger, an invader. They tilled the soil and then moved on. Caesar refers to the annual reallotment of lands among families and clans of the Germans. Later the wandering ceased, the agriculture became intensive instead of extensive.[13] Tacitus describes a shifting from one ploughland to another; the land lies fallow in the meantime. The homeland of the hundred now sees the appearance of village life. In addition to the warrior, the farmer and the serf appeared. The warrior still remained to protect the society from incursion and conquest. Out of these occupations, fighting, farming, and working the ground, together with that of the priest, feudal society and the feudal State emerged.

The authority structure of the tribe was at first one of family and clan. The largest organisation was that of the league of clans headed by a war chief or king. The conquest and settling of strange lands, the defence against invading heathen, demanded a leader in war. But the source of the authority of the war chief was not the blood tie, he was elected. Nor were his principal followers selected by blood; skill in war and devotion to their chief determined their selection. At the same time, the homes of the Teutons became fixed, village life emerged, and the assembly of free men became the political unit. The booty of war in conquered lands was held by the king and distributed among his followers. Each such *beneficium feodum* tended to become a separate political unit. The authority relation therein was one of lord and man or lord and vassal. The man swore homage or fealty to his lord. The *Libri Feudorum* defined the obligations of the man in some detail; he must secure his lord from harm, maintain secret his private concerns, preserve his possessions from injury, and not hinder the obtaining of any advantage by him. The lord engaged to defend and maintain the man. The tie between the two was the most binding of all and its breach an act of 'unfaith' that destroyed the relationship.

Land was held by virtue of this relationship, the man was a

[13] E. Jenks, *op. cit.*, pp. 152–153.

tenant of his lord and held his lands in tenure. Eventually the free man who had no lord commended himself to some lord for protection and all land was held in feudal tenure.

The lord had his court where he administered justice, the profits of which he pocketed. Attendance at the court and military service, at first rendered by the free man who held land because he was free, were rendered the lord by the free man who, in feudal times, was free because he held land. The man was a part of the lord's armed forces and a suitor at his court because he was the lord's tenant. This relationship between lord and man has been called contractual by legal historians, probably because of the voluntary aspects of the ceremony attending its creation. But it was more than contractual, it was a role-relationship of the most binding and deeply felt kind.

Each lord had his own domains and also had certain rights of military service and attendance at his court as against his tenants thereon. The resulting system of authority was coextensive with the society—the *feodum* or fief. Each lord could by his *ban* summon his tenants to war but could not so summon *their* tenants. He had to rely on the exercise of their *ban* to bring their followers to his host. The lord had the *ban* but not the *arrière-ban*; not even the king had the *arrière-ban*.[14] Nor could the king legislate for the under-tenants of his lords. The king and his vassals would meet in the king's court where the vassals might by oath agree to legislate for *their* tenants. At this stage the king's authority did not directly extend to all members of the feudal state.

The organisation of feudal society was thus a relatively simple one. While skills had proliferated in the specialised roles of the warrior class, craftsman and tradesman, the lord and his court was the focus of authority and the king's authority was that of a lord.

English Law

The development of the system of feudal law to that of a modern State can perhaps best be told by way of the story of the growth of English legal institutions, with occasional glances at corresponding institutional growth on the continent. The task, as in the case of the Roman State, was to transform a system of

[14] *ibid.*, p. 83.

law based on an agricultural society to that of a mercantile and industrial society, and to make the structure of authority of the State coextensive with the life of the national society. The tributaries that finally flowed into the majestic stream of the common law were many: courts of the county, courts of the church, courts of the merchant's guilds as well as courts of the king. All eventually were brought into a single system declaring the common law of the realm. The king's peace and the king's law spread through the land as society changed from a feudal to a commercial structure. The king spoke in his curia, in his council and finally in the Parliament of the three estates of King, Lords and Commons.

The Anglo-Saxon kingship found England in the formative stages of feudalism. The kin relationship and the lord-man relationship existed side by side. The latter had not yet become attached to the land. A man could 'go with his land' and commend himself to another lord. He could alienate his land without breach of his feudal faith. But more and more the structure of legal authority came to recognise the social fact of dependency on the land. The land was for administrative and law enforcement purposes divided into shires, the shires into hundreds and each became the situs of a court. The king appointed the shire reeves or sheriffs and they were responsible to him. The king could levy the national taxes, and their collection was not farmed out and made a source of private gain as in France. The king was aided by administrative officials, such as his Chancellor, and a secretariat of clerks. A treasury office existed. The king could render justice, sit as a court, and protect against robbery and wrongs.

The Norman Conquest brought to the kingship of England not only a successor to the Anglo-Saxon crown but a conqueror. This fact was to have profound consequences in enabling the centralisation of authority and the creation of a modern State long in advance of the continent.

The king had his council, his *curia regis*. It appeared in two forms, but the forms were without consequence as to authority; each had equal authority, for they were but different forms of the same institution. One form was the great *curia regis*, later termed the *magnum concilium*, called into meeting only occasionally, and was composed of the tenants-in-chief, the principal officers of State and the members of the king's household. The other form was the small *curia regis,* which was composed of those tenants-in-chief who were in attendance on the king or then at court, together with the king's officers. The latter was always in session and from it, as from a fissiparous organism, the royal courts, fiscal and administrative agencies were created. In this sense a meeting of the council comprised a meeting of the King's Bench, the Common Bench, the Exchequer, the Chancery, the War Office and the Wardens of the Marches. By the beginning of the fourteenth century we have an assembly in which the members of the council were joined by the remaining tenants-in-chief, citizens and burgesses. This meeting of the three estates of the realm was Parliament and this body handled, among other things, legislation, taxation, audience of petitions, and judicial business.

The first step in the unification of England following the conquest took place in the historic oath at Sarum in 1086. As the Anglo-Saxon chronicle put it, King William summoned 'all the landowning men of property there were over all England, *whosoever men they were,*'[15] and made them swear oaths of fealty to him over all other men. The king's authority now ran directly to all men and not indirectly through the various levels of sub-infeudation. He could summon to his army not only his tenants-in-chief but their vassals as well. He had the *arrière-ban* as well as the *ban.* The analogue of the *civitas* of Rome appeared.

The next step was to make that authority manifest in the ways of peace as well as of war and to establish a unified system of legal institutions and a common law throughout England. The paths to the accomplishment of this step were many—the constitution of the king's courts, the development therein of secular instead of magical modes of proof; the search in all courts for a common law based on the 'custom' of the realm; the solution of the problem of growth of the law to fit a changing society not only through the concept of a common law for the whole of England but a law of equity which would reflect the king's conscience and mercy; the expansion of the king's justice into the local districts and local courts; the growth of the concept of the king's peace to establish order throughout all England

[15] *ibid.*, p. 93.

and to protect men not only against violence but against negligent and other injury; the use of the king's writ or command by his Chancellor and by Parliament to provide new legal remedies which would solve multiplying problems in deviant behaviour as the character of society changed and as its interdependency spread from the manor to the breadth of the kingdom and, finally, overseas; the development of legislative as well as judicial institutions and the recognition in law of the new form of corporate organisation which became the source of strength of an industrial England. We can speak only briefly of some of these.

The roots of the king's peace are deep in history. Each man had his *mund,* his peace. An interference with his *mund* was a *mund-bryce,* a breach of *mund. Mund* and *frith* were separate aspects of the same relationship, the relationship of a man to his household and the persons and things under his control. A taking of or injury to his wife, children, slaves or cattle was a *mund-bryce,* a disturbance in his house a *frith-bryce.* From the standpoint of the individual, here is the source of the modern complex concept of *property.* From the standpoint of the king, here is a well-spring of law itself. For the king too had his *mund* or peace and for breaches of that peace the subject could seek justice of his king; the king could hear the pleas of his subjects to the crown. The king's peace was at first personal, but towards the close of the thirteenth century the peace of the king became the peace of the kingdom when on the death of Henry III there was proclaimed the peace of the absent Edward. The pleas of the crown were many; premeditated assault, robbery, theft punishable with death, murder, rape, street breach, treason, default of justice were but some of the pleas listed in *Leges Henrici Primi.* But we subtly shift from the criminal to the civil law when any wrongful use of force, however slight, became a trespass *vi et armis et contra pacem domini Regis.* Finally, through the writs of trespass and other writs emanating from the Chancellor, we have the procuring of control over all litigation by the crown, though the proliferation of writs becomes subject to the control of Parliament. In the reign of Henry II it was proclaimed that no man need answer for his freehold without a royal writ. The ownership of land itself, the most important form of all property, came under the control of king.

The judicial functions of the *curia regis* split into the King's Bench, the Common Bench or Court of Common Pleas, the Exchequer and, eventually, Chancery. This is not the place to enter into the niceties of their respective jurisdictions, but the King's Bench was a court held theoretically before the king himself and having jurisdiction over criminal matters and trespass, that mother of actions; the Common Bench was the court for disputes between subjects and also cases of trespass; Exchequer was at first a court for matters concerning the royal revenue, but under the rivalry of the courts for jurisdiction it later entered into the work of the other two courts, while eventually Chancery emerged and, in its sphere of equity, even prevailed over the courts of the common law.

We turn now to that historic term, the common law. The king's courts and, indeed, all courts of the land as they were brought within the royal system of justice, sought for the answer to cases brought before them in the 'custom' of the realm. This was not the narrow, rigid custom of a particular locality but, as Glanvill put it, custom 'founded on reason.' Here we have the element of free inquiry, present in the Roman law in the growth of the *jus gentium*, which is essential to the growth of a law which will be closely integrated with the ways of life of a changing society. With this vital principle established for the decision of cases and with the new modes of proof by witness instead of compurgation and ordeal, with the use of the jury, with resort to equity as the grooves of the common law became ruts for decision, with the development of established norms for decisions by judges through the principle of precedent, we reach the judicial institutions and judge-made law of the modern state.

We have already spoken of the emergence of Parliament as the law-creating or legislative body, drawn from the principal elements of the national society, the three estates. Its enactments at first reflected in their form the forces that created them, the charter reflecting a grant or conveyance from the king out of his prerogative, the assize, the provision, the ordinance reflecting more of the principle of consensus or agreement, and finally the statute reflecting petitions emanating from the whole commons to the king, containing, by the fifteenth century, the exact terms of the legislation to be enacted and leaving no choice other than that of accepting or refusing the bill as a whole. Eventually, even that choice disappeared and the king must proclaim the bills of Parliament.[16]

One other significant task remained, that of recognising in law the economic organisation which supplanted the *feodum* as the central unit of social structure as society changed from a feudal to an industrial one. Here, as always, the social fact emerges and has to be dealt with by law. In the Middle Ages it was the town, the guild, the church, the monastery, the convent, which were the forms which group life took. The town and the merchants' guilds developed their own laws and courts. All accumulated property and power. The property thus held was withdrawn from feudal levy and thereby represented a loss to the royal treasury. The power of the towns and the guilds represented isolated islands around which royal power and the common law had to flow. The royal weapon in the resulting struggle for supremacy was the writ of *quo warranto* and the means of regulation the royal charter. A vigorous use of the writ searched out those who claimed office, franchise or liberty and required proof of their warrant thereof. The charter at first recognised only a *communitas*, an aggregate body but not a corporate body, but by 1445 Henry VI's charter to the borough of Southampton recognised that 'the town shall be for ever incorporate . . . and . . . shall be one perpetual community, incorporate in word and deed . . . and shall have perpetual succession . . . and that they may plead and be impleaded' and acquire and hold property.[17] The writ and the charter together meant that such powerful groups as these could not exist without royal franchise, that the group was *un corps* or a body and that only the king could create such a body. But this last statement was only the major premise for a number of minor premises that had to be drawn in a multitude of cases before the modern concept of the corporation and its status in law could be worked out. Two landmarks in this history may briefly be noted. Lord Coke's decision

[16] See generally on the history of feudal and English law, C. K. Allen, *Law in the Making*, 1946; A. T. Carter, *A History of English Legal Institutions*, 1910; E. Jenks, *op. cit.*, and *A Short History of English Law*, 1912; W. S. Holdsworth, *A History of English Law*, 1922–1938, 12 Vols.; F. W. Maitland, *The Constitutional History of England*, 1909.

[17] Quoted in J. Goebel, *Cases and Materials on the Development of Legal Institutions*, 1946, p. 342 at p. 343.

in the *Case of Sutton's Hospital*[18] dealt with letters patent by James I to one Thomas Sutton granting a licence for the founding of a hospital. The grant, among other things, provided that the said Sutton, the governors and their successors, *etc.*, 'should be incorporated, and have perpetual succession and be one body corporate and politic.' Lord Coke pointed out that 'the incorporation ought of necessity to precede the execution of the licence' and concluded that there were certain essential requisites to the creation of a corporation, namely, lawful authority of incorporation, as by charter from the king or parliament, the persons to be incorporated, a name and a place. When duly created, the incidents of corporate status necessarily and impliedly attached, such as the right to sue and be sued and to acquire property. The second landmark was the change of corporate structure itself from that of a joint venture to that of a joint stock company with the charter of 1661 by Charles I to the British East India Company.[19]

The consequences of the recognition in law of the form of economic organisation known as the corporation will be elaborated later herein, and will indeed become one of the central elements of our inquiry. We now turn to a more detailed investigation of the modern State, the national and the world society and the place of the corporate organisation therein. What we have so far said is essential to the carrying out of that investigation.

18 10 Coke 23a (10 Jac. 1).

19 See generally J. Goebel, *op. cit.*, Ch. 3 for an excellent collection of materials; H. J. Laski, 'The Personality of Associations,' 29 *Harvard Law Review*, 1915, p. 404 and 'The Early History of The Corporation in England,' 30 *ibid.*, 1916, p. 561; F. W. Maitland, 'The Corporation Sole,' 16 *Law Quarterly Review*, 1900, p. 335; J. Dewey, 'The Historical Background of Corporate Legal Personality,' 35 *Yale Law Journal*, 1926, p. 655; O. Gierke, *Political Theories of the Middle Age* (Trans. by F. W. Maitland), 1900, including Introduction by F. W. Maitland; F. W. Maitland, 'Trust and Corporation,' 3 *Collected Papers*, 1911, p. 321. On the corporation in Roman law see also W. W. Buckland, *op. cit.*, pp. 173–179; M. Radin, *Handbook of Roman Law*, 1927, pp. 266–270.

Chapter 3

LAW IN THE MODERN STATE AND SOCIETY

The State as a Concept

If the scientific method be one in which facts are observed, classified, regularities in sequence determined, systematised, postulates and systems of postulates constructed, laws explaining the largest possible relationship between facts formulated, all on a constantly increasing scale of abstraction, the total system constantly expanding and being tested as to validity by verification of deductions drawn from the system, we find little of the scientific method in the approach of the political philosopher. Concepts such as 'State,' 'society,' 'force,' 'sovereignty,' 'will,' are erected without the preliminary step-by-step discipline of determining their factual bases and ingredients. Abstract concepts are made the beginning rather than the end of a system of observations and conclusions. Concepts once adopted are not rigorously adhered to. 'State' in usage becomes identified with 'government,' though it is a fundamental axiom of political theory that they are separate concepts. 'Power' becomes equated with the energy-potential of a system on the one hand, and with 'social force' or 'social power' on the other hand. 'Authority' becomes equated with 'social power' or *sub nomine* 'decision-making' becomes simply 'power.' Hypotheses and concepts are constructed without verification and even sometimes in the face of the world of facts—the 'State' as 'organism' or possessing 'personality' and 'will,' 'corporate personality' and 'corporate will,' are some products of the conceptualistic approach of the political theorist and classical jurisprudent. The political scientist no less than the natural scientist needs abstractions, but the abstractions of the latter, such as 'mass' and 'energy,' are abstractions which synthesise knowledge based on data and their classification. The scientific method is circular, the building up of systems of postulates by inductive methods and their verification and expansion through the testing of deductive propositions. The field of political theory tends to be one in which the postulate is a hypothesis based on primitive and inadequate data and the system of postulates is based on logical deduction and little more.

We must now turn to the terminology and concepts of the traditional discipline concerned with the nature of the State—political philosophy. A useful study for this purpose, written before the current development of the behaviourist school in political science and before the current critical re-evaluation of assumptions and methodology among political scientists—though one must not forget such early contributions as those of Arthur Bentley—is Harold Laski's *The State in Theory and Practice,* published in 1935 and, in particular, its first chapter entitled 'The Philosophic Conception of the State.' Laski, in his early days particularly, made some notable contributions to the growth of political science and the chapter in question is a restatement of traditional political theory as well as a statement of his own viewpoint in that connection. Hence its usefulness for our purpose.

He starts with definitions. A 'society' is 'a group of human beings living together and working together for the satisfaction of their mutual wants.' The term would fit a family, a community, an organisation, almost any social group. The careful and intensive studies of sociologists to define the basic elements of this concept are largely ignored. A 'State' is 'a society of this kind which is integrated by possessing a coercive authority legally supreme over any individual or group which is part of society.' The definition is no longer primarily behaviouristic, the distinguishing characteristic is the internal element or ingredient of 'a coercive authority legally supreme.' The unit is described not by its physical characteristics but by a philosophic assumption. This 'coercive authority' is explained as 'sovereignty.' 'It is by the possession of sovereignty that the State is to be distinguished from all other forms of human association.' So we must look for a group which has within it something which is 'a coercive authority legally supreme.' We will be able to recognise that something when we find it because it will be 'sovereignty.' We must be careful not to be misled when looking for 'sovereignty' because we may instead find 'government' (a new term). 'Government' is not 'sovereignty' because it is not 'supreme.' It is, moreover, all-pervading. 'A municipality is a territorial society divided into government and subjects; so, also, may be a trade union or a church.' We must, therefore, look elsewhere than 'government' for 'sovereignty.'

The State has a 'will' and 'its will is formally, an unchallengeable will, since, otherwise, it could not be supreme'—a result which would of course be fatal to the system of discourse. 'Supremacy' now means 'unchallengeability,' an equivalent rather than a descriptive term. 'The State is supreme . . . because it is formally competent to bind . . . to obedience without itself being bound.' It is characterised by 'the formal legal right . . . to exact and enforce obedience to its orders.'

We need to know a great deal more than we do so far about 'will' and 'legal supremacy' and 'sovereignty.' Somewhere we must find persons who can exercise this 'will of the State' and who possess 'legal supremacy' and exercise 'supreme coercive authority.' When we use these terms we must be able to define behaviouristically what these persons do and what relations they establish with others. Unless we can find 'a body of men who operate in its name the supreme coercive authority of which it disposes' we cannot have a 'State.' 'This body of men is what we term the government of the State.' Yet 'sovereignty' does not lie in 'government,' for 'we must distinguish sharply between State and government. The latter . . . is not itself supreme coercive power; it is simply the mechanism of administration which gives effect to the purposes of that power.' So once again we are left adrift, 'State' and 'sovereignty' cannot be found in the conduct of man.

To recapitulate, the State's will is unchallengeable 'since, otherwise, it could not be supreme.' The State has 'supreme coercive power' but never any body of individuals, for we cannot tolerate the thought of any government composed of men possessing such unlimited power. The power of the government is always limited by the 'constitution.' This 'supreme coercive power' thus becomes a mythical concept identifying a mythical entity. 'It is a power outside and above that of the people as a whole.' For this power to become manifest the 'state' must 'have at its command coercive instruments, separate from the mass of the population, upon whom it can rely to enforce its authority.' The social facts are that when, in a modern national society, armed attack by forces occurs either within or outside the territorial boundaries of the State, certain officials will make certain decisions. As a result of their exercise of the authority vested in their offices, military forces under their authority will use power or energy to repress that attack. This is observable, repeatable, predictable behaviour. But for the political philosopher the explanation is that 'the will of the government' is no longer 'unchallenged' and 'is in danger' and the counter-resort to force by the government is necessary in order that 'the will of the government may prevail.' The niceties of the formal structure of the philosophy must be preserved at all costs, including that of resort to circular reasoning.

With such an introduction to the basic elements of this philosophy, it is not surprising that Laski should confess that 'the relation between the State and law . . . is not a simple one.' The conceptualistic approach is frankly acknowledged. 'Once we accept the idea of the State as sovereign, law can be no other thing than the will of the State.' Once we personify the State, attribute to it the possession of 'will' and 'supreme coercive power,' the logical deduction is that 'law' is its 'will.' The natural scientist might question the logical deduction, and, if it could not be verified factually, question the system of postulates from which it was drawn. If a logical deduction fails to be verified by experimental proof, a considerable recasting of the system of postulates is usually the eventual outcome.[1]

'Supreme coercive authority' has never alone held together any State. The more closely coercion approaches supremacy the less secure the system of authority. When Louis XIV boasted '*L'État, c'est moi,*' the fact was that France was one of the most disunited and disorganised of countries. It has been well said that: 'One may well interpret the French revolution of 1789 not as a reaction to the monarch's misuse of his absolute powers, but rather to his failure to use them.'[2] That is to say, the use of governmental power was directed to support a social equilibrium not corresponding to the true power in society of the respective social groups.[3] When the energy potential of a society is diverted to force as the primary means for preserving social cohesion, the outcome is eventually disintegration. Neither a

[1] H. J. Laski, *The State in Theory and Practice,* 1935, Ch. 1.
[2] F. L. Neumann, 'The Concept of Political Freedom,' 53 *Columbia Law Review* (1953), p. 901 at p. 923.
[3] B. Adams, *The Theory of Social Revolutions,* 1913, Ch. 4.

Stalin nor a Bulganin could make his system of values prevail over that of the peasant and the consumer through coercion alone. The 'political man' governed by force is as unreal a concept as that of the 'economic man' governed solely by economic wants or the profit motive.

An attempt to go behind the traditional façade of concepts to the fundamental aspects of social action, using for this purpose a case study of the legislative process in action, was recently made by Earl Latham in *The Group Basis of Politics,* 1952. His first chapter is significantly entitled 'Group Conflict and the Political Process.' The 'State' is there seen to be an association resembling 'other associations like churches and trade unions.' The resemblance is found in 'the common factor of power.' They are both 'structures of power because they concentrate human wit, energy, and muscle for the achievement of given purposes.' 'The State and other group forms represent power in different packages.' The 'instrumentalities' of the State 'are themselves groups.' So the concept still persists that the 'State' is something else than its 'instrumentalities.' Government becomes 'groups' which are 'instruments.' The definition of the 'State' is that it is an 'association' which represents 'the consensus by which the groups [of society?] exist in mutual relations.' This association 'establishes the norms of permissible behaviour in group relationships and enforces these norms.' It is not made clear what this 'association' itself is, other than that it is composed of 'apparatus' or 'instrumentalities' and that such apparatus or instrumentalities lay down and enforce norms for permissible behaviour. (One might incidentally question why permissible behaviour would need to be enforced.) The 'groups' comprising 'the instrumentalities of the State' are to be distinguished from other groups by 'the characteristic of officiality,' which seems to be a term equivalent to Max Weber's 'legitimacy.'[4]

Both Laski and Latham seek to describe, classify, and systematise phenomena. Laski deals with the phenomenon of force and its institutionalisation; otherwise his domain of discourse is largely one of *a priori* assumptions. Latham concerns himself with the central fact that modern society is

[4] M. Weber, *The Theory of Social and Economic Organisation,* 1947, pp. 130, 324.

largely organised in groups, notes that governmental structure is group structure, identifies governmental structure by the characteristic of 'officiality,' and makes government an instrument for resolving group conflict. The concept 'State' is still not developed except as it becomes manifest in governmental groups.

Yet Latham's approach breaks free of the logical impasse of circular reasoning in which Laski was imprisoned. Latham's definition starts, as all definitions must start, with a viewpoint external to the subject to be defined and each new element introduced in his definition is identifiable by external criteria. His definition, rephrased, might be said to be: A State is a society largely composed of groups of individuals, some of whom are known as the government. The latter is to be identified as groups possessing 'officiality.' The definition further avoids the conceptual difficulties of endeavouring to integrate structure and process, form and flow, position and speed, into a single unit.

Though the question may be raised whether all that has been accomplished is, in last analysis, merely to pour old wine into new bottles—'State' becomes 'government' and 'government' becomes 'groups,' the course of reasoning was one seeking to arrive at more meaningful and usable concepts than we now have.

The definition of the State noted in Chapter 1 [5] could be briefly summarised in the terminology of everyday discourse as including government, governed and boundary. Obviously both government and governed overlap the boundary. The United States government has thousands of officials abroad and there is also a very considerable number of individuals engaged in trade, transport, communication and travel, not to mention the armed forces located abroad. But we like to see pretty coloured compartments on a map and the resulting picture is tidy even if the constant scurrying of individuals across borders may destroy that tidiness when we turn from maps in books to people in life.

Of course, the concept 'boundary' concerns social facts. Officials perform various acts at a boundary. If we take an extra carton of cigarettes across a boundary, we may find it confiscated. If a division of soldiers marches across a boundary without a prescribed preliminary ritual having first been performed by quite a number of officials, the response may be war. The con-

[5] Ch. 1, n. 15, p. 17.

cept of 'boundary' is an operative fact affecting the decision-making of a great many officials, both administrative and judicial.

Then there is the function of 'boundary' in the process of negotiation. As *between States,* the settling of their differences, the working out of their day-to-day relations through diplomacy, requires at least a formal equality of bargaining power. The parties must be equal and, for purposes of negotiation, must come to the conference table as 'sovereign' within their respective territories, that is to say, equally free to do as they wish therein save only for the rules of international law. Thus, in the recent dispute between Great Britain and Iran involving the nationalisation by the latter of the properties of the Anglo-Iranian Oil Company, Great Britain strove mightily to place the dispute in the international forum of the Security Council and the International Court of Justice, where negotiation and adjudication would be between equals possessing equal rights and each equally entitled to consideration, while Iran strove just as determinedly to place the question in the sphere of its domestic jurisdiction where it was 'sovereign.'

There is still another purpose served by the concept of 'boundary.' It serves to identify the particular set of political institutions in which we find the 'government' of the national State. And here we must place ourselves for a few moments in the role of the political theorist. 'Government' was for him a temporal phenomenon because it was identified by its 'constitutional' configuration. 'State' could not be equated with 'government' because when governments fail the 'State' would then disappear. Yet behaviouristically, historically, when a government was overthrown the governed in due course transferred their habits of obedience to new repositories of authority. To restate the course of thinking, a boundary characterised a territorial society, a territorial society was governed by a government, governments might rise and fall but they still persisted in the territorial society, from which the conclusion was drawn that the 'State' was composed of all these elements save only that it existed separately and apart from the 'government' and that the latter was the 'agent' of the former. The 'State' was to be found within the 'boundary' and existed so long as the 'boundary,' in the course of the shifting political fortunes of the 'State,' remained substantially unchanged. When a substantial change in the 'boundary' occurred, much legal learning developed concerning the 'succession of States.' The 'state' was thus a composite of government and governed within a defined territory—all tangible and concrete elements—and was in addition 'sovereign'—something intangible and to be identified only as *summa potestas,* supreme power. When the natural scientist discovered that his concept of the phlogiston did not square with observable facts, it was discarded as a fiction and postulates were substituted in its place which did square with the facts. But the myth of 'sovereignty' as an element of the 'State' still persists.

The term 'political institutions' of the government, as used at the beginning of the preceding paragraph, includes those persons whose commands and decisions enjoy *legitimacy,* with legitimacy being defined as being both formal, *i.e.,* in accordance with prescribed forms and ritual, and a product of *belief* on the part of those to whom such commands and decisions are addressed. For our purposes we can usefully still employ the term 'government' to describe such persons. But government does not function in isolation, the commands of the executive are shaped by a vast administrative machinery and the carrying out of executive decisions are the tasks of huge organisations. Judicial bodies are all-pervading and are found within the administrative sphere as well as in isolation from it. Judicial bodies are in their turn supported by numerous institutions, lawyers, clerks, bailiffs, sheriffs, *etc.* The legislature may in its turn be formally autonomous but it is in fact shaped in its decision making by many institutions, such as the continual pressures of interest groups.

We are now finally in a position to suggest a definition for the term 'State.' Taking our cue from Max Weber, it is to be defined from the point of view of the existence and acceptance of authority, namely, the authority of political institutions believed to be legitimate. The 'State' accordingly comprises (1) all those persons who are habitually influenced in their conduct by belief in the legitimacy of relevant decisions and commands emanating from (2) other persons in carrying out the requirements of their respective roles as members of a territorially identified government, including decisions as to sanctions to be applied in case of behaviour determined to be deviant.

The implications of this definition are that: (1) Instead of a static definition based on a collection of elements, that is, government, society, territory, plus the additional concept of independence, we have a relational concept. (2) The conduct in which the State is eventually manifested is not merely the conduct of a collection of abstract units called citizens, nationals or subjects, it is the conduct found in the vast variety of the roles present in modern society. (3) Since the greater part of the social roles of a modern society spring from its organisational life (by organisational life we do not limit ourselves to the private corporation but rather the universal social structure we have called the organisation), the State becomes that aggregate of power brought about by all the life of a society dependent upon the functioning of its political institutions. (4) The authority of these political institutions, their ability to influence conduct, is a product of the relation of such institutions to the governed. It is an authority which rests upon its acceptance by those under it as well as the force which it can bring to bear upon those whose behaviour is injuriously deviant. Government, being a product of its acceptance by the governed, exists for so long as that acceptance exists. Thus we avoid the conceptual difficulties of defining government by its constitutional law and at the same time base our definition on observable phenomena. (5) A particular government, and hence State, is identified by its relation to a territory. It is not circumscribed by a territory, it is related to a territory. Thus the definition enables the term 'State' still to be equated with the term 'nation,' in which we have the phenomenon of identification by the governed with the nation through 'nationality,' the resulting social drive with all its implications being known as 'nationalism.' The definition enables us to point to the State as a factor involved in relations with other governments and societies also territorially identified. The definition is still congruent with usage in such situations and enables us still to deal with such situations conceptually. We can, for instance, still grapple with problems of State succession. Yet the definition avoids placing ourselves inextricably behind and within the boundaries of the State and enables us to accommodate the phenomena of acceptance of governmental authority beyond State boundaries. (6) By identifying government by its relation to a territory instead of a constitution, the State can still persist and still be identified notwithstanding the overthrow of a government. And that overthrow, in turn, is not a matter of constitutional forms but a matter of human behaviour, the acceptance of authority.

Of course, we should realise the significance of this step. We have, in effect, committed ourselves to a strategy and that fact is going to influence all our subsequent thinking and methodology. We have not sought to describe the State as structure, as arrested motion, in terms of static universals. We have instead chosen the approach of flow, of relations, of a system of on-going relations. We can identify points in that system and describe their location in static terms, if we wish. (As the social psychologist calls role *status*, for example.) But our further exploration must now be in terms of flow and relation.

With such a definition we can first accommodate ourselves to the fact that the law enters into all social relations as the reinforcing element, as 'the leading string, golden and holy' of Plato. We can also accommodate Latham's observation (and what now seems to be a generally accepted fact) that these relations are largely structured into group relations. We can classify these group relations, in turn, into intra-group and inter-group relations. We can examine the problems of group identification and loyalty, the intensification of group values in their members, the problems of multiple-group membership and resulting conflict, and many other problems which are today the central task of government, notably in the labour and trade union field. We can in this setting then classify the relevant law-norms as fiction or fact, and determine the extent to which they are related to the real social problems and forces involved.

The Democratic State

With the application of the adjective 'democratic' to the concept 'State' there is erected a species in the genus. Another species currently referred to is the 'Communist State.'

We should first appreciate that in each case we are concerned with people living and working together, we are concerned with whether or not in so doing they accept the authority of a territorially identified government, and we are finally concerned with the manner in which the government functions and that acceptance is brought about. It is this last question to which we shall now address ourselves.

We previously defined 'democracy' (in pages 15 to 16) as a factor of the participation by a member of a group, who is part of an authority-relation as a 'subordinate,' in the process of decision-making by his 'superior.' When his participation increased to the point of the complete disappearance of the authority-relation itself, there was 'pure democracy.' When participation ceased altogether there was 'autocracy.' When authority remained but there was still participation by the governed in some manner in decision making, we said we had 'democracy.' This concept of participation in decision making was placed in the context of authority exercised in the 'organisation,' shaped by 'values,' and directed to 'goals.'

These elements or constants still remain when we turn to the 'State.' Only 'institutions' known as the 'government' now exercise authority to 'public' instead of 'private' ends, with the resultant 'power' being shaped by the weight accorded the relevant 'values.' The participation of the governed in the process of decision making becomes highly complex. 'Representative government' becomes the means for constantly testing the sentiments of the governed and determining the changes in the priorities of their goals and values as the society in which they live changes. For in a world in which man has multiplied and spread through all its lands, in which markets have constantly expanded as the technology of transportation and communication has opened up new areas, and in which the techniques of co-operation and group action have enabled constantly larger groups and systems of groups to function successfully, the one constant is change.

The value system of the democratic State

It is an extraordinarily fortunate circumstance in the history of western society that it has for the most part taken the individual rather than the group as the focal point of its system of values. For when the group is posited as the basic unit of social action, then such personification of the group as 'group consciousness,' 'group will' and 'group idea' are selected to characterise the purposeful quality of group action and thereby to conceal and prevent the examination and weighing of group purpose from the standpoint of individual values. An earlier and much more pernicious example of the personification of the group was in the proposition of German political philosophers that man finds the highest expression of his personality in the submission of his will to, and identification with, the State. The concept in western thought of the individual as both the end and a means of social action, however, has kept to the fore a constant process of critical evaluation of group conduct. Basic assumptions as to the nature of the individual have undergone tremendous refinement and elaboration under the findings of modern psychology, social psychology, anthropology and sociology. The Benthamite hypothesis of the individual as a social unit possessing uniform characteristics and susceptibilities to pleasures and pains has been supplanted by an awareness that each individual presents a unique phenomenon and problem in personality. The group has been seen to be but a means for the satisfaction of individual demands rather than an end in itself, while individual demands are accepted to be flexible and varied and to be determined as a social fact rather than material to be cast in an authoritarian mould. The individual fortunately has as yet not been viewed in the west as 'organisational man,' that is, a person who has meaning only by virtue of his role in the totalitarian State.

Functioning of the democratic State

We have said that the political institutions of the State serve to maintain the social system in an equilibrium; they are the balance wheel of the society. When conduct deviates from desired norms, when uncontrolled exercise of social power prevents the satisfaction of pressing needs and frustrates the attainment of desired goals, the appropriate political institution intervenes. When a dispute as to goals or as to the priority of values emerges in a familiar, patterned situation, it usually finds its expression in a dispute as to 'rights' and it is the court which becomes the appropriate instrument for making the necessary decision as to priority of values. When social conflict emerges in an unpatterned situation, it will be either the legislature, or the judiciary acting in a quasi-legislative capacity, which will resolve the conflict. Upon the wise intervention, when needed, of the appropriate political institution will depend the successful functioning of the system of relationships which comprise the State.

The State has been defined above as involving but one type

of relation, namely, the authority relation between a territorially identified government and those whose behaviour is influenced by the acceptance of its authority. When, however, we examine this relation in closer detail, it breaks down into a system of relationships. For if the distinguishing feature of the State be the common acceptance of governmental authority, that acceptance finds its expression in the entire life of the national society. The life of the national society is, in turn, largely structured into organisations because only through the organisational form of co-operation is it today possible to satisfy the wants of men. As men multiplied until the simpler family, clan and feudal structures became inadequate to accommodate social action, as techniques of manufacture, transportation, communication and war became so complex and intricate that only through the organisation could effective social action take place, organisations became the characteristic structures of social action.

The government itself, notably in the sphere of the executive, resorts to the organisational structure to satisfy certain human wants. A governmental department or agency exhibits the organisational form as well as the government corporation. However, the democratic State still largely relies upon the so-called private corporation to satisfy the greater part of our wants. Yet the term 'private' in 'private corporation' is increasingly becoming a misnomer as governmental control of the private corporation steadily increases. In any event, the private corporation has always been endowed with a part of the authority of the government in that by the possession of a legal personality it is enabled to command the force of the government when it exercises its rights of contract and property. When it uses the instrumentalities of contract and property to achieve its corporate purposes, it enters into the authority system of the State.

Thus the State is the ultimate organisation of the national society, since it is characterised by a common acceptance of a certain authority and by the fact that its members identify themselves with it. The national society moves to attain its purposes sometimes through governmental organisations and sometimes through private corporate organisations. The political institutions which comprise the government control the functioning of all the relationships of the society, organisational or otherwise, and direct their power to the purposes then deemed important by the society in such a manner as to engender the least friction and loss of energy.

In order that the exercise of the power of the private corporate organisation *vis-à-vis* its members may be regularised and thereby made effective to the fullest degree, each such organisation must have its own system of constitutional law. Systems of constitutional law accordingly become manifest in the collective bargaining agreement and self-imposed, unwritten codes of management techniques. The power of the corporate organisation *vis-à-vis* other organisations must also be brought under law. The external relationships of the corporate organisation must be regulated so that its exercise of the powers of contract and property will be directed towards an effective expression of its social purpose. It is the task of law to preserve the energy created by voluntary participation within the corporate organisation and to ensure that such energy is effectively directed to ends of importance to the society as well as the organisation and, in so doing, not so to dominate by governmental power and direction that frustration supplants significance and disintegration takes the place of cohesion and energy.

Each corporate organisation finds and maintains its own bases of interaction with others, and the interacting, reciprocating relationships thus developed must be regulated. Trader vies with trader, producer with producer, in seeking to maintain a place in the economy and to grow. Law has the function of preserving equality of opportunity in access to the market, both in sources of supply and of sale, of protecting against harmful aggression, and of ensuring the observance of contract. Law in the democratic State does not have the affirmative role of directing the affairs of such organisations. Its function is regulative, protective. Moreover, it is aware of the principle of the limits of effective authority. It seeks obedience through acceptance rather than through fear and terror. It is carefully integrated with the mores and ways of life of the governed. While it commands, it does not dictate.

The individual and the organisation each becomes entitled to self-realisation. The freedom of the individual becomes a freedom to participate in a rich and varied social life. The freedom of the corporate organisation from governmental control and direction permits it in turn freely to select and pursue its ends, and even largely to make and enforce its own internal norms of conduct for its members, though at all times its area of freedom is circumscribed by law. Liberty in the democratic State thus becomes an equation involving a relationship between the government and the organisation, in addition to the traditional issue of the preservation of a 'Bill of Rights' of the individual against violation by the government.

Just as the government is at all times made aware of the principle of the limits of effective authority, of inducing co-operation and loyalty rather than relying primarily on fear and force, so the directing personnel of each organisation become aware, through experience, of the same principle in the conduct of the affairs of the organisation. A considerable technique involving means of communication within the group and internal norms of conduct and sanctions therefore develops. Authority is accepted, as it must be if effective social action is to take place, but in the western democratic State the acceptance of authority takes place under a questioning rather than an unquestioning attitude. Procedures exist for individual and group participation and representation in the process of decision making. Co-operation takes place on a voluntary instead of an involuntary plane and voluntary co-operation becomes the means for the satisfaction of public ends. The result is an unparalleled effectiveness in maximising the energy of the organisation—the human energy of its members and the physical energy of its property.

Control of the abuse of social power in the democratic State

The supplanting of the feudal system by an industrial society freed both the sovereign and the individual from the restraints incident to the code of chivalry, the mutual obligations of fealty and protection between man and lord, and, with the Reformation, from the authority of the Church. The resultant authority or social power of the personal sovereign or king became, in the words of Bodin, *summa potestas* or supreme power or— sovereignty.' The supplanting of the feudal lord by the sovereign power of the national government left the individual to the mercy of the latter. The protection of the individual from the exertion of uncontrolled and absolute social power was accordingly first seen to be a problem involving the limitation of governmental power in matters of vital concern to the security and integrity of the individual. Hence the American Declaration of Independence in 1776, the French Declaration of the Rights of Man adopted by the revolutionary National Assembly of France in 1789, the Bill of Rights annexed to the United States Constitution and the current 'human rights' movement have all sought to protect the 'rights of man' as against political power.

The problem of social power involved in the relationship of the economic organisation with the individual is, however, a problem which law in the western democratic State has only rather recently come to recognise.[6] The first aspect of this problem, the relationship of the economic organisation to the market, was dealt with in the United States by the Sherman Act of 1890, but the second aspect of the problem, the relationship between the economic organisation and its worker, came under the control of law primarily through the instrumentality of contract (*i.e.*, the collective bargaining agreement) and attendant legislation regulating the collective bargaining process.[7] The problem of the relationship between the union and its members as one of uncontrolled social power has been noticed in legal literature only in the past few years.[8] The common law, for example, gave the worker almost no protection from the exercise of the power of discharge by the economic organisation, with all its attendant consequences and deprivations. The regulation of the exercise of that power has come about largely through the collective bargaining agreement, together with the benefits of unemployment insurance and compensation.

Restating this development in terms of the concepts employed in our first chapter, the transformation of society from a feudal to an industrial structure resulted in the creation of persons in authority whose area of freedom in their decision making func-

[6] 'In sum, the great complexes of property and contract which constitute our modern industrial machine, the monopolistic associations of capital, labour, and the professions which operate it, exert under the forms and sanctions of law enormous powers of determining the substance of economic and social arrangement, in large part irrespective of the will of the particular individuals.' L. L. Jaffe, 'Law Making by Private Groups,' 51 *Harvard Law Review* (1937), p. 201 at p. 220.

[7] See Ch. 8 below.

[8] e.g., C. W. Summers, 'Union Powers and Workers' Rights,' 49 *Michigan Law Review* (1951), p. 805, also 'The Right to Join a Union,' 47 *Columbia Law Review* (1947), p. 33.

tion was largely uncontrolled by law. The growth of the democratic State has in part been the development of norms for decision making, delimiting both the area and the manner of exercise of authority. . Certain areas have been excluded altogether from invasion by authority as involving individual 'rights,' whether as against the political institution or the economic organisation. Other norms have regulated the manner of the exercise of authority—norms relating to notice, fair hearing and the like. Thus, authority becomes both decentralised and regularised.

The ancient problem of *quis custodiet ipsos custodes* is solved by the growth of a body of law regulating the performance of all significant roles in the society, including the roles of the governors as well as the governed. The exercise of authority in any situation is subject to the regulation of the judicial institution. Judges are, in turn, subject to the law. They are subject to discipline if they expose themselves to situations likely to affect their impartiality. They must, in the performance of their role, always give due weight to precedent in accordance with the traditional standards of the legal profession.

As we have seen, authority is decentralised into numerous areas of decision making, rather than centralised into a small group as in the totalitarian State. Wherever authority appears, its use is subject to law. The enforcement of law is entrusted to a separate institution, the judiciary. Judges are bound by precedent and precedent thus serves to build up a body of law analogous to that of the *jus gentium* of Rome. Judges will disturb any part of that body of law in only the most exceptional circumstances; judicial doctrine moves interstitially. Conduct that otherwise might be unpatterned and unpredictable thus becomes patterned and predictable. Cohesion and integration of social life takes place. Authority and its product, power, are decentralised and their abuse is subject to regulation either by the legislative or the judicial bodies. The legislature and the judiciary are separate institutions cutting across all society in their control of conduct yet they are themselves subject to discipline and control by virtue of the high degree of institutionalisation of the process of law making and enforcement. Authority and power are not feared because their use is controlled and directed to public ends.

Individual freedom and the democratic State

We have been steadily moving into areas of increasing abstractness and conceptualism. As we become in corresponding measure remote from observable fact, our generalisation and concepts tend to become increasingly intuitive in content. The words selected for communication no longer carry identic content as between the communicants. The term 'public,' for example, has different meanings to the philosopher and the political scientist; 'power' is a term having many hues. The world seen by the political scientist is not the same world as that seen by the sociologist or the psychologist or the lawyer. Perhaps we need a 'field theory' to integrate all of them into a single system, but the lack of identic concepts of rather concrete content hampers the growth of such a comprehensive social science.

We say this because much of what we will presently have to say (and, indeed, perhaps much of what we have already said in this chapter) involves a cross-sectioning from a different standpoint of much the same observations. We also say this because, in this area of the literature, the prevalence of concepts of a highly vague and all-inclusive nature makes the problem of communication a particularly difficult one. We have to move against the dogma of liberal or conservative interpretations in which the interpretations given to terms have a high emotive content, when we employ such words as 'freedom,' 'democracy,' 'liberalism' and the like. When such a system of thought is impliedly attacked, the reaction is likely to be violent.

Freedom, as is often pointed out, has no significance except as a relation. It may be a freedom or absence of restraint *from* something or it may be the absence of any restraint or obstacle *for* doing something. As we noted before, the selection of our starting point makes a great deal of difference in our system of thought. We suggest that the starting point be that of the concept of the 'area of freedom' as used in Chapter 1 above; in other words, that freedom has significance only as it relates to conduct. Conduct, in turn, is usually either a product of role-performance or affects role-performance. Deviant conduct in the performance of an approved role, such as fraud in the process of exchange, deviant conduct manifested in a disapproved role, such as that of the criminal, deviant conduct revealed in the abuse of social power or in domination rather than persuasion, all raise problems of social control. Freedom becomes significant as a value only as its content is shaped by conduct which involves effective and socially approved performance. Freedom must be subject to responsibility within the individual and to the sanctions of authority.

Always present, however, is the threat of social power. As organisations and institutions grow in their control of power, whether they be economic or political, the consequences of their abuse of power similarly increase. The ability to withhold access to the resources of a monopoly, whether that monopoly be of aluminium products or of labour in coal-mines, railroads or the steel industry, the power to withhold access to certain schools in the Southern States of the United States from Negroes, raise issues in the control of power. When any significant quantity of power in society can be withheld from access or use, whether as a pressure in the bargaining process or in access to the benefits of a so-called governmental function, an issue in the exercise of power and of individual freedom arises. For if the individual be denied access, choice or participation in any significant part of the culture, he is denied the very meaning of freedom—if we conceive of freedom as opportunity to participate in the cultural and social life of the society.

Modern society, whether it be structured in the democratic or, as we shall see, in the Communist State, is largely structured in organisations and groups. In the democratic State, the centres of power thus created are dispersed and are controlled by political institutions, the members of which, in the performance of their roles, are subject to a system of rules of law built up through the centuries and enforced by a disciplined judiciary. The problem of social change is handled by the legislature, whose function will be, *inter alia,* the subject of the next chapter. In the Communist State, the unifying element is the Party, and authority is *de jure* centralised in the government and *de facto* centralised into a ruling clique.

The problem of individual freedom is today not solely a problem of the relation of the individual with the government, which was a basic tenet of liberal thought, but it is a product of the authority-relation wherever manifest and a product of the existence of power wherever manifest. In the creation of power through authority the problem of democratic participation in decision making is raised in both the political institution and the economic organisation. In the use of power by persons in authority the problem of individual freedom is raised whenever that power is abused. Individual freedom, in short, has significance primarily as freedom to carry out the various roles which the individual may assume in social life. The area of freedom of each such role is to be defined in conduct—conduct, on the one hand, which satisfies the needs of the individual concerned and, on the other hand, is effectively directed to the attainment of the goals, immediate or ultimate, aimed at. Deviant performances of roles must be continually examined and weighed from the standpoint of the friction they engender and their effectiveness in goal-reaching. The use of social power to frustrate effective role performance must also be continually examined and weighed. Freedom is thus always relative, always to be seen in a situational context, and its meaning to be shaped so as to enable effective and satisfying performance of the particular role or task of the individual involved.

The national society which we call the United States has gone far towards solving the problem which any national society must solve if it is to be politically integrated; namely, that of extending to each individual within the society equality of access to and opportunity for participation in its political institutions. The Roman State, at the summit of its imperial power, for the first time made it possible for the individuals composing it to have access on a basis of equality of its legal institutions. Not until the political distinction between the *quiris,* or member of the *curia,* and the *peregrinus,* or foreigner, had largely disappeared by the extension of the *civis,* or Roman citizenship, to foreigners, could it be said that substantial full equality between the Roman citizen and the foreigner was achieved. The *jus gentium* eventually became not a law limited to relations with or among foreigners, but a general system of rules governing the relations between free men as such. When political and legal rights were enjoyed, not by virtue of gentile relationships, but by virtue of possessing legal capacity, the groundwork for the modern as well as the Roman imperial State was laid. The history of Roman, as well as of English law, is characterised by the supplanting of the individual as a member of a fixed group (in the Roman State in the *gens* and in the feudal state in the *feodum*) with the individual living in a system of free association with others in voluntary groups, with the accompanying recognition by the law of both the individual and the group as legal entities. In other words, both the modern democratic State and the Roman State came eventually to recognise the principle of equality of access to its political and legal institutions for all the members of its national society. However, in varying degrees, the democratic State is still in the process of working out another principle: that of equality of opportunity for participation by all its members in the basic social institutions of its national society.

In various national societies throughout the world today we find that individuals, by virtue of some particular group status or membership, are denied equality of access to basic social institutions. In the Soviet Union, for example, members of the Communist Party apparently enjoy opportunities for education, social growth and advancement which non-members find very difficult to attain. In India, caste distinctions may be legally nullified, but remain as *de facto* barriers to social progress and recognition. In the United States, members of certain races are similarly denied *de facto* access to certain phases of the institutional life of the society.

Efforts to deal internationally with the so-called problem of human rights are substantially frustrated by the existing philosophy by which our world is ordered, namely, that the ultimate and largest repositories of power are the nation-States and that each of these is assumed, as a matter of law, to be sovereign within its own territory. Individuals find protection under the system of international law only through membership in the State. The principle of the diplomatic protection of citizens abroad extends protection to the individual, not as such, but as a member of a State. The treaties of peace consequent upon the First World War erected certain systems of protection for national and racial minorities through the League of Nations, but otherwise failed to come to grips with the problem. Today, the fact remains that the individual oppressed by the government of the State of which he is a member, whether he be kulak, Jew or Moslem, is without recourse internationally as against his State.

The western world posits the individual as the centre of social action but it remains bound by its existing structures of social action which are those of groups and organisations. When group membership raises issues of status or rank instead of role and performance, when group status determines individual rights and privileges, then we are confronted with a failure of society to free the individual for effective social action. For it is our philosophy of freedom that each individual shall be granted the greatest possible freedom of action, that this freedom of action becomes meaningful only through the opportunity to participate fully in the life of the society, and that it is the task of authority and of law not to frustrate this freedom, but rather to preserve its existence and to ensure that it is responsibly exercised.

The Communist State

Perhaps the most significant difference in the position of the individual in the democratic State of the western world as compared with his position in the Communist State of the eastern world is that his choice of the roles which he shall assume in his daily life is relatively free from governmental force and direction. A basic freedom of man in western democratic society is the freedom to participate in the activities of society. In the Communist State, that area of freedom is much more restricted.

The economic organisations of Communist Russia are government corporations, unlike the voluntary, autonomous organisations of the west.

> 'The State is involved in nearly every relationship between the citizen and those who provide the goods and services which the citizen needs. Although many of these relationships are with officials of government corporations administering industry, transport, housing, banking, and distribution rather than directly with a Department or Ministry of the State, the essential State character of one party to the relationship is unchanged. The citizen is, in effect, an employee of the State. He lives in an apartment house owned and administered by the State; he eats in a State-operated dining hall; and his health is cared for in a State clinic. He buys at State stores, attends State theatres, and rides on State street cars and railroads. In addition, there are those relationships which are found even in non-socialistic countries such as with the State tax collector, the police, the prosecutor, and the court.' [9]

[9] J. N. Hazard, 'Socialism, Abuse of Power, and Soviet Law,' 50 *Columbia Law Review* (1950), pp. 448. 449; see also J. N. Hazard, 'Soviet Government Corporations,' 41 *Michigan Law Review* (1943), p. 850.

The term 'government corporation' as used above and its status as a legal entity (*i.e.*, possession of legal personality):

> '. . . does not mean actual economic independence of an enterprise but merely a special method of finance, accountancy and business operation. As observed by Venediktov in 1928, the legal entity is merely a masque over the government agency. A recent characteristic of an agency operating on a commercial basis, given by the author of a Soviet treatise on administrative law in 1946, states the same idea in a more veiled form:
>
> 'An agency assigned to operate on a commercial basis must carry out the assignments flowing from the governmental economic plan, the resolutions and orders of the Council of Ministers, as well as orders and instructions of ministers concerned, while the superior agencies, such as the Ministry of State Control, the State Planning Commission, and financial and banking agencies, supervise the execution by the economic agency of the directives and acts of government administration.
>
> 'Thus, the commercial basis is merely a special method of governmental management of the national economy, securing the execution of planned assignments on the basis of strictly delimited independence of the economic agency regarding its assets and operations, within the limits of the approved plans and established rules of conduct of business.'[10]

Internal discipline within the economic organisation is not a matter of voluntary, contractual relationships and ethical standards, as in the west, but is subject to legal control. Under Article 130 of the Stalin Constitution every citizen is bound to 'uphold labour discipline, maintain an honourable attitude toward social duty, and honour the rules of socialist community life.'[11] Legislation sets forth the obligations of 'labour discipline' in detail.[12] Protection against abuse of power by managers of government enterprises and as well as government officials therefore becomes a problem in law.[13] Contract, instead of its all-embracing role in the western State of energising the produc-

[10] V. Gsovski, *Soviet Civil Law*, Vol. 1, 1948, pp. 405–406.
[11] A. Vyshinsky, *The Law of the Soviet State*, 1948, p. 639.
[12] V. Gsovski, *op. cit.*, p. 816.
[13] J. N. Hazard, note 9 above.

tion, exchange, distribution and sharing of goods and services, is instead limited to the sphere of 'civil legal relations,' which is a much narrower sphere than that of western legal systems, and the production and distribution of commodities is a direct concern of the government.[14]

The area of the determination of policy is left free from legal controls. The political leaders of the State are free to determine the policy to be followed and law becomes the servant for the execution of that policy. Instead of the lively interaction between all groups and classes of society in the framing of policy characteristic of the representative system of government of the democratic western State, policy making and political power is in the hands of a minority. Under Article 126 of the Stalin Constitution the Communist Party is 'the directive nucleus of all the organisations of the toilers, both social and State.' The membership of the Communist Party numbers approximately 6,000,000 or about three per cent of the Russian people. While the principle of the limits of effective authority is no less operative in the Russian system than in any other social system, to the scales of the power of the Soviet government is added the terror of the NKVD, the internal secret police, with the result that more rigorous policies of industrialisation, collectivisation and armament can be pursued than would otherwise be possible. Resistance itself becomes a source of strength to the State, creating a vast labour force of political prisoners.

The authority patterns of Communist Russia are very different from those of the west, relying on social power and constraint to a much greater extent than accommodation and compromise, but, nevertheless, they are marvellously suited for the hostile environment they have had to face. For struggle has been the byword of the existence of the Russian State: protection against foreign attack, the colonisation of Siberia and the east, the industrial and agrarian revolutions, the implementing of Marxian social philosophy, all these have necessitated a monolithic structure of society that can successfully withstand shock after shock and be capable of sustained endurance. The ultimate end which the Communist State seeks to attain is its preservation, not only its preservation as against external military force but also the preservation of its particular authority structure

[14] V. Gsovski, *op. cit.*, pp. 420 *et seq.*

as against change, which the introduction of western ideals and hence western ways of life within Soviet Russia would inevitably produce. The explanation of the authority structure of the Communist State lies in the emphasis given these values by its political leaders. The sources of that emphasis in turn lie rooted in history.

The Roman Empire had entered its decline, the 'Roman peace' had vanished, war, plague and famine had ravaged the provinces, and the Diocletian reforms had been instituted, when the first federation of eastern Slav tribes was established between the Dnieper and the Dniester Rivers in the third and fourth centuries A.D. These tribes were found in the deep forests of the northern East-European plain and a few centuries later became known as the 'Russ.' Essentially cut off from all Western European connections, they became a buffer people and a buffer State protecting Western Europe and its culture from nomadic invasions from Asia. War, famine, and alien occupation became the way of life of the Russ. Wars with the Goths in the fourth century, conflicts with such early Asiatic opponents as the Bulgars and the Avars in the sixth and seventh centuries, the defence of the southern steppes and trade routes from the Turkish hordes beginning in the ninth century and culminating with the fall of Kiev to the Mongol invader in 1240, the sacking and burning of Moscow in 1382 by the Mongols, and the domination of Russia by the Golden Horde until 1480, these were the early centuries of the Russian people.

Until the Mongolian conquest, such political unity as existed was under the power of the grand principalities first of Kiev and then of Suzdal and Vladimir, which after the Mongol conquest further disintegrated into a number of separate units, waging wars against one another and suffering incursions from the steppes. Moscow in time became the centre of political power and Ivan III became the 'Grand Duke of all Russia,' finally throwing off the yoke of the Golden Horde in 1480. Not until his reign were the foundations of the modern Russian State definitely laid to reach the Baltic and the Crimea. European culture did not begin to penetrate Russia extensively until the time of the Romanovs in the seventeenth century. As European influences began to challenge accustomed habits and religious observance, foreigners were relegated to a suburb of Moscow called the 'German suburb,' with the result that the process of Europeanisation became limited to the court and the upper social classes. A considerable breakdown and change in political and social structures took place a century later under Peter the Great, but his educational reforms proved premature. It is significant that language itself proved to be a barrier to communication; the present Russian lay alphabet was introduced by Peter but a literary language had to be created before translations could be understood by Russian readers. The Christian faith was not accepted in Russia until the baptism of St. Vladimir in 988, while in Europe at that time the Roman Catholic Church had already attained great spiritual and temporal power. Frontier conditions of life, isolation from European contacts, continued wars of expansion and of resistance to Asian invasions, fostered an autocratic and powerful central government at first under the 'Grand Duke' or 'Grand Prince' and then under the tsars. The Napoleonic invasion and burning of Moscow brought about a period of reaction under Alexander I, of 'Holy Alliance' fame. Professors were removed from universities and textbooks banned for their failure to conform to scripture (now for their failure to conform to the current Communist Party line). A liberal revolution in army officer circles of 1825, inspired by exposure of some of the young generation of Russians to European culture and political thinking, failed. A Slavophil movement mystically proclaimed the superiority of Russian civilisation to that of the west. But the Russian political and industrial structure was too primitive and weak successfully to resist the west in the Crimean War of 1854–1856, and a brief period of administrative and social reform ensued, the high point of which was the freeing of the serfs in 1861.

European liberal influences still continued to foment a revolutionary movement against which 'temporary measures' and 'temporary rules' for the control of the press were taken in the early 'sixties; these 'temporary rules' remained in force for forty years. By 1896 the revolutionary base had shifted from the liberal groups to include the working classes. In that year the first large strike of working men took place, 30,000 in number. The political and revolutionary philosophy of Marxism was adopted by some of the younger generation of revolutionists and, led by Plekhanov, Lenin and some less militant figures, their views resulted in the effective establishment of the Russian Social Democratic Labour Party by 1903.

The weakness displayed by the central government in the Crimean War led to the reform movement of the 'sixties. The weakness evidenced in the Russo-Japanese and First World Wars led to the revolutions of 1905 and 1917 and eventual seizure of power by the Bolsheviks and their allies in November, 1917. Attacks from all sides, White Russian and 'Czechoslovak' forces in the west, White Russian armies under Admiral Kolchak in Siberia, Allied intervening contingents in the north, General Denikin's and General Wrangel's forces in the south of European Russia, the war with Poland of 1920, the peasant disorders of 1919–1921, the famine of 1921–1922 (which would perhaps have resulted in the starvation of millions of Russians without the aid furnished by the American Relief Association under Herbert Hoover), faced the new government with trials which it was able to survive only through hard and militant resistance on the battlefield and the savagery of the terror at home.

It is something of a paradox that the revolution of the proletariat, which under Marxist philosophy was destined to take place at the apex of the development of monopoly capitalism, when economic and political power would be centred in a few hands vulnerable to revolutionary seizure, took place instead in an essentially primitive, agricultural, peasant society, backward in industrialisation. The answer may be that the structure of minority control established under the tsars and the delayed development of a middle class rendered the substitution of another minority group in the system of authority thus established relatively easy.

While the 'New Economic Policy' and the resumption of trade relationships with the west in the early 'twenties furnished a breathing space in which some measure of economic strength could be established, the industrial shortcomings of over a century of stagnation had to be overcome and the peasant core of resistance to Communism had to be broken before the Russian State, and with it Communist Party control, could be secure. Hence the processes of industrialisation and promotion of collective farms begun in 1922 and still continuing.

The elimination of the market as a means for allocating the productive resources of society into the hands of voluntary, autonomous corporate organisations, the appropriation by political institutions of the phases of decision-making involving policy and planning which are in capitalist society decentralised in the private corporation, the abolition of private ownership and control of the means of production, inevitably and inexorably committed the Communist State to a strategy of centralisation of decision-making and planning in the hands of the Communist Party. A sharp distinction between equality before the law and equal capacity for rights was introduced. As in the days of early Rome, the patrician was the repository of political power with the plebeian having only limited, though constantly expanding, legal rights, so in Soviet Russia the member of the Party emerges as the *civis* enjoying a *jus civile* of privilege and social power. The *jus gentium* of the Russian subject carefully denies to him any effective political power.

The equilibrium of Soviet society is achieved by placing its governors into a tight, cohesive, disciplined group, resting on a base of mass organisations of trade unions, co-operatives, trusts and government corporations, the press, the bureaucracy, the army and the secret police. Where all are nominally equal, little inducement to striving exists. Hence it became necessary to reinforce the authority system of the Soviet State by a system of wage differentials and graded rewards. But the most significant development in the Soviet structure of the State is the ruling class of the Party, cutting across all organisations, recruiting its members from all organisations and groups and infiltrating all of them. 'The totalitarian party is the ruling class in a world of total syndicalisation.'[15] Whereas the co-ordinating forces of organisational life in the west are leadership, authority and law, in the Soviet organisation an additional reinforcing element is added of conformity to Party policy supported by the placing of Party members in positions of leadership and authority and by the system of the secret police.

To the degree that reliance is placed upon force instead of acceptance of policy as an integrating force for a society, to that degree its equilibrium becomes unstable. In this connection, there is a most illuminating episode in the history of the Zulu.

[15] K. Mannheim, *Freedom, Power and Democratic Planning,* 1950, p. 89. See generally S. S. Harcave, *Russia, A History,* 1952; B. Pares, *A History of Russia,* 1953.

Borrowing the social innovation of a standing army from another ruler who had considerably expanded his territory, Chaka, king of the Zulu, made a standing army not only into an instrument of conquest but an instrument of social control. He became known as the 'Napoleon of South Africa' and his power was felt as far north as Lake Tanganyika. The army acquired a superior social status and was freed from economic necessity. It was fed at the king's expense and as many as twelve head of cattle might be supplied daily to a single barracks composed of from 600 to 1,000 men. The norm of obedience to command, however, was ferociously sanctioned. It was to be followed for even the most extravagant of commands. After every battle the officers were obliged to point out the cowards, whether there had been such or not, and these were executed.

In these circumstances, Chaka's subjects became in effect his slaves. They could not render services to any one else and he reserved for himself the monopoly of trade with the whites. Death was the sanction for disobedience to his command.

Such an authority system disintegrates rapidly when those in authority relax their iron control. When Chaka died and control passed to his successors, who lacked his virile personality, the kingdom split up once more into smaller units.[16]

The applicability of this analogy to the Soviet sphere is reinforced by the expansion of that sphere to include cultures ranging from the westernised cultures of the satellite States of eastern Europe, such as Czechoslovakia, Poland, Rumania and Hungary, to the six Moslem republics of the Soviet Union comprising Azerbaijan, in Caucasia, and Turkmenistan, Uzbekistan, Kazakhstan, Kirghizistan and Tadzhikistan in Central Asia. The divisive forces represented by these various cultures are kept under control by the Soviet Union by force and insularisation. The sovietised Moslem peoples are kept carefully isolated from Moslems beyond Soviet borders. Moreover, whole Turkish peoples, for example, the Crimean Turks, have been compulsorily moved from their ancestral homes and have disappeared as an entity. Slavs have been brought into the Turkish community to water down the Turkish elements. The latter are denied access to positions of authority. Though the Turks and other

[16] R. H. Lowie, *Primitive Society,* 1947, pp. 373–376.

smaller Moslem peoples comprise ten to fifteen per cent of the total Soviet population, no member of these peoples has as yet reached the inner circle of power of the Soviet government. In the Turkish Soviet Republics, more than half of the Party members and officials are, as a rule, Russian. It is not surprising, therefore, that 'nationalist deviations' still continue in these Republics.[17]

The consequence of the extension of the Soviet State to include such disparate races, cultures and stages of economic development, the attempt to impose by force a common Russian culture upon diverse races and peoples, the application of restrictive measures and policies against Moslem, Jewish and other dissident races and groups, the closing of the doors to positions of power and esteem to those who are not Russian or members of the Party, the disparity in status between the Party *élite* and the submerged proletariat and landless agricultural worker, is that the Russian system would be peculiarly vulnerable to change through exposure to the culture of the west.

The empires of Rome and Islam were founded upon a common system of law welding the subject peoples together, in each case furnishing greater security, order and justice than the superseded laws. The *jus gentium* of the Roman Empire, created by the skilled jurists of Rome out of the Stoic vision of a system of universal law, was a far more advanced system of law than the *jus civile* of the Roman tribes. The law of Islam, based on the Koran, proclaimed the equality of all the faithful and recognised no divisions between nations, castes or classes. It thereby furnished a means whereby the aspirations of the peoples of the conquered territories of the Islamic empire could be met. Does the Soviet legal system, as administered, furnish a similar protection and advance in the view of the peoples of its conquered territories? Does it provide them full equality and access to political and basic social institutions? Has Soviet policy *vis-à-vis* its subject peoples and peoples of satellite States shown that readiness to subordinate Russian interests to empire interests which is the keystone of a successful imperial policy? In the answer to these questions lies the future fate of the Soviet system.

17 F. W. Fernau, *Moslems on the March*, 1954, pp. 245–254.

Communist China: a State in Transition

Although the geographical limits of China have expanded and contracted during its history of over 4,000 years, its natural geographical boundaries are now rather well fixed. One of the most notable of historical facts is the absorption of all invaders and alien elements into the Chinese culture without essentially modifying it in the process. Its traditional institutional patterns can be traced far back in history, sometimes for as much as 2,000 years. The Chinese civilisation is indigenous, though numerous invasions have fused many races into the Chinese people. Only within the past seventy-five years have the institutional patterns shown marked changes as against the preceding three centuries.

China is a country in which a minority, the gentry, has possessed political and economic power and intellectual leadership. Hence a certain similarity to the Russian structure. But unlike Russia, the central government has intruded but little in the affairs of everyday life. While the economic institutions were 'free enterprises,' so far as their relationship with the government was concerned, entrance into them was a matter of birth rather than of voluntary choice, as in the west. For the characteristic institutions were those of the family and of the clan. The family was not the simple family unit of the west but a unit comprising a father and mother and as many of their descendants, except for married daughters, as possible. And it was from the family which owns but does not cultivate land, the gentry, that government administrators and scholars were generally drawn. The resulting social structure, relatively free from the problems of change in the economic and cultural environment in which it functioned, was extraordinarily stable and capable of resisting the shock of war and invasion.

The introduction of European culture and the process of industrialisation during the past seventy-five years are breaking up the old family patterns of society. The structure of the modern corporation, the services required of a modern State, require values and standards of a universal rather than a particular nature. New members born into the old family groups can no longer find their place within that group when they reach maturity but must establish themselves anew in some occupation and residence outside the family. So established, they can no longer give strong support to particularist family values.

It is a highly significant fact that the Communist Party in China is a Party composed of youth and appealing to the youth thus displaced from old family structures which can no longer satisfy their basic economic and social wants. The introduction of the technology and cultures of the west has created an unrest on which the Communist Party has been able to capitalise with a simple, compact ideology and programme of economic and agrarian reform—a point which it would be well to remember in the application of technical assistance programmes in other so-called undeveloped countries. On the other hand, the task of imposing the Russian pattern of an all-powerful, highly centralised system of government and governmental control of society on the Chinese social system, in which the intrusion of the central government in the affairs of life was negligible, is a task which will be extraordinarily difficult for Chinese Communist leaders to carry out. Communist ideology cannot easily uproot the voluntary patterns of centuries of Chinese culture. The traditional culture of the peasant agricultural establishment and self-sufficient peasant village is now being supplanted by a rational society and economic system. Resistance to such a process of urbanisation and collectivisation under the pressure of a continuing war economy is of course inevitable. Hence the resort to terror and the liquidation of hundreds of thousands of Chinese citizens by the Communists; only in that way can they hope to lift the processes of the Chinese social system out of the deep grooves of the past into the shimmering paths of the Marxist future. A still further obstacle which they must face is that it will not be easy to industrialise, pursuant to Communist theory, a country so lacking in any economic reserve as China.[18]

[18] M. J. Levy, Jr., *Family Revolution in Modern China*, 1949, is most illuminating in this connection.

Chapter 4

THE WORLD SOCIETY

The Nature of World Society

The term 'world society' is here used to indicate the extent to which interaction, interdependency and community have developed in the population of the world.

The term 'society' itself is an abstraction of the social scientist.[1] It is an abstraction which assumes meaning according to the use which we make of it and the data to which we apply it. It is said to refer to an enduring and self-sustaining social system [2] or a plurality of interacting individuals, self-sufficient for their purposes and capable of existing longer than the customary life span of the individuals involved.[3] Other sociological definitions point to additional elements in the concept, including the realisation of unity and of belonging together. Thus, a society is 'a number of people, interacting in a common territory, sharing a consciousness of unity, and participating in a common institutional framework and culture pattern which function to fulfil the condition of man.'[4] Another detailed definition is to the effect that 'A society is composed of a normally constituted population whose members share in the status-prescribed manner of living, co-operate in the chief concerns of life, live in interdependency with one another, think of themselves as belonging together in important respects, and are capable of continuing through successive generations as a unit.'[5]

As used originally in the literature, the term community was used to designate the residents of a defined geographical area 'engaged in interrelated economic activities and constituting a politically self-governing unit.'[6] It was given 'a connotation

1 R. T. La Piere and P. R. Farnsworth, *Social Psychology*, 1949, p. 52.
2 T. Parsons, *The Social System*, 1951, p. 19.
3 M. J. Levy, Jr., *The Structure of Society*, 1952, p. 112.
4 J. W. Bennett and M. M. Tumin, *Social Life, Structure and Function*, 1948, p. 206.
5 E. T. Hiller, *Social Relations and Structures*, 1947, p. 670. See also T. Parsons, 'Society,' 14 *Encyclopædia of the Social Sciences*, p. 231; H. P. Fairchild (Ed.), *Dictionary of Sociology*, 1944, p. 300.
6 E. C. Lindeman, 'Community,' 4 *Encyclopædia of the Social Sciences*. p. 102.

of smallness, intimacy, and interactive unity.'[7] The extent and size of the community, however, is a product of the data. If we conceive community in the functional sense as 'any process of social interaction which gives rise to a more intensive or a more extensive attitude and practice of interdependence, co-operation, collaboration and unification,'[8] we may apply the concept to a population without regard to its geographical size. Usually, however, a community is considered to lie within specific spatial boundaries. Thus an accepted definition is 'any consciously organised aggregation of individuals residing in a specified area or locality, endowed with limited political autonomy, supporting such primary institutions as schools and churches and among whom certain degrees of interdependency are recognised.'[8] The realisation of interdependency and the sense of identification seem essential in the concept of community. 'United by reciprocal relations and bound by a common culture, the members of the community form an 'in-group,' characterised by internal peace, law, order and co-operative effort. Since they assist one another in the activities which gratify basic drives, and provide one another with certain derivative satisfactions obtainable only in social life, there develops among them a collective sentiment of group solidarity and loyalty, which has been variously termed syngenism, we-feeling, *esprit de corps*, and consciousness of kind.'[9] A community may be a society, but not all communities are societies.[10] Whether a community exists depends upon the degree of ecological, economic, cultural, political and moral integration of a given aggregate of individuals.[11]

The technological revolution of the past two hundred years has vastly influenced the organisational life of the world. It has multiplied the occupations of man. It has made possible incredibly rapid transportation and communication. Yet it has left man still within his local community. Each day he assumes his appointed role and travels to and from his home. Periodically he visits his friends, attends his church and repairs to accustomed

7 J. W. Bennett and M. M. Tumin, *op. cit.*, p. 389.
8 E. C. Lindeman, *loc. cit.*, p. 103.
9 G. P. Murdock, *Social Structure*, 1949, p. 83.
10 J. W. Bennett and M. M. Tumin, *op. cit.*, p. 392.
11 L. Wirth, 'World Community, World Society, and World Government: An Attempt at Clarification of Terms,' in Q. Wright (Ed.), *The World Community*, 1948, p. 9.

places of entertainment. Depending on his wealth, an annual vacation may for a brief time enable him to use one of the means of transportation and for a brief period view other countries from the windows of a train or bus or the confines of a hotel dining-room. In short, the face-to-face interactions of individuals are still principally within the local community. Whether one is a local merchant or an employee of a great international corporation, one remains in his home, his place of employment and his local community.

Yet no individual, no organisation, no community and no State exists in isolation. Communities vary as to the character of their labour supply, accessibility of and endowment with natural resources. States vary as to their supply of labour, capital equipment, productive land, mineral deposits, accessibility and climate. Differences in the scarcity and character of these factor endowments inevitably produce trade. No community or society is self-sustaining. Its members may remain at home but the product of their labour is made possible by purchases abroad and is paid for by sales abroad.

It was the teaching of the classic theory of comparative costs or territorial division of labour that foreign trade resulted from comparative differences in cost or advantage resulting from different factor endowments and that, if a country possessing superior advantages would concentrate on the production of those articles in which its comparative advantage was the greatest while a country less advantageously situated would restrict itself to those in which its comparative disadvantage was the least, the result of such specialisation would be to increase productivity and standards of living in both countries through trade between them.

International trade, however, is also a price phenomenon and prices and well as productive capacities vary from region to region. 'Thus it appears that the prices of commodities, the prices of the productive agents, consumers' incomes, the demand for finished goods, and both the demand for and the supply of the agents of production constitute a complex group of interacting and intimately interrelated forces, which, taken all together, mutually determine one another. To no single element in the total situation can causal priority be attributed; each exerts its influence simultaneously with all the others. This explanation of prices has been aptly characterised as one of mutual determination, or, alternatively, as a general equilibrium theory.'[12]

The play of other forces in world markets must also be realised. The intrusion of governmental restrictions, such as licensing systems, exchange controls, tariffs, quotas, subsidies and the like, must also be taken into account. 'Economists may study international equilibrium but this does not mean that governmental officials desire its attainment.'[13]

The forces of 'relative endowment with the productive factors, social conditions of production, economies of large-scale production, and costs of transfer' are forces which are constantly at work and which constantly react upon one another.[14] Foreign commerce is a web composed of many interlacing threads, each creating a stress upon and each being supported by others.

By the end of 1953, the trade of the world had a volume of over 75,000 million dollars.[15] Before the Second World War, over nine-tenths of the world trade had centred in five groups of countries: (1) the tropics, (2) the United States, (3) other regions of recent settlement in the temperate belts, (4) continental Europe, and (5) non-continental Europe. This trade was not a bilateral affair, it was not neatly balanced directly between any two countries. It was a multilateral trading system. Trade balances were settled through a world-wide system which also provided for the service of foreign investment of European creditor countries, particularly the United Kingdom. After the First World War, the functioning of this system was supported by United States capital exports. As these capital exports began to dwindle after 1928 and creditor countries began to repatriate their liquid funds, the functioning of the system was disturbed. After the financial crisis of 1931, many countries sought to balance their foreign transactions by import restrictions. The spread of this practice and consequent retaliation resulted in the replacement of multilateral by bilateral trade. Yet, inherently, the diversity of the means of production of the countries of the world leads to a multilateral pattern of trade embracing the world.[16]

[12] P. T. Ellsworth, *International Economics,* 1938, p. 93.
[13] S. Enke and V. Salera, *International Economics,* 1951, p. 258.
[14] P. T. Ellsworth, *op. cit.*, p. 133.
[15] Contracting Parties to the General Agreement on Tariffs and Trade, *International Trade* (Geneva), 1954, p. 6.
[16] League of Nations, *The Network of World Trade* (Publications, II. Economic and Financial, 1942. II, A 3), pp. 7–10.

The impact of the War upon the countries of Europe varied. By the end of 1947, Europe's working population and productive capital were up to the pre-war level. Germany emerged with greater manufacturing capacity. Perhaps one-fourth of Italy's industry was damaged. In France, war damage fell largely on transport and social capital. Damage to industry in the United Kingdom was negligible and its output increased during the war. Poland became a new industrial country. Many of the smaller countries of north-west Europe showed considerable economic development. The poorer countries in southern and south-eastern Europe have not, however, attained the same rate of development in employment and investment.[17] The cleavage between eastern and western Europe and the change in the economies of the former created most considerable difficulties. Western Europe lost its creditor position and the supply of much essential foodstuffs and raw materials which had to be found elsewhere. The dollar area proved largely to be the substitute supplier, thereby enhancing the dollar shortage of western Europe. Yet the United States did not provide a market of commensurate scope. Its imports were notably of primary goods while tariffs prevented it from becoming a market which could absorb the required imports of manufactured goods, if a balance in payments were to be achieved. The loss of foreign investments, the lessening of opportunities to earn dollars indirectly through trade with other regions selling in the dollar area, the considerable increase in the price of primary goods required by western Europe compared with the failure of the prices of its manufactures correspondingly to advance, were other forces leading to the precarious trade position of western Europe.[18] Although there has been some lessening of the dependence of world trade outside the United States upon its import balance with the United States,[19] the problem of the dollar shortage remains a major problem in international trade.

The underdeveloped countries are similarly exposed to the fluctuating forces of a world economy which they can do little to control. They are dependent on the export of raw materials

[17] United Nations, *Economic Survey of Europe Since the War* (U.N Doc. No. E/ECE/157), 1953, pp. 1–9, 81.
[18] *ibid.*, Ch. 2.
[19] United Nations, *World Economic Report*, 1953–1954, (U.N. Doc. No. E/2729, ST/ECA/30), 1955, p. 91.

for a substantial proportion of their income. The rather extreme fluctuations in the prices of primary commodities in world markets have led to correspondingly wide fluctuations of their income and, in addition, have made it difficult to budget an orderly programme of economic growth. Attempts to free themselves from their dependence on the sale of primary goods in the world markets by local industrial expansion have produced internal dislocations in their economies. The increased industrialisation generated a rise in total money incomes which in turn led to an increased demand for consumer goods, especially food. These goods, however, were not forthcoming in a sufficiently increased supply to prevent inflation. Indeed, the expanded foreign exchange earnings were in considerable measure used to import foodstuffs. Yet the underlying social demand for imports of capital goods will continue to press upon the industrialised regions and to compete, in the latter, with the demands of rearmament and expanding economies.[20]

As was pointed out at the beginning of this discussion, the fortunes of countries are not only a product of their native endowments but also of fate in that, thrust into a world economy, they become subject to the vicissitudes of a world economy. Prices, foreign exchange and foreign investment influence trade as well as the factor of comparative advantage. The fall of prices for primary goods since 1951 has forced their producers to cut down their imports of manufactured goods from industrial areas. The deficit in the dollar trade of Western Europe was balanced by United States economic assistance. Of late, the availability of competing goods at competitive prices from non-dollar countries has increased. This fact, and probably the influence of governmental pressures and controls, has resulted in a considerable shift of trade channels.

The monetary disorganisation of the earlier post-war years has accelerated the emergence of patterns of regional trade. There has been a strong intensification of trade between each industrial region and that non-industrial area which, for monetary and other reasons, is most closely connected with it. This tendency is most marked in the trade in manufactured products.[1]

[20] United Nations, *World Economic Report*, 1951–1952, (U.N. Doc. No. E/2353, Rev 1, ST/ECA/19), 1953, p. 14.

[1] Contracting Parties to the General Agreement on Tariffs and Trade, *International Trade* (Geneva), 1954, pp. 5–23.

As we move from the fortunes of particular countries to overall patterns, trade has not grown as rapidly as world production and the share of world output entering international trade was smaller during the post-war years than in the decade following the First World War.[2] This is particularly true of manufactured goods. Yet this very increase in productive power renders each industrialised country and each underdeveloped country increasingly at the mercy of the impersonal forces of world economy.

The United States, for example, has had an enormous increase in productive power yet its strength rests upon a substratum of imports and exports whose significance is more qualitative than quantitative in its economy. The strategical significance of many of its imports looms large. It depends in varying degree upon imports of such basic metals and minerals as copper, iron and steel, lead, zinc and petroleum. It relies heavily upon imports of antimony, cadmium, chromite, cobalt, manganese ore, tin, mica, graphite, nickel and platinum. The metallurgical, electrical products and chemical industries would be crippled without imports of such raw materials. For example, the United States produced one per cent of the free world's production of nickel and consumed 68 per cent of the total supply. It consumed about one-half of the primary platinum produced annually in the world and relied upon imports for most of this. It produced in 1952 21,216 tons of chromite as against imports of 1,700,209 tons. Its total production of antimony ore in 1952 was 5,571 tons of which 90 per cent came from one mine, as against imports of ore and metal of 26,291 tons.[3] A United States official has said: 'We must import ninety per cent or more of such strategic minerals as nickel, tin, tantalum, mica, chomite, industrial diamonds and quartz crystal. In addition, we regularly import forty per cent or more of a dozen other vital minerals among them cobalt, mercury, bauxite and lead.'[4] The United States 'consumes about half the materials of the free world and is the major single importer of most materials.'[5]

[2] *ibid.*, p. 5.

[3] Commodity Research Bureau, Inc., *Commodity Yearbook 1953*. 1953, pp. 47, 65, 77, 82, 101, 189, 201, 209, 225, 248, 255; Staff Papers Presented to the Commission on Foreign Economic Policy, February, 1954, p. 253.

[4] Address of Assistant Secretary of State Morton, October 27, 1953 (Dept. of State Press Release No. 595, October 26, 1953).

[5] President's Materials Policy Commission, *Resources for Freedom*, Vol. I, 1952, p. 59.

As a consequence, many supplying countries in the free world are heavily dependent upon American markets for their economic stability. In 1950, Chile sent 71 per cent of her total copper production to the United States, Cuba sent 52 per cent of her sugar, India 45 per cent of her manganese, Indonesia 28 per cent of her rubber, and Canada 80 per cent of her newsprint, 72 pe1 cent of her nickel, 62 per cent of her lead and 64 per cent of her lumber production.[6] The effect upon their economies of the stopping of United States defence and stock-piling purchases is obvious.

In the field of exports, rice, cotton, wheat, dried fruits and tobacco are still important in the export of agricultural commodities while heavy machinery, pharmaceuticals, lubricating oil, sulphur, copper, sulphate, and carbon black are important industrial commodities relying on export markets.[7] The United States has authoritatively been characterised as 'the world's major source of capital, equipment, technology, and management skills, all essential to promote material production and general economic advancement in less developed areas.'[8]

If atomic war between the United States and Soviet Russia should occur tomorrow without a blow being struck or a bomb being dropped in politically neutral countries, such are their economic ties with the west or the east that, as a consequence of the decimation of the warring powers, disaster would visit them as well.

The United States consumes more raw materials than it produces and its dependence on imports of materials will increase with the growth of population and the increase of standard of living. It has been estimated that the population factor alone will add 25 per cent to the needs of the United States in the next fifteen years.[9]

In the United States three basic forces are now at work: (1) a constantly increasing need for raw materials from abroad to maintain a constantly expanding economy in a State whose domestic resources are constantly being depleted, where they are

[6] Staff Papers Presented to the Commission on Foreign Economic Policy, February, 1954, pp. 253–254.

[7] *ibid.*, at p. 254.

[8] *op. cit.*, note 5 above at p. 59.

[9] Commission on Foreign Economic Policy, Report to the President and the Congress, January 23, 1954, p. 39.

not already substantially lacking or exhausted; (2) a constantly increasing need for foreign markets to maintain a market equilibrium and to find outlets for surplus productive capacity; and (3) a constantly increasing need to find foreign outlets for national income available for investment if (a) an expanding economy is to be maintained and (b) the 'dollar-gap' is to be closed and kept closed.

Throughout the world the growth of nationalism, resistance to colonial control, and desire for industrialisation, are phenomena of terrific force in the underdeveloped States and areas. The 600 million people of South-east Asia, the 170 million people of Latin America are committed to policies of industrialisation and expansion of production, and similar demands are emerging in Africa and the Middle East. Behind the Iron Curtain, including China, the drive towards industrialisation as a means to national power and military strength is also only too evident.

In short, the United States may be independent in the sense of classic political theory but it is no longer independent either in the pursuit of its political policies or in the functioning of its economy. It has reached the point where its increasing strength can only come from the increasing strength of its neighbours.

Import and export transactions do not magically appear on the pages of governmental reports nor are they isolated transactions in fixed market places to which individual buyers and sellers repair. They become institutionalised in the sense that organisations repeatedly and continually engage in the purchase and sale of the commodities and services which go to make up international trade. Each transaction may be discrete and isolated but each is also part of a stream of transactions executed by established organisations for which capital investment in varying sums is required. The western State has largely delegated to the private corporate organisation the carrying out of the economic phases of its activities, and it is through the management skill and capital equipment of corporations engaged in foreign trade, transportation and communication that the transactions of international trade and the currents of trade development are brought into being.

The transactions of international trade involve the meshing of a vast number of organisations, many of them of great size. They are the means whereby each of these organisations maintains its existence in the economic world. From them flow the monetary rewards by which they can command the continued participation of their members through the distribution of profits and the payment of wages. They are the indicia by which the purpose and nature of each organisation may be determined. These transactions cannot be resolved into the simple, primitive patterns of conduct of individual buyers and sellers in a single market place; they take place through the functioning of corporate organisations cutting across State boundaries. These transnational corporations become a part of the national life in each of the countries in which they operate. Their employees are for the most part citizens of each such country and their economic product becomes statistically a part of the economic product of each such country. Yet, as a social system, the transnational corporation is a discrete organisation having a life of its own in that it embraces a series of functions all co-ordinated by a commonly accepted authority. In other words, 'international trade' is the product of institutionalised patterns of conduct primarily found centred in the transnational corporation and in other organisations of an established character.

The day of the individual trader in foreign trade is past. The conduct of foreign trade today requires the co-ordinated teamwork of specialists in currency exchange, taxation, tariffs and customs procedure, foreign law and the like. Substantial capital funds and equipment are necessary. Great ingenuity and 'know-how' are required to break through the barbed-wire of trade barriers. Management must be supple and flexible in conforming corporate policy to the national policy and mores of each of the countries in which the corporate organisation functions.

The government of each State of course seeks to control its international trade, but the requirements of each national society are such that the end of economic self-sufficiency, to which such control is nominally directed, can never in fact be achieved. The resources within the boundaries of each State in fact become less and less a means for its survival and more and more a support for a world economy. The demand of each national society that its standard of living not only be preserved but raised, the necessity to provide for constantly increasing populations, the preparation for and conduct of war, all these, which have become part of the life of the national society, are thrusting each national society at a constantly accelerating pace into an interdependent world system. The illusion of economic self-sufficiency may still persist, but the emerging social fact is the interdependence rather than the independence of States.

The world system of economic relations and the economic interdependency of States which we have been describing may figuratively be characterised as a composite of horizontal and vertical structures of social action, with the horizontal forms of action comprising the organisational life of the world society in the economic sphere, and with the vertical forms of action comprising the several States past whose borders this organisational life flows. Yet such a description of data is more misleading than helpful, for it is but another instance of our tendency to personify and spatially identify States. The vertical elements in such a characterisation are a product of still other misleading ways of using data, firstly, our tendency to regard the territorial border of a State as a wall instead of an operative fact affecting the behaviour of a very considerable number of governmental officers and employees, including the armed forces, and, secondly, our tendency to objectify the authority system of the State as a vertical relation between superior and subordinate or, geometrically, as a pyramid of authority. When social scientists, at least in some branches, can free themselves from thinking in terms of such fictions and analogies, when the limitations of their concepts and abstractions as descriptions of the relevant data are more rigorously investigated and kept in mind by those who use them, then social science will indeed have made a great stride forward.

Once again, in our effort to describe the nature of world society, using that term in the loose sense indicated at the beginning of this chapter, it is as well to begin with human behaviour.

Psychology has been described as 'the science of adaptation, its determinants, its modalities, and motivations, and of the mental and emotional phenomena that accompany the vicissitudes of adaptation.'[10] The human individual is born with certain basic needs. To satisfy the forces of hunger, love, vanity and fear, the individual will, with others of his group or society, engage in institutional performances directed to self-maintenance, self-perpetuation, self-gratification and religion. Thus any society

10 A. Kardiner and others, *The Psychological Frontiers of Society*, 1945, p. 5.

will exhibit institutionalised activities directed toward supplying food (hunger impulse), shelter (heat and cold avoidance), war (aggression and anxiety or fear), and marriage (sex impulse).

Yet human motivation cannot be so neatly compartmentalised. Any one social institution is a complex phenomenon characterised by a number of basic impulses and a variety of derived drives. Marriage, for example, is a complex of patterns of behaviour which are a product not only of the sex drive but also of the hunger drive and the avoidance of anxiety.

The human individual is always born into a society and a culture. The former term refers to a group of individuals possessing the distinguishing characteristics noted at the outset of this chapter. The latter refers to their distinctive ways of life. Any society will posses common themes of behaviour in that its members will engage in behaviour directed toward the satisfaction of the basic human drives. For each human organism continually finds its behaviour shaped by situations in which its impulses are aroused and by those in which they are satisfied, with drive supplanting drive as satisfactions succeed one another. Moreover, there are the common elements of the physical environment which are the succession of night and day, the seasons, meteorological and geographical phenomena, flora and fauna, and the human anatomy and physiology itself.[11]

Beyond these common factors, however, each society develops its own 'historically derived system of explicit and implicit designs for living,' its 'historically created selective performances which channel men's reactions both to internal and external stimuli.'[12] The culture of a society is concerned with its conventional patterns of behaviour, with the manner of performance of its social institutions. It is concerned with conduct which is not determined by personality and individual initiative but is determined instead by the traditional or institutional patterns of behaviour.

Each individual, then, must learn, and channel his action in conformity with, the traditional cultural patterns of his society. He comes to accept its specific configuration of beliefs, attitudes and values and to perform its traditional roles.

Interaction between individuals is a product of adjustment,

[11] G. P. Murdock, 'The Common Denominator of Cultures,' in R. Linton (Ed.), *The Science of Man in the World Crisis*, 1945, p. 123.

[12] C. Kluckhohn and W. H. Kelly, 'The Concept of Culture,' *ibid.*, at pp. 98, 84.

of a concensus upon a common objective, of ability to communicate with one another, of ability to co-ordinate their performances or behaviour toward the common goal, and of the successful meshing of their performances, whether such performances exhibit similarities or interlocking dissimilarities. So long as culturally shaped performances result in a reduction of the drives which initiated them, so long as such performances produce satisfaction instead of frustration and internal conflict, cultural change will not be stimulated. Interaction between different cultural groups is not likely to lead to cultural change when the product of that interaction is mutual satisfaction. When contracts or social interaction between societies marked by different cultural systems are limited to the exchange of goods or services which each can offer, the symbiotic relationships thus established are not likely to produce cultural change in view of the satisfactions which they afford.

For example, in the Nilgiri Hills of India there were found four culturally and linguistically distinct tribal groups, the Toda, the Badaga, the Kota and the Kurumba. The sorcerers of the Kurumba were often called in by the Kota, among whom were smiths, and the Badaga, who were agriculturalists. The transactions usually took place outside the village limits. Kota musicians served in the Toda major ceremonies but were not allowed near the Toda dairies in which the sacred buffalo were kept. The supply of specialists from neighbouring groups thus produced stability rather than conflict and change.[13]

Whether inter-cultural contacts produce cultural readaptation and change is, accordingly, in part dependent upon the incentives to learning which such contacts produce. Stated more comprehensively, whether such contracts will produce change will depend upon the kind and relative number of the individuals engaged in such interaction, the conditions under which the interaction takes place, including the incentives to and opportunity for learning, that which is learned, and the results of the process within each group and in their subsequent relations.[14]

13 D. G. Mandelbaum, 'Cultural Changes among the Nilgiri Tribes,' 43 *American Anthropologist* (1941), p. 19. See also E. J. Lindgren, 'An Example of Culture Contact without Conflict; the Reindeer Tungus and Russian Cossacks of Northwest Manchuria,' 40 *ibid.* (1938), p. 305; R. Redfield, 'Culture Contact without Conflict,' 41 *ibid.* (1939), p. 514.

14 M. J. Herskovits, 'The Process of Cultural Change,' in R. Linton (Ed.), *op. cit.*, p. 143; A. I. Hallowell, 'Sociopsychological Aspects of Acculturation,' *ibid.*, p. 171.

Organisational interdependency thus tends to perpetuate cultural diversity, for only a small proportion of the members of a transnational organisation is likely to be exposed to a different culture inasmuch as the organisation in its overseas operations draws a very considerable portion of its staff from nationals of the various countries. The relative few who leave their home country maintain continuing cultural relations with their country through home leave, reading, correspondence and the like. Within the home country itself, the individual's interactions are still in part a product of his culture and are only slightly shaped by the fact that the impersonal, massive forces of world trade creates a substratum upon which his welfare is based. So far as the national society is concerned, if it can endure by virtue of the trade relations with other groups which it has established, there is, as we have seen, little stimulus to change its ways and to borrow from other cultures.

In each national society, then, face-to-face contacts are largely within the community and only infrequently with members of other national societies. Even where such contacts exist, the stimulus to change and the adoption of common value-systems and ways of behaviour is not strong. Indeed, there may be cultural disparities within a national society as great as those existing between different national societies.

The world has yet a great distance to go before it will possess anything like that degree of integration characteristic of the local community or that consciousness of unity and of belonging together, as well as the planned co-operative behaviours characteristic of a society. This is not to say that there are not unifying forces at work. Creative thought in science and art knows no national boundaries. The common core of learning shared by western industrial civilisation tends to produce common perceptions and values among different cultures. Heterogeneous cultures in some nations come to share a common, mass culture, though such mass cultures tend to find their common elements in the more surface aspects of life.

The question of law as a unifying force for world society as here described will be considered later. To complete our picture of world society, we must now turn to the functioning of the State in that society.

The State in World Society

In pages 54 to 62 we explored in some detail the concept of the State and suggested a behaviourist definition for it. In this section an attempt will be made to lay down a series of propositions towards (1) explaining the emergence of the State as a structure of social action, (2) describing its place and function in the history of man, (3) indicating some of the fundamental changes to which the State system must adjust itself and their consequences for national policy, and, finally, (4) pointing out some of the inherent limitations of the State as a means for creating a world community. Before doing so, however, it is useful to recall some of the points already made.

(1) Power is energy. Power is the energy potential which two or more persons in association with one another can create. In this sense 'power' is neither good nor bad; it is merely energy or force which is the product of group action.

(2) Power is a product of group behaviour and the use of physical equipment by groups. Whether it be the family, the clan, the tribe, the *feodum,* the organisation or the State which is chosen to be the unit of social action, power is a product of the action of the group utilising the necessary elements of the physical environment and capital or physical equipment under its control.

(3) Power is a product of purposive and institutionalised behaviour. Individuals coalesce into groups to attain common ends or purposes. On the one hand, their ways of behaviour become repetitive and institutionalised as workable solutions of common problems are found and, on the other hand, the group itself emerges as a result of such purposive and institutionalised behaviour. Through such co-operative behaviour power is created.

(4) Since power is a product of group behaviour, its creation is dependent upon the principles governing effective group performance. The term 'group' has been used to indicate a collection of individuals of varying numbers which becomes separated out from other individuals in society by the performance of institutionalised patterns of behaviour. So long as its members are in working, functioning relationships with one another, the group exists and power or energy is created by it. But the emergence of groups and the continuance of their performance are governed by their own principles, including the following:

(a) In a free society a group does not exist unless the satisfactions afforded its members by participation in its activities outweigh those offered by competing opportunities to participate in other groups. While habit, custom, standards and tradition as well as reason determine individual action, in general, when the satisfactions afforded by membership become slight, a group drops apart.

(b) Among these satisfactions are a certain degree of observance of group norms by the members, a certain degree of effective performance of group roles and a sense of locomotion toward the attainment of group goals. The rules of the group which are important to its members must be generally observed, the performance of group roles by their incumbents must be reasonably predictable, and the result of group action must be sufficiently significant in the eyes of the members for the group to endure.

(c) The performance of the leadership role is critical. The requirements of the role of leader as envisaged by the group must be filled by him to a reasonably satisfactory degree, and any failure to do so must not be too prolonged if the group is to continue.

(d) Another important element is that each member of the group must have the sense of being accepted by and belonging to the group. If the group is to continue, there must be an identification by the member with the group and an acceptance by the group of each such individual member.

(5) The group which (a) is exclusively dependent upon communication by word or act to give the cues for the performance of its members and (b) involves the performance of highly predictable and concrete sequences of behaviour, is of a limited size. Groups of a permanent character which are working directly with and upon their physical environment and are engaged in modifying or changing it in some way do so in highly concrete and fixed sequences of behaviour. Most of the time the requirements of the task itself will provide a visual cue for the desired conduct. For the rest, signals or commands suffice. An effective team or small group probably cannot exceed six or eight in number, though it may be larger in number if we view it from the standpoint of responsibility instead of control.

(6) Organisations are groups which are not so exclusively dependent upon personal media of communication and which are concerned with more generalised and abstract types of behaviour, *i.e.*, the determination of purpose and the planning and the carrying out of purpose, and hence are not limited to a small number of members. In the organisation we are concerned with sequences of human behaviour the content of which varies from the highly abstract to the highly concrete and with written media of communication as well as communication by sound and act. The size of such groups is not so much limited by physical as by other factors.

(7) The emergence of large groups is first of all a product of situations demanding mass action. In a stable fishing and agricultural community in which the danger of attack by others is lacking or remote, group action will be largely directed to fishing, agricultural, family and religious purposes. Such groups are for the most part small groups, though ritualistic activities may call for the performance of most of the community. The carrying out of larger enterprises, notably attack and defence in war, requires the utilization of the whole available manpower of the community.

(8) The emergence of larger groups is a product of leadership. In the small group the leader acts as the arbiter of disputes and symbol of the admired virtues of group membership and behaviour, as well as a director of performance of group conduct upon the appropriate occasion. When, however, the group task does not involve the performance of highly concrete and predictable sequences of behaviour and instead requires the planning of behaviour in the light of most novel and complex situations, and when, in addition, the group task requires a considerable number of persons for its accomplishment, the leadership function becomes vital.

(9) The emergence of larger groups is a product of law in the sense of conformity with norms of behaviour regarded as binding. Even the small group is held together by certain norms of behaviour, departure from which is regarded as most serious and reprehensible. The modern industrial work group, for example, has its own productive norms which may or may not coincide with those of the efficiency engineer, but which, in fact, powerfully influence the individual performance of the members of the

group and the survival of the group itself when the work situation is radically changed. Those enterprises which call for the larger group are usually accomplished by a number of smaller groups and teams, the individual members of which perform varied and specialised tasks or roles. The organisation of these smaller groups and units into a co-ordinated system requires not only leadership, as we have seen, but approved norms of behaviour. Those norms which are not merely permissive but are compulsory or binding in the view of the group may be regarded as law in its most elementary form. For all groups, both large and small, a common norm may well be: Follow the command of your leader when it is situationally appropriate.

(10) The emergence of larger groups is a product of the development of the concept of authority. One ingredient, and perhaps the most important, in the concept of authority as it has developed in modern society is that it involves the leadership role just stated. But authority carries with it other elements as well. It determines, and is reinforced by, status; those exercising authority have a higher status than those who are the subjects of authority. It is reinforced by the legal institutions of society; when those exercising authority are within their delegated sphere of authority, persons under their authority are subject to various penalties permitted by the legal system in case of a failure to obey authoritative commands—so goes the customary legal ritual.

In behavioural terms, however, the existence of authority may be determined when the giving of directions or commands by certain persons to others is followed with a high degree of predictability by the carrying out of such directions or commands by their addressees.

In terms of organisational structure, authority involves the delegation to a person of the duty or responsibility to accomplish a certain task or function requiring the co-ordinated activity of others, and the vesting in such person of a certain degree of influence over the imposition of available sanctions towards ensuring that such task or function is carried out.

In terms of law, authority involves a certain ability or power to call into play the forces of the legal system to support directions or commands.

Hence, the concept of authority is a product of a far more advanced and complex social structure than that of the primitive tribe or clan. It is, in short, a product of the modern State and corporate organisation.

(11) The modern State is the largest effective group yet to emerge and its existence is a complex of many forces and elements. As social scientists we are beginning to know something about the small group; we are just at the point of starting our investigation of the organisation; and we have some studies in political behaviour and public administration which throw new light on the nature of the State. What we shall presently have to say about the State as a group is, therefore, most tentative.

If we do not attempt to define the State in terms of structure but instead in terms of human behaviour we can perhaps come to a more accurate understanding of its composition and functioning than is afforded by classic political theory and its assumption of the existence of sovereignty or supreme power. So considered, in this work the State has been defined to embrace all those who accept the authority of a territorially identified set of governmental or political institutions. The State basically involves a relation between those who exercise such authority and those who accept such authority and are influenced thereby in their conduct. The sum total of all those in such a relationship constitutes the membership of the State.

Yet the members of the State are not individual units; they are the occupants of many roles. They are the governors as well as the governed, they are members of corporate organisations having authority or influenced by authority, they are buyers, sellers, miners, seamen, airmen, members of armed forces, members of families and travellers. Whoever and wherever they may be, whether within or outside the territorial limits of the State, they exercise or they accept the system of authority of the State. They belong to the State as its nationals. They identify themselves with the State in the spirit of nationalism. Their fortunes are tied up with those of the State. They rely upon and fear its system of sanctions. The State makes life possible and worthwhile for them in a world of hostility and insecurity.

(a) The State represents an organisational structure of social action necessary for the effective functioning of the modern industrial society. As families multiplied and emigrated to new lands, as the art of war became more and more an art requiring special skills and personnel, as the king as a leader in war and peace supplanted the chief and body of elders, as the rudimentary forms of the courts and law-making bodies emerged as specialised institutions to regularise the handling of certain functions of leadership formerly reposing in the chief and the elders, as the mystic relationship between lord and man took the place of the gentile bond of the clan, we find the feudal State emerging. Men tilled the soil, traded and fought wars in the tribal as well as the feudal society, but the group structure and characteristics of the feudal society were different and more complex. No longer were the family and the clan and the gathering of the clans the principal means of association for work and war. There were many men and many families not necessarily related by blood. War was no longer the occasional foray by the horde equipped with primitive weapons. The warrior class with its specialised roles, together with the farmer and the priest became the three basic ingredients of the feudal society. The conduct of war brought forth the *organisation* of knights, bowmen and specialists in the siege and the assault, and the defence essential for the protection of the farmer, the trader and the priest. The expansion of trade to constantly wider and distant markets brought forth the *organisation* of traders into trading companies and groups that lacked only the invention of the grant of corporate charter and legal personality to transform them into the modern corporate organisation. The necessity of resolving intra-group and inter-group conflict and giving direction to the blind forces of voluntary co-operation brought forth the manor courts, the county courts, the *curia regis* and the expansion of the *curia regis* into the courts and legislature of the modern State. The continued development of the art of war rendered obsolescent the feudal army and tie between lord and man. The Oath at Sarum laid the groundwork for the eventual establishment of the national army and for the proliferation of skills all under the direction of a single commander or authority which modern warfare requires. The fealty of the man to the lord was supplanted first by allegiance to the king and then to the national State. The mystic bond between lord and man was supplanted by the fanatic spirit of nationalism and patriotism.

There are three forces which led to the creation of the modern State, the necessity of the organisational structuring of the military force of society and the necessity for the organisational structuring of its commerce and economy, conjoined with the necessity for specialised institutions to handle the governing of conflicting groups. The feudal State represented those solutions involving the ordering of men in groups which enabled an equilibrium to be reached in the light of the conditions of feudal society. The modern State represented another working set of solutions responsive to the conditions of modern industrial society and war-making.

The effective functioning of the organisation as a structure of social action requires identification and loyalty on the part of its members. It requires that the universalist values incident to the government and the economic organisation supplant the particularist values of a kinship or feudal society. To the degree that such identification, loyalty and value attachment develop in any national society, to that extent does it become a viable State.

(b) The State is a product of the concept of the legitimacy of its system of authority. In the modern State authority is accepted not only because it is purposively exercised, that is, directed towards reaching goals important to its members and to its survival, but also because of belief in its legitimacy. The commands of one's superiors, when they are exercising their roles of authority and are within the limits of such roles, are accepted because they are regarded as legitimate and supported by the appropriate legal sanctions.

So long as the system of authority of the State was for the most part found within its territorial borders, relatively little conflict in the legitimacy of the exercise of authority by governmental organs arose. As the nationals of the State travelled, traded and settled abroad, however, they found themselves in the territories of other States and subject to other systems of authority regarded as supreme within their territorial boundaries under the concept of sovereignty. The hypothesis of the supremacy of the territorial sovereign served two purposes in the growth of the modern State. First, it expressed the concept that the particular national society should be free to determine its own destiny and to pursue its own interests and ways. Second, it minimised inter-State conflict because it set up territorial lines of demarcation beyond which the exercise of State authority ceased to be legitimate. Thus legislative intervention within the territory of another State was a violation of the latter's rights under public international law and a nullity under private international law.

The concept that the State, as a legal and political entity, was confined within its territorial boundaries was largely consonant with the facts of State life, since within its boundaries were found its predominant sources of national power and life. War might damage but it did not destroy the national society. It might lead to the disappearance of the State in the sense that the particular national society might be brought under the authority of one or more other States. Under the new authority or sovereignty of the victor State or States, the life of the particular society went on. Since there was no fundamental change in the conditions of life of the national society, it could continue to exist so long as it was within the system of authority of *some* State.

(12) Since the State represents an adjustment to the conditions and demands of modern industrial society, it will continue so long as its structure responds to existing conditions and demands. The one constant is, of course, change. The feudal State was the response to the conditions and demands of feudal society. When that society ceased to exist, the feudal State became a part of history. When the violence of feudal society was replaced by the king's peace of England, when national supplanted local markets, when organisations for manufacture and trade supplanted local guilds and individual craftsmen, the modern State emerged.

We are now, however, faced with fundamental changes in the structure and relationships of States and these are creating great stresses for which an adjustment must somehow be found.

The modern era has witnessed both an enormous development of capital and a spreading diffusion or decentralisation of capital. Agrarian and trading societies have been transformed into industrial societies. An industrial revolution has spread from England to western Europe and the United States and is now transforming Russia, Japan, Canada and other States. While the diffusion of capital is spreading to still other States, they are demanding that its pace be accelerated and that their peoples share in the rise of living standards and spread of learning and skills which seem to be concomitant with industrialisation.

Partly as a result of the emergence of the demand just stated, and partly as a result of other forces, including the failure of resident foreign nationals to integrate themselves with the local community, and the failure of some business interests to give due recognition to the value of local contributions, there have developed, notably in Asia and Africa, forces of nationalism, anti-imperialism and anti-colonialism.

In advanced industrial societies, there have developed demands that the benefits of a constantly growing technology be spread throughout the society and that the delegation of the conduct of economic enterprise to the voluntary, autonomous corporation provide a reasonable degree of security to the employee and to the trader who supplies his wants.

The depletion of national resources, the proliferation of consumer demands, the technological necessities of modern warfare, the pace of geological discoveries outside the national borders of sources for replacing exhausted local mineral reserves, the expansion of national to international markets, the resulting spread and growth of economic, political and military organisation beyond State borders to the territories of other States, mean that no State is in fact independent but exists and functions because of its ties with the rest of the world. We pursue the myths of national independence and sovereignty in a world which has in fact become interdependent. We adhere to these myths when the fact has emerged that the destruction of the social fabric of one State by atomic warfare would have enormous economic and social consequences in other States who look to it for markets and supplies for domestic industry. The expansion of national power had been made possible by the international expansion of the sources of that power.

Yet the fiction of sovereignty, or the supremacy of the power of the State within its territory, still continues to influence State conduct. Morris Cohen once said that fictions may be a convenience but we must not let them become our masters. Within the borders of the western democratic State sovereignty is no longer a negative, but is instead a positive concept. Sovereignty exists in order that the purposes of the national society may be achieved. However, States still postulate no external limitations upon sovereignty except those of international law. States still assume that governmental policy may be shaped without regard to its effect outside the State borders, not realising that the external effects of policy may vitally affect national interests and strength. While the physical boundary of the State serves a useful political role, it is increasingly becoming of less consequence in the economic and social relationships of States.

War and the threat of war were powerful forces in the creation of the modern State. War, as well as peaceful commerce and intercourse, must be regarded as a practice of States. While war ravaged, it did not destroy. It might result in the disappearance of a particular State in the political and legal sense, but it did not destroy the society found within the confines of the vanquished State. Today, however, atomic warfare means national suicide for the belligerents and economic catastrophe for the neutrals. Moreover, within each national society the political fact is that there is a great weariness of war, a great fear of war and a great demand that a way be found to turn the enormous power now allocated to the ways of war to the satisfaction of the demands of peace.

National power today is a product of technological progress and discovery as well as the organisational revolution in the ways of men. The solutions which man has been able to bring forth in increasing the quantity of power at the disposal of each human being are a product of the spirit of free inquiry. Our whole social fabric, our ways of living and working together, our accumulation of scientific and social technique and capital equipment, are a result of the secularisation of human thought and inquiry. The separation of church and State, the freeing of scientific inquiry from the deadening hand of the Inquisition and from the control of the State, these are the victories in the history of human thought which have brought forth the renaissance of science in the modern era.

The principle of intellectual freedom, which made it possible for man to provide for increasing populations and thus to defy the Malthusian law, to work out new ways of ordering his life in association with others and to enlarge his cultural horizon, is today under an increasing threat. In Soviet Russia it has reached the point of controlling not only the arts but also certain of the sciences—though those concerned with the technology of war have apparently escaped the ideological control of the Communist Party. In the free west there have, however, developed at first subtle and now increasingly open attacks upon the principle of free inquiry.

If we are to bring about peaceful change in a world which is constantly changing, if we are to have rational instead of irrational and violent solutions of problems of social conflict, if we are to find workable solutions for the practical problems which confront us, whether they be in the social or the physical sciences, we must preserve unimpaired the heritage of free thought and inquiry bequeathed to us by those who suffered under the Inquisition and the Star Chamber. A threat to the spirit of free inquiry, thought and expression, wherever it appears, is a threat to the scientific method which created and supports our civilisation.

It is the function of the political institutions of a national society to take cognisance of the facts influencing the source and use of national power. The spirit of free inquiry must control their investigations and decisions. The shape and direction which they give to the vast forces of the State must be dictated by the relevant facts. The authority which they possess must be responsibly exercised to the end of fostering and preserving the welfare of the people.

The movements towards industrialisation, agrarian progress and political and social reform which are now transforming this world are movements which neither the governments of the peoples concerned nor any other country can stop. They may delay or momentarily divert these movements but they cannot prevent them. Their force is irresistible. Even in the Soviet sphere, we must look for and await the time when the freedom of the individual to choose his associations, to determine his government and its policies, and to pursue his thoughts and religion will finally break through a system of force. A system of authority which is dependent upon force for its survival is a system which is inherently weak, for its extreme allocation of the available power of the community to the instruments of coercion means a State laggard in the satisfaction of the wants of its members; it means an energy potential which is lower than that created in an atmosphere of acceptance and understanding; and it means an unstable social system supported not by conviction and loyalty but by fear, and vulnerable to the ideas and fuller ways of life of its neighbours. The use by a State of its power must take account of the social changes taking place elsewhere in the world if it is to have the maximum effect in influencing the policy of other States to desired ends.

A democracy whose foreign policy is shaped by legislative control of the purse strings often finds that solutions for the problems confronting it in its foreign relations are not governed by the principle of achieving the maximum effect with a given quantity of power but by whether the solution happens to fall within the area of defence or within other areas less politically favoured. The value of national survival leads the legislature to shrink from vetoing the allocation of national power to military channels. The value of national welfare, however, is of much less influence when the solution falls in the category of foreign aid.

The only criterion for the determination of policy should be: Will the proposed use of the available part of the national power best foster the national interest as against other proposals? If aid by the United States to others serves its national interest, it should not be cut off because it is 'aid' and not 'defence.' A proliferation of political and military pacts, without economic and social ties to support them, may prove to be as fruitless to prevent aggression as the network of treaties with which France sought to protect herself after the First World War. An exclusive reliance upon military power, instead of other forms of power which may be more suitable for the purpose, such as economic and social aid in South-east Asia, may result in Communist control by subversion instead of aggression. The United States extended nearly three billion dollars in military aid to the French in Indo-China. Would a greater emphasis upon economic aid, internal reform and recognition of political demands have been more likely to achieve its objective? Might not considerably less than three billion dollars have been required to achieve its objective of a free Indo-China, if policy had been less rigid and more ready to select other than purely military measures?

It is a fundamental principle of national policy that each State must exercise its power so as to preserve its sources. For example, the United States appears to have at its disposal the greatest accumulation of power the world has ever seen. To those accustomed to think of States as being territorially defined, it would seem that the exercise of this vast power by the United States would be subject to no limitations except such as it might choose to regard as binding it, such as the principles of international law. But its power is a product of the fact that it is a world power, its sources of power are those of the world as well as those found within its national borders. Since it is from the world that it draws its power, it is to the world that it must direct its policy. If it is to preserve the avenues to power, it must keep them open. It must work with others and not seek to dominate them. Respect for others, not force, must be fundamental in its foreign policy. Humility in the exercise of its responsibility for the use of our power, not arrogance, must be its outlook.

Each State, including the Soviet, must eventually accept the fact that atomic warfare means national suicide. Perhaps the greatest tragedy of the post-war era has been the failure of the Soviet Union to accept an international system of control over the use of atomic power. Yet the obdurate fact remains that atomic warfare would be a betrayal of the interests of the citizens of Soviet Russia, since there can be no victory for any belligerent in a war which is nothing more nor less than national suicide. It is on this fact that the States of the west must continue to rest their policy and to endeavour to bring Soviet leaders to a common solution of their common problem.

Finally, as Kurt Lewin remarked, a State can be intolerant only of intolerance. Intolerance which strikes at the principle of free scientific inquiry undermines the foundation upon which western civilisation was built and the western democratic State erected. Fear and insecurity in a world of change should not carry us to the point where we destroy this ultimate source of strength and power.

The State is the largest structure of effective social action which man has been as yet able to create. Its survival will in the last analysis depend upon the ability of its leaders to recognise the basic forces now at work in the world, to adopt policies responsive to the pressure of these forces, and to bring about an acceptance and understanding of these policies upon the part of the members of the State generally.

(13) The State is subject to certain inherent limitations as a means for integrating world society. The State, as any social system, has its own equilibrium and its own space of free movement.

An individual, no less than a mechanical measuring device, is limited in his potentialities for perception. The same situation will be viewed differently by the different actors in it. The same behaviour may be virile, brusque, threatening or aggressive, according to the interpretation of the particular observer. Yet some aspects of a situation, for example, the question, 'How many were there?' are much more likely than others to produce uniform perceptions because of the training of the observers and the lack of emotive influences in the stimuli.

The physical scientist is likely to find a wider area of agreement on concepts with his brethren than the social scientist. The latter shares a more considerable store of common knowledge with his colleagues than say a popular columnist. The latter has a greater degree of sophistication than the well-known 'man in the street.'

The speed and accuracy of modern means of communication has not been accompanied by a corresponding increase in the sharing of common perceptions by the members of the various national societies. While the various fields of science have in varying degree become internationalised, the individual, even if he be a scientist, has not kept pace in his learning with the increasing complexity of the problems bearing on his social environment. Ortega y Gassett brilliantly points out that:

> 'The convulsive situation in Europe at the present moment is due to the fact than the average Englishman, the average Frenchman, the average German are *uncultured:* they are ignorant of the essential system of ideas concerning the world and man, which belong to our time. This average person is the new barbarian, a laggard behind the contemporary civilisation, archaic and primitive in contrast with his problems, which are grimly, relentlessly modern. This new barbarian is above all the professional man, more learned than ever before, but at the same time more uncultured—the engineer, the physician, the lawyer, the scientist . . .'[15]

In the national press the selection of facts to be reported seems to be increasingly subject to cultural and political pressures. Indeed, the world situation is increasingly described through reporting the views of officials expressed in emotive terms. The appreciation of other cultures and the demands of other societies increasingly comes to be viewed from a national instead of a universal viewpoint. It may be, as Kardiner holds, that specific cultures

[15] J. Ortega y Gassett, *Mission of the University*, 1944, p. 59.

tend to produce certain basic personality structures, yet it is an utter distortion of this observation to cast the American, the Englishman, the Frenchman and their respective countries into type categories of the most rudimentary form. The skilled anthropologist or social psychologist cautions that any attempt to describe a mass culture is necessarily highly impressionistic and can only suggest its largest configurations, values, assumptions and type situations. Yet, individually, most of us are quite ready to personify nations and depict the typical native. Thus, for most of us, the truth about the rest of the world increasingly becomes pure fantasy or fiction. Truth ceases to be universal or international and instead becomes the captive of national forces.

Governmental policy is a focal point, a point of balance, of many forces. Interest groups impinge their pressures upon any point where decision-making takes place to a substantial degree, whether this be in the legislature, the government department or the determination of a party platform. Those who are vested with authority are a product of these forces and their conduct is shaped by a constant evaluation of the relative strength of these forces. The leaders of a society are a product of their culture and share its particular historical configuration of values.

Beyond this, those who shape the foreign policy of a State must constantly keep in mind the sources and limitations of the national power, determine the nature and strength of the shifting forces affecting the policies and alignments of other States, and decide upon those measures of national policy which will have the greatest probability of accentuating selected elements of those forces so as to tilt the policies of other States in desired directions.

Viewed as a factor in decision making, the national self-interest is the primary factor influencing the foreign policy of any one State. The determination of that policy, however, is confined to those limits determined by the relative intensity of the various values shaping the national culture, the conditions determining the perceptions of the citizenry, and the relative strength of the various interest groups. Leaders cannot always select that policy which will best promote the national interest because of the foregoing limiting forces upon the determination of specific measures of policy.

As a consequence, those who are vested with the determination of foreign policy will always tend to evaluate measures designed to promote a world community upon the basis of whether they promote the national interest, and also whether they do not unduly disturb that balance of forces which has thrust the particular group of decision makers into power. The two criteria do not necessarily lead to the same decision.[16]

This chapter should not close nor the succeeding chapter begin without a reference to the brilliant and magnificently organised lectures of Professor McDougal at The Hague in 1953.[17] Professor McDougal takes a global view of those bodies who are 'participants in the world arena' and points out that these include not only the familiar 'nation-states' but also international governmental organisations, transnational political parties (whose characteristics he defines), transnational pressure groups, transnational private associations and the individual human being. He suggests, among other things, that each of these be studied from the standpoint of its bases of power, practices and effects achieved. He submits that their practices must be studied from the standpoint of policy or, more particularly, the goals or values to which the decision makers or persons in authority in the various bodies direct the energies of such bodies. He proposes eight basic concepts as a comprehensive set of 'goal values,' namely power, respect, enlightenment, wealth, wellbeing, skill, affection and rectitude. With extraordinary sweep, he offers a new perspective within which traditional international law may be placed and a means for synthesising it with other traditional fields of study, such as international organisation and international relations.

16 See generally in connection with this chapter D. Schindler, 'Contribution a l'étude des facteurs sociologiques et psychologiques du droit international,' 46 *Hague Recueil*, 1933, p. 233 at p. 297 *et seq.*; Th. Ruyssen, 'Les caractères de la communauté humaine,' 67 *ibid.*, 1939, p. 125; J. S. Reeves, 'La communauté internationale,' 3 *ibid.*, 1924, p. 5; J. Stone, *Legal Controls of International Conflict*, 1954, pp. 37–45; G. Schwarzenberger, 'The Frontiers of International Law,' 6 *Year Book of World Affairs* (1952), p. 246.

17 M. S. McDougal, 'International Law, Power and Policy: A Contemporary Conception' 82 *Hague Recueil* (1953), p. 137.

Chapter 5

LAW IN THE EXTERNAL RELATIONS OF GROUPS

Law in the External Relations of Groups

When the fishing group of which we spoke at the beginning of Chapter 1 returned to shore, it would find a number of members of some inland village waiting to receive bundles of fish to be carried home. The inland village in turn supplied the fishermen with vegetables. An elaborate ritual was built up for the process of the exchange, which was characterised by a system of mutual obligations deviance from which was sanctioned.[1] At page 97 above we referred to the interchange of specialised goods and services which took place among certain tribes of the Nilgiri Hills in India.

In still other ways the relations between groups become fixed. Hobhouse observes that: 'Often an open and honourable declaration of war is insisted upon, as among the Kaffirs, and in early Rome. The persons of envoys are, as a rule, respected, and often women are employed for this purpose. Agreements are understood and bad faith is condemned. We even hear of instances in which the use of poisoned weapons is avoided, and in which permanent injury to property is avoided.'[2] Among the Greeks, feuds were replaced by *spondae,* which developed into alliances, usually of a defensive character.[3] A rather elaborate system of agreements between the Greek city-states developed, consisting largely of treaties of peace, alliance and confederation and even including agreements for the protection of citizens of foreign states analogous to the modern treaty of commerce.[4]

We have used above a new term, 'agreements.' We have in so doing referred to conduct which is a product of the leadership function and of authority and which, in addition, involves interactions between members of different groups, neither of

[1] B. Malinowski, *Crime and Custom in Savage Society,* 1926, pp. 22–23.
[2] L. T. Hobhouse, *Morals in Evolution,* 1924 (?), p. 236.
[3] *ibid.*, p. 257.
[4] A. Nussbaum, *A Concise History of the Law of Nations,* 1954, p. 6.

which accept the authority system of the other. To the basic norm of 'Obey the command of your leader,' we now add a new norm, *pacta sunt servanda,* or 'agreements must be observed.'

Instead of co-ordination within the group, a function of leadership, we now have co-ordination of behaviour of members of different groups. Instead of a system of relationships within the group towards reaching the group goal, we have an interlocking system of relationships between groups towards reaching a common goal. Instead of leadership exercised within the group, we have leadership exercised in the process of negotiation between the representatives of different groups towards arriving at a new and mutually accepted objective and ways for reaching that objective. Instead of fixed behaviour, we have planned or social behaviour creatively determined by the leaders of two or more groups.

Now such external relations may themselves become the concern of specific roles within the organisation and performance thereof may become highly predictable. However, the investigation to be made in this chapter is directed to the function of the basic norm *pacta sunt servanda* as a creative force for the co-ordination of multi-group action in new channels. We will also briefly discuss in this connection the role of legislation and statute in the resolution of group conflict and the co-ordination of human effort in the national society. This inquiry is felt to be a necessary background for the topic of law in world society which is taken up in the next chapter.

Role of Negotiation and Contract

If it is to exist in society, the economic organisation must establish relations with other organisations and persons which will give it access to the power they control and thereby co-ordinate the respective systems of power to common ends. It must find a lodging-place in a market. It must establish a substantial system of relations with a market from which it can derive its support and thereby bring about the continued participation of its members. This system of relations with a market is the product of a continuing stream of transactions. Each transaction is, nevertheless, a discrete event. Out of all the potential transactions available to the parties, their concurrence in or choice of this particular transaction must somehow be brought about. The process by which a transaction or a series of transactions between the parties is brought into being is the process of negotiation. In each case the conflicting or divergent interests of the parties involved are bridged by a new and mutually acceptable hypothesis for the co-ordination of their activity. Negotiation thus involves co-ordination through consensus rather than through leadership and authority. When negotiation succeeds in formulating the new hypothesis and that hypothesis is accepted by each party as a guide for conduct, the resulting co-ordination in the activity of each of the co-operating parties is made more effective in reaching their respective goals because the power potentials of each are united towards reaching the agreed new goals.

Negotiation is that process by which two or more parties arrive at a consensus for the co-ordination of their activities. It involves the joint search for a new hypothesis for such co-ordination, and the acceptance by each party of that hypothesis as a guide for conduct. The joint search is not only an exploration on the technical level to lay down the patterns of behaviour which shall characterise future interactions between the parties, it is also a process in which the value attachments of the parties are reshaped. Through discussion, education, and even through fatigue in the course of the negotiations themselves, the process of negotiation redefines the value systems of each party and thereby enables them to formulate complementary rather than conflicting patterns of behaviour and to devote their joint power or energy towards reaching a common goal.

Contract or agreement is the end-product of the process of negotiation. It establishes new, complementary, interacting relationships between the parties involved. Such relationships may be relatively short-lived or they may be of lengthy duration. While they exist, the activities of the parties in question are directed to a common end. Contract is thus the instrument for bringing about the performance of the various internal functions of the economic organisation (*e.g.*, the employment contract and the collective bargaining agreement) and the performance of those external relationships necessary to the continued life of the organisation (*e.g.*, contracts of purchase and sale). That is to say, contract primarily deals with either the internal or external relationships of the organisation. It is the consensus concerning common ends and the means to such ends which characterises the concept of contract. Negotiation is the process by which that consensus is arrived at, while law seeks to ensure that the relationships thus envisaged shall remain a social fact and their breach appropriately repaired.

In the preceding discussion, we used the term 'parties' to indicate those persons who were brought into a co-operating relationship through negotiation and contract. When one such person is that fictitious legal personality known as the corporation, however, care must be taken that this personification of the corporation does not mislead. In terms of human behaviour, the making of a contract by a corporate organisation is the making of an authoritative decision that certain members of the organisation shall engage in specified forms of behaviour. This decision is authoritative; first, in the sense that it is made by a person who has an office within the corporation of a kind which will enable his decision, evidenced in the established form and ceremony, to be reinforced by the appropriate governmental institution and, second, in the sense that such person within the organisation will, by virtue of his office, and his decision in the performance of his office, call forth the described behaviour on the part of the members in question of the organisation when the content of that decision is communicated to them. Obviously, we do not need to repeat all this whenever we refer to the making of a contract by a corporation any more than the mathematician needs to repeat $a \times a \times a$ when he wishes to express the concept a^3. But we must always remember the content of our concepts when we use them, and not let fictions which we adopt for the sake of convenience become realities.

To say that a corporation has freedom of contract is to express a legal assumption or hypothesis governing the bargaining process rather than the social facts under which bargaining takes place. Just as the individual has his space of free movement restricted by the requirements of the role which he may at the time occupy, so the economic organisation may be said to have its space of free movement limited by the situation in which it finds itself. Within the domain of law, the corporation has a freedom to contract substantially equivalent to that of the individual. There are relatively few types of economic endeavour which the corporation as such may not pursue. The practice of the professions is, for example, barred to it—though the large law firm or large medical clinic is in fact a corporate organisation lacking only the formal certificate of incorporation. The modern corporate charter and the corporation law of the State are designed to promote, rather than to limit, corporate enterprise and the legal forms which corporate organisation may take.

The negotiator for the economic organisation approaches the bargaining table endowed with formal freedom of contract and right of property on the part of the organisation which he represents. Yet, as a matter of social fact, this freedom of contract may be illusory for one who must negotiate with a monopoly. The space of free movement of the corporate organisation must be viewed from the standpoint of the economic opportunities open to it. The range of activity open to the giant corporation of today, financed largely by its own accumulated funds, having numerous market relations in a diversified line of products, is much broader than that, for example, of a small corporation, limited to a single product and to a single local market for that product, such as a retailer.

Both the corporation and the individual have superimposed upon them the rules of law governing the bargaining process. Law intervenes to repress the use of contract for criminal or illegal purposes. It intervenes to control the conditions of bargaining and to restore the balance between the parties following the use by one of them of fraud or duress. It does not condemn parties to carry out otherwise formally valid contracts brought about through mutual or obvious mistake. The use of economic power is regulated to a very considerable extent by statute, through the antitrust laws.

The law allocates the disposition of the facilities and resources of the corporate organisation to those persons who may legally act in the name of the juristic personality known as the corporation. The law stops at the wall of the corporate entity; the meaning of property *within* the organisation itself is ignored. It is left to the organisation to determine *who* shall decide *what* is to be done with the facilities and resources comprising the organisation's 'property' and by whom it shall be done. Property may, at first blush, be thought to be communal within the organisation itself, but just as modern anthropology has destroyed the myth that property was necessarily communal in a primitive society and became individual in character only in an advanced society, so upon further examination 'property' in an organisation becomes the means by which those in authority within the corporate organisation make effective their control of the differential degree of access by its members to its facilities, and reinforce the authority of their commands to their subordinates. Thus, a direction that *this* working group shall use the bank wiring room and the equipment therein implies that the *other* members of the organisation shall not interfere with it. 'For, considered from a functional point of view, property rights are institutionalised means of defining *who* may control various classes of valuable objects for a variety of present and future purposes and the *conditions* under which this power may be exercised . . . property rights are not only an integral part of the economic organisation of any society; they are likewise a co-ordinating factor in the functioning of the social order as a whole.'[5]

In the modern industrial society the concept of property not only relates to the *use* of the facilities and products of the organisation but also to the *withholding* of their use. The legal ability to withhold access to the facilities and products of organisation not only becomes a means for controlling the internal functioning of the organisation itself but also becomes at times an element of constraint in the bargaining process.[6] Property is the starting point for negotiation, in that access to the facilities and power of the organisation can be withheld by the negotiating authority until satisfactory terms for such access are worked out in the contract.

Role of Legislation and Statute

Not all group conflict can, however, be resolved by negotiation. In the economic sphere, the market, as a means of utilising the resources of the society and directing them to the satisfaction of the needs and goals of its members, may break down. Undirected and purely voluntary group activity often fails to satisfy the wants of the members of the State. Leadership in the national

[5] A. I. Hallowell, 'The Nature and Function of Property as a Social Institution,' 1 *Journal of Legal and Political Sociology* (1943), pp. 115, 133.

[6] J. R. Commons, *The Legal Foundations of Modern Capitalism*, 1924, pp. 24–64.

society may require a decision that some new co-ordination of its activity is necessary if it is to continue to survive and grow in a changing environment. The function of providing that leadership is formally lodged in the legislature, but is in fact found in all the affiliated institutions of committees, committee hearings, drafting reference bureaus, trade associations, lobbying groups and even administrative agencies and organisations within the executive branch of government itself. In the democratic State, the process of legislation is carried on by legislative representatives selected by procedures and continually subject to pressures which will make them sensitive to the attitudes and demands of the groups affected by proposed legislation. The final basis for the accommodation of the divergent interests involved and for calling forth new patterns of conduct to satisfy emergent demands in the national society is the statute which, as a manifestation of both authority and compromise, finds acceptance as well as obedience among the governed.[7]

It was an extraordinarily fortunate circumstance in the development of the democratic State that its authority system was conceived to be a relation between the government and individuals, with corporate groups being treated as if they were persons, instead of a relation between the government and corporate groups. The felt values of individuals instead of representatives of corporate organisations or trades unions shaped the goals of government, and a more stable equilibrium of the forces of the society was thereby reached. The legislature could shape national policy in the national interest, the general welfare did not become identified with the welfare of, for example, General Motors. The consequences of the dictatorship of the proletariat or of the corporate groups of the Fascist State is inevitably a control of power to particularist rather than universalist ends and a reliance upon force instead of consent to establish authority and social equilibrium.

That is not to say that group pressures do not operate upon either the voter or the legislature. Each voter belongs to many

7 'But the legislature is, for all that, the only institution developed by man through the centuries which preserves individuals against gross invasion of their private rights and guarantees some minimum of benefits to all groups alike in their struggle for survival and supremacy,' T. V. Smith, *The Legislative Way of Life*, 1940, p. 91; see E. Latham, 'The Politics of Basing Point Legislation,' 15 *Law and Contemporary Problems* (1950), p. 273, and *The Group Basis of Politics*, 1952.

different groups; the character of his memberships varying with his status in society. His resultant demands are shaped by the perspectives of his particular social environment.[8] The legislature is in turn subjected to group pressures and demands, and tends to be selected by those groups which control the party machinery and mass media of communication. Nevertheless, the resultant system of authority in the democratic State rests on a broader base than that of the mass-organisations of the totalitarian State. It rests on a base of participation of the citizen in decision making which permits a social equilibrium to be established with much less diversion of social energy to the use of force than is the case in the totalitarian State.

Legislation, administration and law

The distinction has been advanced that administrative regulation prescribes in advance the obligatory rules of conduct, while legal regulation establishes these in retrospect.[9] The administrative regulation, to employ the terminology of Chapter 1, defines elements of responsibility in an area of freedom, while law is usually thought to be formulated by the judge *after* deviant behaviour occurs and *after* the parties in conflict have freely resorted to the judge to resolve the conflict from the standpoint of public purpose. In this sense legislation and administration are both phases of decision making involving policy or co-ordination of human activity to objective goals, legislation establishing the broad policies which administration in its turn successively redefines into constantly more concrete sequences of human behaviour. Legislation, administration and adjudication thus flow into a single stream of law, legislation and administration defining the course of the channel and adjudication removing the lesser obstacles.

Role of Diplomacy and Treaty

The analogous process in the international scene is that of diplomacy and the analogous end-product the treaty.

The rule *pacta sunt servanda* is a rule of international law. Among the expectancies included in the office of a head of state

[8] W. Lippmann, *An Inquiry into the Principles of the Good Society*, 1937, p. 254.

[9] K. Mannheim, *Man and Society in an Age of Reconstruction*, 1940, p. 298, citing W. Lippmann, *op. cit.*, p. 316 *et seq.*

is the expectancy that a decision made by him in the performance of his office, expressed in the established form of a treaty and carried to completion by certain established ceremonies, will be communicated to the members of his State whose behaviour will be affected by the content of such decision and will be followed by their performance of the specified behaviour. This happens with a sufficient degree of uniformity to enable us to predict social behaviour on the basis thereof, and to say that it is a principle of international law that international agreements, duly made, are binding. Yet we must remember that international law is, for the most part, limited to rules regulating the performance of governmental officials of a great many kinds and varieties, including not only heads of States and foreign ministers but officials of lesser importance, members of the armed forces, border officials, and so on. We shall go into this question in greater detail in the next chapter, but for the present we wish to point out that international law has not reached the point of development where the control of deviant behaviour is institutionalised in specific offices or bodies. It has not, for example, become institutionalised in the sense that there are supra-national political institutions which may be expected to intervene and apply sanctions to behaviour in conflict with decisions made by governmental officials expressed in the form of a treaty, save only to the extent that the proper governmental officers may have duly consented thereto in advance.

International law is a law of co-ordination in that, by regulating the conduct of governmental institutions and officials, it regulates certain phases of the exercise of power by States. It affords governmental officials a formal freedom in negotiating treaties analogous to the freedom of contract of the corporate officer under domestic law. The space of free movement of the State in establishing continuing relationships with others by agreement is limited by the necessities of its political situation, as is the private corporation by the necessities of its economic situation. The foreign minister of a satellite State of eastern Europe has formal legal capacity and freedom to negotiate treaties with Soviet Russia or any other State, but his space of free movement in so doing is limited by Soviet policy as expressed in the current Communist Party line.

Negotiation between officials vested with authority to decide upon the content of inter-State relations proceeds from the assumption of 'sovereignty' or the complete formal equality of legal capacity and bargaining power of each party. Another term for this theoretical or formal equality flows from the personification of the State and its endowment with the eighteenth century philosophical concept termed the 'will.' The psychological validity of this concept as applied to the person is no longer accepted. As applied to the State, it is pure symbol and myth, serving in this connection to describe the formal assumptions governing the initiation and manner of performance of the process of diplomacy.

In the absence of any superior authority controlling both the process of negotiation and its outcome, as between 'States,' we necessarily find that all the elements of the power of each of the bargaining parties are brought to bear upon the bargaining process. Just as economic power is used as a means of achieving social power as between parties possessing unequal power in the domestic sphere, so in the international sphere national power, *i.e.,* access to the economic power of the State, and with it an implied reliance on force itself, are used as elements in the bargaining process between 'States.' We have in each of the two preceding sentences used the term 'States' strictly in accordance with customary usage, but have in each case placed the term in quotation marks to indicate that the real participants in this bargaining process must be identified and to avoid falling into the semantic trap of personifying the State. Agreements between 'States' are reached by many officials, in the United States by the President, members of the President's 'office' in the name of the president, the Secretaries of State, of the Treasury, of War, Navy, etc. The form of such agreements is infinite, treaty, agreement, exchange of notes, act, statute, *aide-memoire*, *modus vivendi,* and the rest.[10] But in many cases, particularly in those involving the broad issues of national policy, the element of force is present as a counter in the bargaining process.

If duress or threat of force is used, it will not invalidate an international treaty. Force and the threat of force are in fact, even though concealed by punctilio and form, approved conditions of bargaining; they are *de facto* international relations.

10 M. V. Jones, 'International Agreements other than "Inter-State" Treaties,' 21 *British Year Book of International Law* (1944), p. 21.

Thus, no weighing of the respective national interests in a spirit of free inquiry and give-and-take shapes the content of the resulting treaty. No law steps in to control abuse of power, as in the domestic scene. Equilibrium and agreement are reached by an evaluation of the respective strengths of the national powers involved. The resulting compromise represents a balancing of forces rather than a pure balancing of interests. Negotiation between representatives of different States does not change the value systems of such States when force is an authorised instrument in the bargaining process. And when a party's command of force changes, as it inevitably does in a changing world, the agreement reached through force ceases to rest on its former foundation.

'We must negotiate through strength,' is the ever-present cry. The government of a State is the repository of its instruments of force, and force is used by officials to achieve particular national ends rather than the universal ends of world order. The law of nations is a law controlling the conduct of those officials in certain limited ways, as we shall see in the ensuing chapter, instead of a *jus gentium* brought about by world political institutions. Force, not reason, remains as a means for settling deeply-felt conflict. Instead of channelling conflicting patterns of conduct into complementary ones, which is the function of negotiation or legislation, war seeks to change through force and destruction the conditions giving rise to the conflict, to establish agreement or consensus by changing the power relations of the parties. Conflict then ceases to be manifest as a political problem, though it may still remain as a social problem. The cause may be a 'lost cause,' but it may still remain as a submerged 'cause' or unsatisfied demand.

In other words, the value systems of national societies may remain unchanged or may, indeed, even become sharpened in their intensity by war. An equilibrium based on force or 'balance of power' is constantly being overthrown as the repositories of force wax and wane in their strength. Today, for example, the United States is at the peak of world strength. Yet its strength is increasingly being based on access to raw materials and trade outside its borders. Within its borders, groups such as petroleum producers, clamour for exhaustion of national reserves as against reliance on foreign supplies—and hasten the day of national poverty or lack of power. Outside its borders another system of national power, that of the Soviet Union, is rapidly closing the gap in the command of atomic military power. Finally, the border as a symbol of defence from attack, as an operative fact in any decision to repel invasion, has largely ceased to be effectual in providing a shield behind which the national society can be a base of operations. With mobile atomic warfare conducted by jet planes and guided missiles, the fabric of the national society faces substantially total destruction on the outbreak of war. Planning of national policy must take account of all these aspects of power-relations between States, both present and future.

The foregoing description of the relations between States ignores the fact that many agreements are reached realistically, with an appreciation of mutual self-interest, and thereby rest on solid ground instead of the shifting sands of force. It ignores the many phases of international legislation which survive wars. It ignores the fact that the process of decision making by the officials concerned cannot be reduced to a simple mathematical evaluation of the element of force. Enlightened, long-term viewpoints shape the content of decisions in much of international relations. Yet the total structure or design of national power controlled by the State must be preserved, if necessary, by force. In the domain of foreign policy, force is an element involved in its shaping.

Force as an ingredient of national power must today be re-examined. A classic statement of power politics is that of von Clausewitz: 'War is thus an act of force to compel our adversary to our will.'[11] The atomic war of today does not stop short of bending our adversary to compliance with our policy through force, it totally destroys both our adversary and us. Force is carried to its logical absolute in atomic war. Its use overrides even the most basic of all values, that of survival. That is the terrifying fact confronting not only the governors but also the governed in the modern State. The political and legal institutions of national societies must be reshaped to prevent that imminent fact from becoming real.

To revert to our theme by way of summary would at this point be an anti-climax. Yet we must needs go on. We must say that negotiation looks to the creation of continuing relation-

[11] K. von Clausewitz, *On War*, 1943, p. 3.

ships between persons, including 'juristic' persons or organisations, law to the preservation of those relationships. Negotiation eventuates in the contract in the national sphere and the treaty in the international sphere, law concerns itself with the binding quality of the contract or treaty so created. Negotiation establishes functional relationships, law buttresses those relationships when deviation threatens social order. Negotiation creates new orders of relationships, law prevents their breakdown. Negotiation and law each has its role in the international order, and law cannot well take the place of negotiation when the latter is frustrated. While legislation is to some extent supplanting contract within the modern service State in creating new institutions and relationships, international legislation can today only most timidly occupy this role in the international scene. For, instead of the problem of the accommodation of group interests within the national culture faced by internal domestic legislation, international legislation must satisfy the divergent demands of many different national cultures and in so doing must rely on the consent of all the parties concerned.

CHAPTER 6

LAW IN THE SOCIETY OF STATES AND IN WORLD SOCIETY

THE SOCIETY OF STATES AND INTERNATIONAL LAW

AN anthropologist, E. A. Hoebel, recently said, 'The emergence of world law waits on the coalescence of a genuine sense of world community . . . Without the sense of community there can be no law. Without law there cannot for long be a community.'[1] In Chapter 4 we explored the concepts of the world community and the world society and the place of the State in world society. It will be the purpose of this section to explore certain hypotheses which have been used as a basis for classifying, organising and conceptualising certain observable data found in the relations between those groups known as States.

The behaviour of States in their relations with one another reveal patterns of practice followed by government agents just as there may be found in the behaviour of the occupants of any organisational role. As such behaviour becomes institutionalised and predictable, certain conduct involved in the role performance is regarded as obligatory. It is not only conduct which is expected by the performer of the complementary role but it is conduct to which he feels he has a right. Certain norms of conduct develop which define rights and expectations and obligations. Other norms of conduct develop as a response to deviant behaviour. Behaviouristically, we would define the law of nations as comprising those institutionalised rules for behaviour which indicate the content or permissible limits of behaviour of a government agent in the performance of his role in situations, one or more constituent elements of which are characterised by the fact of their identification with another State, that is, by the fact that other actors involved therein are government agents or members of another State or that territory or property involved therein appertains to another State or its members. Described in terms of deviant behaviour, a violation of the law of nations occurs when the behaviour of a government agent in the perform-

[1] E. A. Hoebel, *The Law of Primitive Man*, 1954, p. 332.

ance of his role so far departs from the expectations developed through custom in the performance of his role in situations of the foregoing character as to lead to the reaction that his conduct is outside the proper limits of his role. The impact of such rules upon any individuals involved in such situations and their status or position under such rules will be discussed in pages 140 to 145 below.

It will be observed that the latter definition does not state in whom the reaction occurs that the conduct in question is outside the proper limits of the role. In the structure of the modern State we say that the executive, meaning usually the foreign office, determines when such deviant conduct occurs on the part of a government agent of another State. It will also be observed that the latter definition is not phrased in terms of the violation of a right of another State. The conduct in question may have the effect of merely being treated as null, as in the case of a failure to follow established forms in the creation of a treaty obligation. On the other hand, it may result in an injury to an important interest of another State, thereby acting as a stimulus to still other responses on the part of agents of the second State.

Viewed in such a context, the rules of law become a product of the social action involved in a type of situation. They help to define the situation and the appropriate conduct therein by the actors. Law is a product of custom, but custom of a very specific kind in concrete and recognisable situations. Law does not concern the conduct of the abstract entity of the State, but the conduct of persons who are the repository of legal authority in the State when such conduct involves relations with the government agents or members of another State. International law so conceived remains positive international law, in that inductive techniques still remain the means for discovering its rules, but in the search for such rules it is freed of the fiction that States are its subjects.

The root of the difficulties implicit in the classic definition of international law as obligatory rules based on custom governing the conduct of States in their relations with one another lies in the personification of the State. Max Huber, in a perceptive study written as early as 1910, pointed out that the term 'international' in English is derived in part from the word 'nation,' which is used in the sense of a politically organised people or State, and hence 'international' signifies the relations between States and not between nations in their ethnical or cultural aspects. The term 'nation' was, however, to be understood in its latter sense in the German tongue. He remarked that the problem of international relations was one which has many aspects, the most important of which were sociological, psychological and biological. While a comprehensive approach to the problem was required, international law, fluctuating between natural and positive law, largely overlooked its sociological foundation. International law dealt with peoples only through the ethnographic-geographic framework of the State. It was the State which was governed by the rules of law. What was needed, however, was a clear understanding of the sociological as well as the legal nature of the society of States.[2]

Yet even Huber failed to carry through the logical implications of his observation that the use of the term 'international' involved a subtle shift from the social unity of the nation to the political organisation of the State, and hence referred to relations between States so understood rather than to the relations between nations in the broadest sense of that term. For him, the society of States and the will of its members remained the bases upon which the law of nations rested. No individual State can escape the consequences of its membership in the society of States and its subjection to its rules. As well as for groups of individuals as for the individual himself, the highest good remained the personality.[3] Though the term 'nation' implied more than a politically organised society, the world society was found in the society of States and its law in the relations between the political institutions of the several States.

Our eventual task must be to point out the categories of law and types of institutions regulating the life of world society and not merely the behaviour of the governments of States. If the State is a complex or a relation involving the governed as well as the governors, we must look to all the external relations of this group, whatever their form, if we are to describe the role of law in world society. Yet, as Max Huber was on the threshold of discovering, were it not for the fact that even he was a captive

[2] M. Huber, *Die Soziologischen Grundlagen des Völkerrechts*, 2 *International-rechtliche Abhandlungen*, 1928.
[3] *ibid.*, p. 101.

of the tenets of his discipline, international law shrinks from erecting its system of law on such a basis and instead confines its inquiry and hence its scope to the behaviour of government agents when dealing with agents or nationals of other States. Such patterns of practice, *sub nomine* 'the practice of States,' become the body of international law.

In last analysis, whether we start from the classic concept of the State and move therefrom to the conduct of the political institutions of the State in their relations with those of other States, as the source of law, which is the approach of classic positive international law, or whether we start from the individual and thence move to those particular individuals who are under the national law of a State charged with making governmental decisions in situations involving the members of other States, which seems to be the approach of those international lawyers who posit the individual as the ultimate subject of international law, in both cases, as we have said, we are concerned with essentially the same behaviour of the same kinds of person in the same types of situation. The differences between the two schools lies in how the behaviour is explained or conceptualised. Our point of view is essentially that a more precise terminology is necessary in both approaches and that when such a terminology is employed the doctrinal differences between the two schools become meaningless and evaporate. We learn through trial and error as well as trial and success.

The State as a Subject of International Law

It has been said that 'every system of law that has attained a certain degree of maturity seems compelled by the ever-increasing complexity of human affairs to create persons who are not men, or rather (for this may be the truer statement) to recognise that such persons have come and are coming into existence, and to regulate their rights and duties.'[4] We have hitherto traced the emergence of the association or organisation in the history of Roman and English society and the corresponding recognition of such collectivities as juristic persons in Roman and English law.[5] This was a convenient fiction which enabled the collectivity

[4] F. Pollock and F. W. Maitland, *The History of English Law*, Vol. 1, 1899, p. 486.
[5] Chap. 2, above

to become subject to the system of law in question. If the task of law be, among other things, to render human conduct more predictable than it would otherwise be, it was essential thus to regulate the conduct of great organisations of human beings. It was also necessary to define the persons who would be authorised to act in the name of the legal entity known as the 'corporation,'[6] for this was a power which could not be extended to each member of the organisation. When the official deemed to be appropriate for the purpose acted, the collectivity was bound and its property stood surety for its obligation. In the course of time courts and legislatures laid down in detail the circumstances in which individuals acting in their corporate roles would entrain corporate responsibility. As various configurations of operative facts involving the corporate fiction became set in familiar patterns, the law applicable to corporate action effected through the individual roles within the corporation became relatively fixed and predictable. The fiction became ritual while the law controlled, as it always must, specific human behaviour.[7]

The fiction of the personality of the State, with its attendant fiction of sovereignty, however, led to the erection of a glittering structure of conceptualism from which we are now just beginning to free ourselves.

The fall of Rome marked the emergence in the west of the feudal world of warrior, priest, free farmer and serf, with the trader for the most part confined to the local market. But by the beginning of the seventeenth century man was colonising the new world and engaged in a rich trade in the east. (It was in 1602 that the United East India Company of the Netherlands was formed.) An east to which a Columbus and a Marco Polo once ventured forth was now tied by trade with the west. A society which was once confined to the hundred was on its way to becoming a part of the world.

The system of authority to control this rich life of trade and intercourse was not found in the Roman State, which had once ruled much of the western world, but instead in a new ordering

[6] *Daimler Co. Ltd.* v. *Continental Tire & Rubber Co., Ltd.* [1916] 2 A.C. 307; J. H. Beale, *A Treatise on the Conflict of Laws*, Vol. 1, 1935, pp. 769–770.

[7] See S. Timberg 'Corporate Fictions: Logical, Social and International Implications,' 46 *Columbia Law Review* (1946), p. 533.

of authority, the nation-State. The warrior chief became the prince, the king, the sovereign. The prince and his entourage, once known as *lo Stato* in the Renaissance, faded into the background of history and the modern State emerged as sovereign. A personal sovereign became impersonal and absolute. The State was separate from the prince, it was a *personne morale,* a juridical person, and even separate from the government through which it spoke.

States are many, that is to say, each State has failed to keep pace with the expansion of its economic organisations beyond its political borders. The end of the Thirty Years' War with the Peace of Westphalia of 1648 has been taken to mark the final step in the emergence of the modern system of States under the authority of a consensual system of international law.[8] The tragedy of this step lies in the fact that the system failed to provide the necessary means of control for the real social system even under the conditions of the world of 1648. Centuries of bitter wars for colonies and trade ensued. No one State was successful in achieving world or even continental dominion, however, and the world remained one in which trade and communication flowed past State boundaries and the *jus gentium* of the Roman citizen became a *jus inter gentes* or a law of nations. The final consequence of the cleavage between the national State and the world society today seem to be at the point of pushing western civilisation into oblivion.

It is quite obvious that the collections of individuals who compose the entities known as States cannot, as such, become the subject of the rules of law arising out of what we so loosely call inter-State conduct. The individuals who are the subjects of a State do not act as a mob or as a pure democracy; they act, as we have seen in Chapter 2, through political institutions. We usually say that the relations between States are handled by officials known as heads of State, foreign ministers or secretaries of State and diplomatic officers and the like. But this is only a partial truth. There are many institutions and organisations through which inter-State relations exist. For example, there are the relations between the armed forces of States. In war, great

[8] L. Gross, 'The Peace of Westphalia, 1648–1948,' 42 *American Journal of International Law* (1948), p. 20; K. Wilk, 'International Law and Global Ideological Conflict: Reflections on The Universality of International Law,' 45 *ibid.* (1951), pp. 648, 660–661.

bodies of individuals are engaged directly and indirectly in applying force to a foreign State. In peace, military attachés and sometimes armed contingents are located in the territory of another State. Travel organisations carry individuals from the territory of one State to that of another. Trading and shipping organisations transport goods across State boundaries.

Yet the social fact that the State exists, not in the abstract, symbolic language of the political theorist or jurisprudent, but in the concrete, behaviouristic sense in which we have described it, of course has profound significance in shaping the law. For law must take cognisance of the enormous power which the social structures known as States exert. It must find a hypothesis to govern their relations which will enable their co-existence with a minimum of friction and will allow each a maximum of freedom. That hypothesis was found in the concept of sovereignty and its corollary concepts of independence and equality of States.

The personal sovereign of the early nation-State was, nominally at least, subject to the imprescriptible and universal system of natural law. But when the personal sovereign became the impersonal government the last formal restraint on the exercise of State power was removed. Yet, if we speak of this fact only in national terms, this freedom from restraint was nothing other than a statement of the goal of pure, absolute freedom in which each nation might pursue its own destiny and select that form of national life which gave it, if not the maximum of satisfactions, at least the minimum of social equilibrium and order.

The internal supremacy of the State, that is, the concept that the space of movement of the whole people was unlimited, was essential for a dynamic, rapidly changing national society. So conceived, sovereignty was a most useful hypothesis or basic concept. Sovereignty, however, was by hypothesis indivisible; it could brook no limitation upon its absolute supremacy either from within or without the State. As has been shown in preceding chapters, this too was a useful though imperfect starting point for a system of postulates to govern the relations between States. If each State be acknowledged by all others as supreme within its territorial sphere, a simple principle for purposes of administration would be established to take care of the problems of inter-State friction inevitably arising out of social intercourse across

State borders. No cause for complaint by the officials of one State could *ipso facto* arise by virtue of any exercise of governmental authority within another State's borders, save only as specific instances of conduct might, through mutual consent and uniform practice, become violations of a legal right. Also, if each State be acknowledged as supreme within its territorial sphere, a mutually acceptable starting point for the process of negotiation would be furnished, as has been seen.[9]

It was further necessary to have a concept which would locate the ultimate repository of power, so far as inter-State relations were concerned. Some governments were substantially supreme within their own territories, yet lacking in authority to conduct inter-State relations through customary, legitimate channels; they were, for example, protectorates. The concept of independence or capacity to conduct foreign relation was, as has been shown,[10] made an additional criterion for defining the State from the standpoint of international law.

So much for the criteria of Statehood. It now becomes necessary to trace the emergency of the concepts of the society of States and the law of that society.

The founders of international law lived in a world which accepted the existence of natural law as a given, and not to be questioned, fact. This was a higher law to which all mankind was subject. While with Grotius this higher law rested directly upon the individual and was thus directly binding on the conscience of rulers and thence upon States, later writers personified the State itself, postulated States as composing a society distinct from the society of men within States and as being subject to a system of law also separate and distinct from the systems of municipal law within States. The law of nations, deriving its roots and strength from the natural law, was considered to be universal, immutable and obligatory in the society of States.[11]

With the emergence of the modern positive school of international law, the law of nations still remained universal and obligatory; States still remained persons; there was still a society of States; but the law no longer necessarily remained immutable, for its roots were no longer found in the eternal verities but in

[9] E. D. Dickinson, *The Equality of States in International Law,* 1920.
[10] See p. 17, above.
[11] See W. Schiffer, *The Legal Community of Mankind,* 1954, Chaps 1–4.

custom or practice, and custom or practice may change. Hence the search of jurists for new roots to support the validity of international law. These have generally been found in the concept of common consent, whereby States are endowed with wills and substantial uniformity of practice becomes evidence of the existence of the convergence of the wills of the States members of the society, whereupon the resulting rule becomes binding independent of consent thereto by any particular State. When the binding character of the rule rests upon common consent, there is of course no conceptual difficulty in finding rules of law flowing directly from express consent, as in the case of treaties. The juridical validity of the system has also found its expression in such formulae or fundamental hypotheses as 'the will of the international community must be obeyed'[12] or 'States ought to behave as they have customarily behaved.'[13]

The positivist school of international law made the State the sole subject of international law, and the resultant system of law is accordingly called *inter*national law or the law of nations. It is a legal fiction which has worked reasonably well, since it is related to a unity of action in the national government and the national society which is reasonably identifiable as a social fact. Scientific methodology has been used to develop the content of the principles of international law, inasmuch as positivism requires that specific conduct of specific government officials be examined to determine whether any rule shall be deemed to exist. For example, a foreign minister of one State determines that national interest, on the basis of reciprocity, demands recognition of a claim or demand presented by the foreign minister of another State. Both the demand and the action pursuant to the demand are placed on the basis that they are required by 'law.' A series of such 'precedents' will establish a 'customary' rule of international law. Or an international treaty may be arrived at on a basis similar to that of the provision in which the early statute was sometimes couched, namely, that of compact. The rules laid

[12] H. Lauterpacht, *The Function of Law in the International Community*, 1933, p. 421.

[13] H. Kelsen, *General Theory of Law and State*, 1945, p. 369. Professor Corbett notes that 'Kelsen's "States must behave as they have customarily behaved" seems to be only a verbal variant, equivalent to "The will of the international community, as manifested in the customary behaviour of States, must be obeyed."' P. E. Corbett, *Law and Society in the Relations of States*, 1951, p. 308, n. 20.

down in the treaty will also become law governing the conduct of specific persons in each of the signatory States. In short, international law is a body of rules which patterns and renders predictable the behaviour of various government officials and individuals. Sometimes individual behaviour which is non-official may enter into the operative facts upon which official decisions are made, as in the case, for example, of that phase of international claims known as the 'responsibility of States' or as 'denial of justice.' Piracy, the slave trade, blockade running and carriage of contraband are other examples of non-official individual conduct entering into the decision making of officials patterned by the rules of international law.

The law thus created does not flow from separate supra-national political and legal institutions. It is a *jus inter gentes,* a law developed through practice and custom, based on the necessity of working out rules to govern the existence in a single world of a number of systems of authority and resultant systems of power lodged in national States, and to control, by a variety of institutions and means, the conduct of both officials and private persons. An alien is injured and is denied justice in the courts, an alien's property is expropriated, an alien is thrown into jail, a local official fails to act in an administratively approved fashion, a group of aliens is sent to a concentration camp, an alien is denied entry to the national territory or is expelled from the national territory, an official engages in negotiation with his official counterpart in another State, an agreement is reached between them, the agreement is broken, certain officials or governmental bodies decide that military force shall be applied against another State, these are some of the specific patterns of human behaviour with which international law deals *sub nomine* the 'State.'

When we come to examine the policies of governments which are *not* subject to the rules of international law because they fall within the sovereign sphere of domestic jurisdiction, we see even more clearly how international law is a *jus inter gentes* instead of a *jus gentium.* The areas of competition between national societies are outside the orbit of law, save only as voluntarily assumed treaty regulations may control such competition. International law governs treaties only in the formalities and modes of their execution, the time when and the circumstances in which they become binding, and their interpretation. The treaty relationship is one voluntarily assumed and may be terminated at will, subject to the risk of war. Success in war may validate such a termination in the treaty of peace and may also result in the imposition of new relationships, including the incorporation of conquered territories by the victor, which are likewise legally binding even though imposed under force of arms. Economic warfare, trade discriminations, export and import controls, the behaviour of cartels, access to raw materials, the treatment of minority races and groups, the solution of population pressures, the communication of ideas and the travel of individuals across State boundaries, are all outside the scope of law and left to sovereign determination as a matter of domestic jurisdiction. Human rights are respected and enforced only as an incident to the process of diplomatic protection of citizens abroad. To procure universal protection for human rights, resort to the promises of treaties rather than to a system of law and regularised sanctions is the best that can be had to assure minimum standards of decency for oppressed groups.

When the popular complaint is voiced that international law is not law, its zealous defenders will demonstrate that it is law, that it is respected, observed and regarded as binding within the areas of State conduct with which it deals. Yet there remains the fact that as a system it fails to regulate those relations between States which are most productive of tension and conflict. This failure, however, is not to be laid at the door of the system of international law itself but is rather the result of the conditions which brought the system into being. For international law, no less than any other system of law, is the product of its environment. When that environment became inter-governmental relations instead of inter-State relations, the structure and substance of international law became fixed.

The subject-matter of international law is a product of the fact that the system of law took State personality as its starting point. At first the sovereign or head of State was the mind and voice of the State. Later the political institutions of the democratic State were substituted in place of the personal sovereign. Consequently, a considerable part of international law is derived from the implications of the concept of the State itself. Was the Inca State encountered by Pizarro or the African and Asian

States found by early European explorers entitled to recognition as subjects of international law? When did a secessionist or revolutionary movement establish a new State? Who were the members of the society of States? How was a new territorial grouping of individuals to be brought into this society? Did a new grouping have legal rights or duties? Did it succeed to any of the rights and obligations of the State formerly in control of the subjects of the territory? Did it have a right to recognition as a State by the existing members of the society? What were the legal consequences of recognition as a State? What were the legal consequences of a revolutionary overthrow of a recognised government? Of the recognition of such a revolutionary government? In the course of history new States and new forms of government were born and died. It was accordingly inevitable that a large part of international law should concern itself with the legal consequences of this process.

Possibly the rules of international law stretching farthest into the past concern the ritual of communication and the protection of the channels of communication between governments. Who may speak to whom and how? What government officials are immune from the exertion of legal power by another State?

The physical fact of the territorial boundary of the State has an enormous number of legal consequences. How is it determined? Where are the limits of national power on the high seas, bays and rivers? In what circumstances will the authority of the State validly extend to new territories? How will it affect the exercise of power by government agents, including customs officials, coastguards and armed forces?

Then there is the great body of law finding its origin in intergovernmental agreements. What are the rules governing the making, interpretation, binding quality and termination of treaties?

The fact that the State is a relation between the government and the governed and that many of the latter find themselves in the territories of other States has numerous legal consequences. In what cricumstances does the treatment of an alien become the subject of international rights and duties?

War is a relation between States, and war occurs when complex and skilled organisations created and maintained by governments and under the authority of governments are authorised to apply their measures of force against one another and against the members of other States. Will the fact that war is waged violate a legal right? Will the manner of its conduct? To what extent may force be applied to States which are not engaged in the conflict as belligerents? What legal relations are affected by war and to what extent?[14]

In the western democratic State the relationships of commerce, travel and intercourse, which are termed the ways of peace, are not generally regarded as part of the government. They are largely the concern of the private corporate organisation or, in any event, of individuals, and of organisations treated as if they were individuals. The legal relations stemming from this type of social action have, therefore, historically fallen under the control of private or municipal law rather than international law. We shall have something to say later about the role of private international law or conflict of laws and the role of commercial treaties in this connection. International law, however, intervenes only in order to establish a certain minimum standard of justice for the treatment of aliens by governments. It does not otherwise, except for treaties, try to regulate these relationships.

The delegation of the economic phase of State life to private enterprise, the postulate that the legal control of such enterprise was a matter of domestic jurisdiction, the placing of such control within the sphere of the supreme power of the sovereign, meant that each State was largely left free to formulate its own policies in shaping its international trade, to determine what goods and what persons should be permitted entry within its territory and the conditions under which such entry should be permitted. It has meant that competition between States in the economic sphere has not been regarded as subject to legal control.

The Individual as a Subject or Object of International Law

So long as we confine our description of the rules of international

[14] An excellent summary of the rules of international law and the forces shaping their growth will be found in P. E. Corbett, *Law and Society in the Relations of States*, 1951. For a largely doctrinal account of the historical development of international law, see A. Nussbaum, *A Concise History of the Law of Nations*, 1954. Another valuable study is P. C. Jessup, *A Modern Law of Nations*, 1948.

law to observable sequences of human behaviour, and determine how different sequences of behaviour involving conflict between persons who are members of different States affect decision making by the relevant State officials, we are not troubled by the conceptual problem of the jurist as to whether the juristic entity, the 'State,' is the subject of the system of rules of law thus found in concrete human behaviour. We are not concerned whether these rules belong to a separate body of law, brooding and omnipresent, called international law, or whether they are national or municipal law. We are only concerned with segregating the predictable from the unpredictable in human behaviour and, in particular, in the behaviour of the officials and other persons involved.

Individuals are always involved in any 'law' problem, they may be involved in an organisational role and context or in a personal role and context. It is stating the obvious to say that we are concerned with specific human behaviour when we have a 'law' problem. The specific rule of law may be addressed to the individual acting as a pirate or as an applicant to an international tribunal, or as a police officer, judge or minister of State, all depending on the operative facts of the particular 'law' problem from which the rule eventuates. Moreover, all rules of law are purposive, they are directed to lessening friction and maximising the use of human energy to attain desired human goals. In this sense, the individual may be said to be the end or the beneficiary of the system of law. The jurist, however, deals less with the observable facts of human behaviour and more with concepts distilled out of generalised aspects of human behaviour, which he erects into a system of postulates which may, under the principles of logic, be dealt with as if they too were concrete and observable entities. The 'State' is thus endowed with 'personality' and a 'will' and 'supreme coercive power,' is made the repository of a system of rights and duties developed by and applicable to specific human institutions and behaviour, while the system of law thus erected between States is itself concretised as an entity separate and apart from the human institutions by which it was made manifest.

The system of discourse of the traditional international lawyer is to the effect that international law comprises a body of rules ascertainable with reference to the behaviour of States, that either States or individuals must be the subjects of this system of law, that individuals obviously cannot be, and hence States must be the exclusive subjects of this system of law. The concession is made that the individual may be the object of the rules, even that he may be the ultimate beneficiary of the rules, and it may sometimes be conceded that some rules may apply to his behaviour as an individual, but the traditionalist never concedes that the individual *qua* individual can invoke or become the subject of the rules of law. Other jurists point to the numerous instances in which the individual *who is not acting as a state official,* or bodies or groups of individuals *who are not acting in a public or governmental capacity* become involved in the making of rules of international law (*i.e.*, become part of the operative facts in some international precedent or decision) and draw therefrom the conclusion that the individual must be the real or ultimate subject of international law, which conclusion they usually reinforce with the additional propositions that the State can only act through individuals and that all law must necessarily be concerned with sentient individuals anyhow.[15] In other words, there are those jurists who make the State the sole subject of international law, those who make the individual the ultimate subject of international law, and those between the two who would make the individual (1) the object, or (2) the end or beneficiary, or (3) the addressee of rules of international law. An enormous literature has grown up and some jurists have become skilled in its classification and analysis and in dealing with the resulting concepts.[16]

Concepts in law, as in any other field of learning, have usefulness only so long as they are demonstrably based on human behaviour and enable us correctly to handle sequences of human behaviour. Concepts based on certain sequences of facts have

[15] An exhaustive list of instances in which individuals may be said to be the subject of specific rules of international law is set forth in G. Manner, 'The Object Theory of the Individual in International Law,' 46 *American Journal of International Law* (1952), pp. 428, 434–436.

[16] A most complete classification of doctrine and literature on this topic will be found in Manner, *op. cit.* See also H. Aufricht, 'Personality in International Law,' 37 *American Political Science Review* (1943), p. 217; V. Idelson, 'The Law of Nations and the Individual,' 30 *Transactions of the Grotius Society* (1944), p. 50; P. C. Jessup, *op. cit.*, p. 9 *et seq.*; H. Lauterpacht, *International Law and Human Rights,* 1950; H. Lauterpacht, 'The Subjects of the Law of Nations,' 63 *Law Quarterly Review* (1947), p. 438; 64 *ibid.* (1948), p. 97.

usefulness only in dealing with repetitions of such sequences. Concepts based on legal fictions have usefulness only in their immediate contexts. A concept that the individual is the subject of international law based on a classification of some, but not all, of the rules of international law has validity and usefulness only in the particular segment or group of rules from which the concept was drawn. The logical absurdity of the conclusion that the individual is the ultimate subject of international law can be seen if the full syllogism be stated. Any system of law must involve subjects (*i.e.*, persons or bodies to whom such rules apply whether as rights or obligations), (some) rules of international law apply to individuals, therefore, individuals, not States, are the subjects of international law. A course of reasoning which might be said to be more in accordance with facts and logic would be: Any system of law must relate to concrete sequences of individual behaviour involving interaction with other concrete sequences of individual behaviour, such concrete sequences of individual behaviour possess meaning only in their situational aspects, some situational aspects involve conduct and relationships cutting across State boundaries or involving members of different States; the term international law may be applied to the content of the decisions made by the relevant officials of the government concerned in dealing with such conduct and relationships under the belief or conviction that they are bound by legal norms so to decide. The official in question may occupy any one of the widest variety of roles. He may be an official in the Foreign Office, an officer in the armed forces, a legislator, a judge, a police officer, or a customs official. As the required behaviour in the performance of his office falls through repetition into fixed patterns, his official behaviour becomes predictable in given types of situations. The institutionalisation of such behaviour will of course lead to other institutionalised responses on the part of other persons affected thereby. Treaties will be signed and ratified in accordance with established custom, the relevant officials of each State acting their traditional roles. A military aircraft of one State crossing the border of another without consent, a public vessel of war overstaying its permitted period in the harbour of a neutral in time of war, an alien thrown into jail without due process of law, each will lead to predictable responses on the part of various officials of the second State. Individuals such as pirates and contraband-runners will find their behaviour leading to institutionalised action on the part of officials whose role it is to act in such situations. Other individuals may refrain from being pirates or contraband-runners because of the predictable behaviour of such officials and their command of instruments of force.

International law thus conceived falls into a system of rules of conduct for State officials indicating, as does any system of law, that behaviour which is permissible, obligatory or prohibited in the given situation. In each type of situation in which such rules for behaviour have developed, those with whom the official interacts will expect that he will perform in accordance with the relevant rules. Sometimes those in whom such expectations will exist will be the officials of other States, sometimes they will be merely private individuals. If those expectations are frustrated by deviant behaviour, then such deviant behaviour will give rise to still other institutionalised responses on the part of yet other State officials. Whether such other responses will be in exercise of a legal 'right' will depend on the facts of the particular situation. If an individual without any official capacity be primarily affected by such deviant behaviour, his 'rights' can be enforced only through such 'official' institutions and procedures as have developed for that purpose. If the person affected be an official of another State, his 'rights' *in the performance of his role* can similarly be enforced through certain established 'official' institutions and procedures. The description of the permissible, obligatory or prohibited official conduct in situations involving members of another State, and the indication of the official conduct to follow upon deviant official behaviour in such situations, constitute the science of international law. Thus, neither 'individuals' nor 'States' are the subject of international law, for neither term points with sufficient precision to the persons whose behaviour in the performance of their role is governed by the rules of this system of law.

Whenever an official in making a decision is affected by the fact that the situation being dealt with involves elements identified with another State, as, for example, the fact that an actor therein is identified as a member of another State, rules of international law come into play. These rules will indicate the manner of performance of his official role necessary to insure the legal validity of his acts or to comply with the expectations of the persons who will be affected by his decision. So long as he stays within his area of freedom in the performance of his role as circumscribed by the law, his acts will entail legal consequences according to the nature of the particular situation, that is to say, they may involve the discharge of a duty, the exercise of a privilege, or the creation of new legal relations. When he steps outside his area of freedom with deviant behaviour, his acts may be a legal nullity or they may possibly result in the creation of a new juridical situation.

It will be necessary to define with greater precision the nature of the legal relations involved in situations presenting questions of international law. A 'right,' for example, may involve merely an expectation of official conduct of a certain nature or it may refer to the official behaviour necessary to prevent a new juridical situation from being created unilaterally (*i.e.*, protest, reservation of legal position, application of sanctions, *etc.*). The ascertainment of the facts which are to be deemed important for purposes of decision making in all such situations, the legal significances of such facts as they bear on human conduct and the description of the legal consequences flowing from decisions of officials in such situations are the concern of the science of international law.

Determining the subjects or persons affected by the rules of international law is quite a different matter from determining the subject matter of those rules. In ascertaining the content of the rules of international law we are concerned with the behaviour of a limited number of persons in limited situations, namely, the predictable behaviour of government officials in situations one or more constituent elements of which are characterised by their identification with another State. The persons affected by such official behaviour in such situations cannot, however, be so neatly categorised. They will vary widely in their roles. They will not necessarily be an official of another State. They may be an owner of a farm located at a river boundary, a smuggler, a traveller, a resident alien, a corporate officer or a member of the armed forces overseas. Many persons other than government officials will find their conduct circumscribed and determined by the rules of international law. Though those rules may be limited in content, they will nevertheless affect the legal relations of many individuals.

Consequences of a Behavioural Approach to International Law

Adherents of the view that only States are subjects of international law, as well as those who contend that the individual is the real subject of international law jointly subscribe to the fundamental tenet of the positivists that the rules of international law are based on custom or the practice of States. Positivism made possible a scientific approach to the study of international law when its rules were conceived to be derived from precedent instead of the law of nature.

Yet a law based on custom is a law always laggard in meeting the problem of change and in dealing with new situations. Old custom may become inappropriate behaviour under changed conditions. A basic norm of the Cheyennes was that material goods, even though private property, should be generously shared with others. Hence, the taking of a horse by a friend of the owner reflected custom. But horses had become a kind of property peculiarly important to their owner. For this reason the proper persons in the tribe made a new rule for conduct: There shall be no borrowing without an asking.[17] Only slowly can custom bring forth such a rule. On the other hand, departure from customary behaviour may indicate a desirable innovation rather than conduct to be repressed. To the extent that the science of international law is faithful to its fundamental tenet, to that extent it will tend to be a rigid rather than a flexible body of law. Positivism was not, however, always faithful to its fundamental tenet.

If writers on international law were to confine themselves exclusively to State practice, and to practice as widely spread among States as theory would require to demonstrate the needed consensus, the rules of international law found in treatises would be considerably less detailed than they now are. International precedent may be the best but it is not the only admissible evidence in support of profferred rules of law. The decisions of international courts may also be cited and will in fact be accorded great weight. The views of writers may lend an

[17] K. N. Llewellyn and E. A. Hoebel, *The Cheyenne Way: Conflict and Case Law in Primitive Jurisprudence*, 1941, p. 127; E. A. Hoebel, *The Law of Primitive Man*, 1954, p. 143.

apparent solidity to an asserted rule. Finally, the fundamental assumptions of the discipline, in particular the hypotheses of sovereignty, independence and equality of States and all of their logical deductions, have had an enormous influence in shaping the content of the rules. The outlook of the individual scholar also shapes his appreciation of the data and statement of the rules.[18]

Yet departure from the purely inductive method is not necessarily to be condemned. For the most part, it may be said to illustrate the juristic method at work, the examination of juridical situations and the application of legal analysis and reasoning to their solution. As conflict arises between the governments of different States, its solution must be found in rules which will serve their mutual interests and take cognisance of the relevant facts of interdependence and co-operation, rather than be found by logic starting from the major premise of sovereignty.

The legal advisers of foreign offices are constantly faced with new and baffling problems. Situations arising out of the day-to-day external relations of States do not often find a ready answer in the relevant practice of States. Yet law impinges thereon, and alternative rules of law may be asserted as applicable to the particular situation. Varying legal approaches are possible and each must be weighed. The legal adviser must always examine the doctrine and decide upon the scope of action open under the established doctrine, and weigh the relevant rules of law applicable to the possible choices of policy which might be adopted.

When a scholar finds himself confronted with a problem on which the past practice of States can throw but little light, he may nevertheless formulate a rule which he believes should be applicable and bring such reasoning to bear in support thereof as may be possible, as well as such evidence as may be available. When a legal adviser is faced with such a situation, however, it is immediately cast in terms of freedom of action: What latitude for decision will the relevant rules afford? Yet the situation will in due course lead to a decision on the part of the appropriate government officials. Would it be possible for the scholar to examine the responses on the part of all the govern-

18 See G. Schwarzenberger, 'The Inductive Approach to International Law,' 60 *Harvard Law Review* (1947), p. 539; H. Lauterpacht, 'Codification and Development of International Law,' 49 *American Journal of International Law* (1955), p. 16.

ment officials concerned, that is, those of the several States involved in the conflict? Could these be examined within the context of the whole situation with a view to determining what new values may be emerging in inter-State relations, and the extent to which a new consensus on the requirements of role behaviour in such a situation may be developing?

It may be desirable to adopt an entirely new approach towards determining the rules of international law. Since they must always be rules applicable to the conduct of government agents in the performance of their roles, rather than to those vast organisations and fictional personalities called States, perhaps they might be regarded, in a very broad sense, as a form of administrative law. Need international lawyers, in their search for rules of law, emphasise those cases in which disputes have arisen between States and a rule of law has been conceded to apply? May not obligatory norms for behaviour be found otherwise than in situations involving deviant behaviour? May not international lawyers go directly to the examination of the expectations implicit in the roles themselves? Might they not resort to a technique of comparative law to determine a consensus in the laws of the several States which would reveal that which is obligatory therein? Might they not take as starting point the function and purpose of the particular role under investigation? For example, under present conceptions there seem to be little legal controls over the initiation of war. Yet, given the conditions of modern war, can any government officials be said to serve the interests of their State when decisions are made resorting to war as an instrument of policy?

If we look to the conduct of officials instead of the practice of States, if we place these officials in their organisational setting, if we examine the system of responsibility and authority of which they are a part and determine their freedom of action in the functions of leadership and the exercise of authority, given the value priorities of the society and the social pressures exerted upon them, we may then be in a position where we can predict the likelihood of any given rule of international law coming into being. We would then discover that 'custom' or institutionalised behaviour does not often furnish ideal norms against which deviant behaviour may be measured. States vary in their national interests. Some States are at the threshold of industrial development, others are highly industrialised. Some are maritime, others land-locked. Some are creditor nations, others are debtors. Some have colonial interests, others have but recently emerged from a status of colonialism. Some find a quasi-community in a common religion and written language, others in the tenets of international communism. Some are democratic, others totalitarian. On many issues, therefore, no consensus is likely to be reached on the basis that it is 'law.' In a world of diversity, there are few universals.

The search for the rule of law in international relations must be a search which will realistically face the fact that international law as custom will not furnish either a set of principles or a technique which can effectively deal with many of today's problems. It must face the fact that the approach of treaties or international legislation may provide a minimum set of rules making possible a workable system of international trade, travel and intercourse but that it fails to provide a means for dealing with highly charged international rivalries and competition. Some possible directions which the search for the reign of law might usefully take will be indicated in the next section.

Law in World Society

Private international law

We have hitherto noted that the State was classically considered to be an entity composed of a sovereign government and a permanent population within a defined territory. As such, its external relations might involve events transpiring outside the State borders or they might involve relations with members of another State, depending upon whether one viewed the State as a territorial entity or simply as a form of social organisation. Classic international law did not purport to govern all the external relations of a State, but only those which were the preoccupation of the government itself. International transactions involving individuals or corporations became the concern of international law only when a government agent had intervened therein in a manner prohibited by custom or treaty.

Let us now take a recent international dispute of considerable magnitude as a basis for illuminating the manner in which the various forms of law impinge upon the life of the world society. Such a case was the dispute between Iran and the Anglo-Iranian

Oil Company in which the governments of a number of countries, and Great Britain in particular, interested themselves.

Oil was found in Persia, now known as Iran. To bring that oil to the world markets, wells had to be dug, pipe lines laid, a refinery built, docks and storage facilities constructed and tankers built. These physical activities were called into being by a host of contracts and legal documents, including a corporate charter, shares of stock, loans, bank deposits, purchase contracts, employment contracts and the like. Contracts were signed in London, in Teheran and other capitals, in ports, and elsewhere and were performed throughout the globe. The enterprise took the form of a concession agreement between Persia and a private corporation. Persian oil could have been sold in the world market as crude petroleum but instead Persia became through contract interested in a joint venture or enterprise with the Anglo-Iranian Oil Company. Where otherwise Persian profits from its oil would have been limited to the fluctuating value of crude oil on the world market, now it shared in the profits from an integrated enterprise. Where, otherwise the Anglo-Iranian Oil Company would, in its refining and distributing functions, have been at the mercy of the world market for its supply of crude petroleum, it was now assured of a stable and continuous source of supply. For the whole technology of the oil industry is dependent on a continuous, never-ceasing flow of oil. Oil cannot be stock-piled or handled in batches; it flows.

Thus Persian oil moved into the markets of the world and energised factories and motor cars as a result of the functioning of the Anglo-Iranian Oil Company and other organisations with which it became linked through transactions formalised in contracts. These transactions often contemplated action in a number of states. The contracts by which they were formalised often involved negotiations in different States. There was no *jus gentium* applicable to such inter-State transactions or *praetor peregrinus* to decide them, as in the days of Rome. Nor was there a world-wide Law Merchant to be applied to such transactions by the Courts Merchant, as in the Middle Ages. International law was not applicable thereto because it related to the rights and duties of States rather than private persons. What law was to govern transactions cutting across State lines and occurring in more than one State? What law was to govern foreign transactions?

The answer seemed obvious. 'Any contract which is not a contract between States in their capacity as subjects of international law is based on the municipal law of some country.'[19] The world knew only these two forms of law and the disjunctive syllogism pointed to the municipal law of *some* country as governing any transaction between private persons. For 'an agreement is not a contract, except as the law says it shall be, and to try to make it one is to pull on one's bootstraps. Some law must impose the obligation . . .'[20] In other words, when events occurred it was felt that they must be governed by some law.[1] The question was which law.[2]

Why is it that the occurrence of all events must be governed by 'some law,' *i.e.*, the law of some one State? What is law in this context? Is it any thing else than the 'prophecies of what the courts will do in fact?'[3] Can we think of rules of law independently operating upon events as they transpire? When we say that as a result of certain events new legal relations have come into being, are we not in fact saying that, if these events were properly brought before the courts of a certain legal system, they would so determine? Yet, when a case is brought before a particular court is there anything other than the requirements of justice itself which makes it necessary that that court shall decide the case 'as if' it were the court of some other legal system? Is there anything inevitable, unavoidable and inherently necessary which drives the court to apply the 'law' of some other legal system? Upon what basis is it demonstrable that: 'Some proper law must have governed the juridical situation at the moment of its occurrence; the effort of the court is to determine what that law was; and that involves a question of the power of some particular law to extend to and rule the juridical situation?'[4]

19 *Case Concerning the Payment of Various Serbian Loans Issued in France. Case Concerning the Payment in Gold of the Brazilian Federal Loans Issued in France,* Permanent Court of International Justice, Ser. A, Nos. 20–21. Judgment of July 12, 1929, p. 41.

20 *E. Gerli & Co., Inc.* v. *Cunard S.S. Co., Ltd.,* 48 F. 2d 115. 117 (2d Cir. 1931). See also dissent of Justice Holmes in *Farmers' Loan & Trust Co.* v. *Minnesota,* 280 U.S. 204, 216–218 (1930).

1 J. H. Beale, *A Treatise on the Conflict of Laws,* Vol. 3, 1935, p. 1965.

2 See the perceptive analysis of E. E. Cheatham, 'American Theories of Conflict of Laws: Their Rôle and Utility,' 58 *Harvard Law Review* (1944), p. 361.

3 O. W. Holmes, Jr., 'The Path of the Law,' 10 *ibid.* (1897), pp. 457, 460.

4 J. H. Beale, *op. cit.,* p. 1965.

The assumption that there must be in the nature of things some proper law governing any event at the moment of its occurrence was a consequence of the territorial concept of the State. Since the State was a composite of a sovereign government, a people and a definite territory, the law of that State was necessarily territorial. In the classic pronouncement of Chief Justice Marshall: 'The jurisdiction of the nation within its own territory, is necessarily exclusive and absolute; it is susceptible of no limitation not imposed by itself.'[5] Events transpiring within its territory were subject to the operation of its laws and no other State should fail to recognise the validity of such legal consequences.[6] Whether such recognition was compelled by comity or by the existence of vested rights, whether such recognition imported a juristic act of the local law, with such local law regulating the foreign transaction by rules identical with those of the foreign State, the underlying assumption was the territorial nature of law.[7] Consequently, the principles of conflict of laws have the purpose of settling 'conflicts of legislation and conflicts of jurisdiction in space and in time.'[8]

With the last statement we have introduced a new concept, that of 'jurisdiction,' which must also be explored. It is a concept used to indicate the limits of legal power of a governmental organ. The principles of jurisdiction define the 'power of a sovereign to affect the rights of persons, whether by legislation, by executive decree, or by the judgment of a court.'[9] It 'means the power of a State to create interests which . . . will be recognised as valid by other States.'[10] Thus 'for every situation dealt with in the conflict of laws there is some one and only one "law" which has "jurisdiction," *i.e.*, power, to determine what legal consequences shall be attached to a given situation.'[11]

5 *Schooner Exchange* v. *McFaddon,* 7 Cranch 116, 136 (1812).

6 Thus Justice Holmes in his dissent in *Farmers' Loan & Trust Co.* v. *Minnesota,* 280 U.S. 204, 216–217 (1930): 'No one would doubt that the law of Minnesota was necessary to call the obligation into existence. . . . The continued operation of that law keeps the debt alive. . . . When such obligations are enforced by suit in another State it is on the footing of recognition, not of creation.'

7 For a discussion of the relevant theories, see E. E. Cheatham, *op. cit.*

8 E. Bartin, *Principes de Droit International Privé,* Vol. 1, 1930, p. 69.

9 J. H. Beale, 'The Jurisdiction of a Sovereign State,' 36 *Harvard Law Review* (1923), p. 241.

10 American Law Institute, *Restatement of the Conflict of Laws,* 1934, s. 42.

11 W. W. Cook, *The Logical and Legal Bases of the Conflict of Laws,* 1942, p. 7.

Whether the situation arose wholly within the territorial limits of one State or within the territorial limits of two or more States, the task of any court dealing with the situation was to find the proper law to which it should be allocated for purposes of decision. Since all systems of municipal or State law were territorial, logic dictated that there must necessarily be some one system properly applicable to any given situation. Was the premise true, however, that all systems of law were territorial?

To support the premise it was pointed out that 'The foundation of jurisdiction is physical power,'[12] and that 'The State legislates for and with respect to its territory because it is its domicile, its physical base, its centre of operations, the indisputable sphere of action of its coercive power.'[13] Yet territory should be regarded as 'the object and not the limit of the dynamic function of law. To make all law territorial is to forget that the State is composed of other elements and, in particular, is above all else an association of individuals.'[14] The subjects of a State travel, marry and settle abroad. They make contracts and engage in transactions involving conduct in several States. Corporate organisations establish offices, plants and buying and selling agencies abroad. Government officials and agencies become located abroad. These subjects, organisations and officials are considered to 'belong' to their State and, in certain respects, to be under the legitimate authority of their State. Law need not always be considered as territorial. The theory of personal jurisdiction increasingly broke down the principle of exclusiveness inherent within the territorial theory of jurisdiction.[15] For it is intellectually possible to conceive of law as being personal. Such a conception prevailed within the territory of the former Roman Empire and still persists in parts of the world today.[16] Law can operate only upon persons and affect only the behaviour of persons. In some situations, indeed in most situations, territory enters implicitly or overtly as an operative fact in determining the content of a decision by a government agent. Yet in other situations jurisdiction existed in respect of

[12] Justice Holmes in *McDonald* v. *Mabee*, 243 U.S. 90 (1916).

[13] A. S. de Bustamente y Sirven, *Derecho Internacional Privado*, Vol. 1, 1931, p. 176

[14] *ibid.*, p. 177.

[15] P. Arminjon, *Précis de Droit International Privé*, 1925, p. 92.

[16] A. Nussbaum, *Principles of Private International Law*, 1943, pp. 6–7.

the person alone, notably as in the case of nationals of the sovereign found abroad.[17]

On the one hand, reciprocity and fear of retaliation were powerful restraining forces dampening desires to expand the national sphere of control to other territories.[18] On the other hand, even more powerful forces pressed the sovereign to seek exceptions to the territorial theory, as national life expanded beyond State boundaries. It was considered that jurisdiction *in personam* would justify commands to perform or refrain from the performance of acts abroad,[19] though such commands must be made with due regard for the law of the foreign sovereign.[20] For example, a State could not punish a person otherwise subject to its jurisdiction for committing an act in another State done pursuant to express governmental authority,[1] nor could the courts of a State order the performance of an act abroad which was contrary to the law of the foreign State in which it was to take place.[2]

The limits of national power underlying the territorial theory were restated with considerably greater sophistication in the principle of effectiveness, namely, 'that a judge is not competent

17 *Rose* v. *Himely,* 4 Cranch 241, 270 (1807) (Marshall, C.J.): 'It is conceded, that the legislation of every country is territorial; that beyond its own territory, it can affect only its own citizens'; *The Apollon,* 9 Wheat. 362, 370 (1824); J. H. Beale, *op. cit.,* Vol. 1, pp. 291, 314; *Restatement of the Law of Conflict of Laws,* ss. 62, 63. For applications of this principle see: *United States* v. *Bowman,* 260 U.S. 94 (1922) (criminal prosecution); *Cook* v. *Tait,* 265 U.S. 47 (1924) (income tax); *Blackmer* v. *United States,* 284 U.S. 421 (1932) (to give testimony); *Skiriotes* v. *Florida,* 313 U.S. 69, 73 (1941) (application of State criminal statute to acts of citizens on the high seas); *Vermilya-Brown Co., Inc. et al.* v. *Connell, et al.,* 335 U.S. 377, 381 (1948) (Fair Labour Standards Act); *Steele et al.* v. *Bulova Watch Co., Inc.,* 344 U.S. 280 (1952) violation of Lanham Act occurring as a result of acts abroad by United States citizen residing in United States); *State of Netherlands* v. *Federal Reserve Bank of New York, et al.,* 99 F. Supp. 655, 665 (S.D.N.Y. 1951) (violation of Trading with the Enemy Act, as amended, s. 5 (*b*)).

18 *Lauritzen* v. *Larsen,* 345 U.S. 571, 582 (1953): 'But in dealing with international commerce we cannot be unmindful of the necessity for mutual forbearance if retaliations are to be avoided; nor should we forget that any contact which we hold sufficient to warrant application of our law to a foreign transaction will logically be as strong a warrant for a foreign country to apply its law to an American transaction.'

19 *Restatement of the Law of Conflict of Laws,* ss. 94, 96; J. H. Beale, *op. cit.,* Vol. 1, pp. 431, 415.

20 *Rickey Land and Cattle Co.* v. *Miller and Lux,* 218 U.S. 258 (1910); J. H. Beale, *op. cit.,* Vol. 1, p. 281.

1 *Nielsen* v. *State of Oregon,* 212 U.S. 315 (1909).

2 *Restatement of the Law of Conflict of Laws,* s. 94.

to pronounce a judgment if he cannot enforce it within his own territory.'[3]

Cognisance was taken of the fact that transactions or a series of related events might occur in more than one State. Put in its simplest form, any 'person who causes an act to be done within a foreign territory thereby submits himself, in so far as the legal results of his act are concerned, to the law of that territory.'[4] Thus a court having personal jurisdiction over the defendant could enjoin him from doing acts outside the territory which had the effect of injuring property within the territory.[5] In a more refined form, the rule was stated thus: 'If consequences of an act done in one State occur in another State, each State in which any event in a series of acts and consequences occurs may exercise legislative jurisdiction to create rights or other interests as a result thereof.'[6]

The hypotheses upon which conflicts were resolved between governmental organs of two or more States in the application of penal law evidence a similar history. While 'the territorial principle determining jurisdiction by reference to the place where the offence is committed . . . is everywhere regarded as of primary importance and of fundamental character,'[7] a series of additional theories was elaborated.[8] Consequently, it was affirmed that there are no '"rules" of reasonably definite content, established by international law, so regulating international relations that it is always illegal for a State to apply its criminal law to the acts of foreigners committed abroad.'[9]

[3] G. C. Cheshire, *Private International Law*, 1952, pp. 101–102; see also J. H. C. Morris (Ed.), *Dicey's Conflict of Laws*, 1949, p. 22.

[4] J. H. Beale, *loc. cit.*, n. 9, p. 152 above, p. 253; J. H. Beale, *op. cit.*, Vol. 1, pp. 315–316, 322.

[5] *The Salton Sea Cases*, 172 Fed. 792, 813 (9th Cir. 1909).

[6] *Restatement of the Law of Conflict of Laws*, s. 65.

[7] Harvard Research in International Law, 'Draft Convention on Jurisdiction with respect to Crime,' 29 *American Journal of International Law* (1935), Supp., pp. 439, 445; see W. E. Hall, *A Treatise on International Law*, 1924, pp. 261–264; C. C. Hyde, *International Law Chiefly as Interpreted and Applied by the United States*, Vol. 1, 1945, p. 727.

[8] 'Second, the nationality principle, determining jurisdiction by reference to the nationality or national character of the person committing the offence; third, the protective principle, determining jurisdiction by reference to the national interest injured by the offence; fourth, the universality principle, determining jurisdiction by reference to the custody of the person committing the offence; and fifth, the passive personality principle, determining jurisdiction by reference to the nationality or national character of the person injured by the offence.' Harvard Research in International Law, *loc. cit.*, p. 445.

[9] W. W. Cook, 'The Application of the Criminal Law of a Country to

The so-called objective territorial principle was developed in both Great Britain and the United States.[10] Under this principle, as stated by Justice Holmes:

> 'Acts done outside a jurisdiction, but intended to produce and producing detrimental effects within it, justify a State in punishing the cause of the harm as if he had been present at the effect, if the State should succeed in getting him within its powers.'[11]

John Bassett Moore stated that:

> 'The principle that a man who outside of a county wilfully puts in motion a force to take effect in it is answerable at the place where the evil is done, is recognised in the criminal jurisprudence of all countries.'[12]

Another basis for extraterritorial jurisdiction was found in the need to protect important national interests from injury. As stated by the Harvard Research:

> 'A State has jurisdiction with respect to any crime outside its territory by an alien against the security, territorial integrity or political independence of that State, provided that the act or omission which constitutes the crime was not committed in exercise of a liberty guaranteed the alien by the law of the place where it was committed.'[13]

Acts Committed by Foreigners Outside the Jurisdiction,' 40 *West Virginia Law Quarterly* (1934), pp. 302, 327; see also G. W. Berge, 'The Case of the S.S. "Lotus,"' 26 *Michigan Law Review* (1928), pp. 361, 381–382: 'When such a respectable number of nations make claims of varying degrees of extravagance, it is difficult to say that the matter is settled'; W. W. Cook, *op. cit.*, n. 11, p. 152 above, p. 15.

10 Harvard Research in International Law, *loc. cit.*, pp. 487–488; W. E. Beckett, 'The Exercise of Criminal Jurisdiction over Foreigners,' 6 *British Year Book of International Law* (1925), pp. 44, 53.

11 *Strassheim* v. *Daily*, 221 U.S. 280, 285 (1911).

12 J. B. Moore, *Report on Extraterritorial Crime and the Cutting Case*, 1887, p. 23, 1887 *For. Rel. U.S.* 757, 771; to similar effect see Report of Committee of Experts for the Progressive Codification of International Law, Criminal Competence of States in Respect of Offences Committed Outside their Territory, January 29, 1926, Publications of the League of Nations. V Legal 1926 V 7 C. 50. M. 27. 1926. V.—Report by J. L. Brierly as Rapporteur. For a notable international case affirming the authority of a State under international law to punish an act committed by an alien on the high seas resulting in the death of nationals of the State, when the cause of such death was the sinking of a ship of such State as a result of a collision with a foreign vessel of which the alien was an officer, see *Case of the S.S. 'Lotus,'* Permanent Court of International Justice, Ser. A., No. 10 (September 7, 1927). The circumstances that 'the offence produced its effects on the Turkish vessel and consequently in a place assimilated to Turkish territory' was noted by the Court, *ibid.*, p. 23.

13 Harvard Research in International Law, *loc. cit.*, p. 543, Art. 7; see L. Oppenheim, *International Law,* Vol. 1, 1955, p. 331.

The corporate fiction became another means for the extra-territorial extension of criminal or other jurisdiction. The employee or other agent of a corporation may perform acts abroad which result in the commission of a crime when the 'corporation or other juristic person . . . had the national character of that State when the crime was committed.'[14] Foreign corporations may be brought within the jurisdiction of the forum with increasing facility under easing standards of 'doing business' in the forum.[15] When personal jurisdiction over the corporation is found to exist, all its acts wherever performed may theoretically become subject to control. The spreading effect of these doctrines as they affect corporations engaged in international trade is evident.[16]

The hypothesis that all law was territorial was a hypothesis congruent with fact, so long as the facts dealt with by a court occurred within the territorial confines of only one State, although not necessarily the State of the forum. The moment, however, a transaction or contract had contacts with two or more States, the determination of its proper law became a creature of pure logic and mechanical jurisprudence in proportion as the contacts with such States multiplied. From the standpoint of the business-man, the transaction was one transaction even though it spread through several States. From the standpoint of the judge, however, the transaction was to be compartmentalised into the laws of several States dependent upon the place of offer or acceptance, the place of performance or delivery, the place of the occurrence of the last act in a series of acts necessary to the creation of a legal relation, and so on. Maxims such as *lex loci contractus, lex ioci solutionis, lex rei sitae, locus regit actum, mobilia sequuntur personam* formed the basis for the choice of proper law. Policy, in the sense of convenience and justice, might well influence the creation of the rule determining the choice to be made but whether the law finally applied to the dispute was a

14 Harvard Research in International Law, *loc. cit.*, p. 519, Art. 5.

15 *United States* v. *Scophony Corporation of America, et al.*, 333 U.S. 795 (1948); *United States* v. *Imperial Chemical Industries, Limited, et al.*, 100 F. Supp. 505, 511 (S.D.N.Y. 1951); cf. *International Shoe Co.* v. *State of Washington*, 326 U.S. 310, 316 (1945).

16 See *British Nylon Spinners Ltd.* v. *Imperial Chemical Industries Ltd.* [1952] 2 All E.R. 780 at 782 (C.A.), referring to *United States* v. *Imperial Chemical Industries, Limited, et al.*, 105 F. Supp. 215, 229 (S.D.N.Y. 1952).

wise or sound solution of the dispute was purely coincidental, for in determining the law to be applied the content of that law was never material and was never revealed until the choice of the proper system of law had been made. Whereas the *praetor peregrinus* or the Court Merchant could look at the facts of the dispute and apply the best rule for resolving the controversy and controlling future conduct of a similar nature, a court dealing with a similar controversy today has no such freedom to mould the law to the facts. A suggestion that the court be at least allowed to open the books of the several systems of law which might be applicable, and select that rule which would best fit the case has received but slight approval.[17] A proposal that a simple formula be adopted in connection with the Uniform Commercial Code which would extend the application of the proper law to all related phases of the transaction,[18] has likewise been persuasively criticised on the ground that no simple formula can provide a just solution in the variety of cases which must be handled by the technique of conflict of laws.[19]

It is submitted that the initial hypothesis upon which the system of conflict of laws was erected is incorrect. Law is not territorial; it is a product of human behaviour. The circumstances that in most situations it is just that the expectations of the parties in situations taking place in or predominantly connected with the territory of one State should be deemed to include the expectation that the law of that State would be applied thereto in case of conflict, does not necessarily lead to the conclusion that in *every* situation there *must* be some one and only one proper or governing law. When a court is confronted with an inter-State transaction, there is no reason why in the first instance it should not be able to apply such rule of law as seems best in the light of the facts. Where the transaction is strongly localised in one of several States, it may well decide to select the law of that State as the basis of decision. However, this result need not flow from the nature of things, from a major premise of universal application that there must be some one

17 D. F. Cavers, 'A Critique of the Choice-of-Law Problems,' 47 *Harvard Law Review* (1933), p. 173.

18 See H. F. Goodrich, 'Conflicts Niceties and Commercial Necessities,' *Wisconsin Law Review* (1952), pp. 199, 203.

19 M. Rheinstein, 'Conflict of Laws in the Uniform Commercial Code,' 16 *Law and Contemporary Problems* (1951), p. 114.

proper law governing every transaction. Rather, the inquiry of the court in an inter-State transaction should be: What decision will best serve the interests of security and stability in international transactions of this nature and carry out the expectations of the parties? In answering that question it should be free to turn to the law of any of the States with which the transaction is connected for guidance, or to make its own rule as did the *praetor peregrinus*. The answer to that question should be made in the spirit of free inquiry which is essential to the judicial method. In that spirit the court should be free to examine the law of any or all of the States with which the transaction is connected. It should not, however, be compelled *ipso facto* to apply any such law. Rather its approach should be that of the *praetor peregrinus,* seeking that rule which will best solve the dispute and adopting the foreign law only when it meets that test. The search for certainty and justice through the application of mechanical rules for the choice of law can never succeed, whether those rules be expressed in simple formulae or in a highly complex and detailed code of regulations. The moment that a court finds itself powerless to deal directly with the facts of a case and decide it on its merits, at that moment it ceases to be an intelligent instrument of social control.[20]

The consequences of the system of private international law are that it has compartmentalised into the territories of the several States transactions which are international in scope, and to which a truly *jus gentium* or Law Merchant should be applied. It has cloaked with the conceptualism of territorial sovereignty and jurisdiction the interdependent life of world trade, communication and intercourse. It has treated international facts as if they were national and has perpetuated a national viewpoint where an international viewpoint is needed. Because its fundamental thesis is inherently a fiction, treating international facts 'as if' they were national, it has led to a conceptualism and unpredictability in the legal process which has hampered the planning of international transactions. Hence, international business has resorted to other solutions in order to render more secure its transactions, namely, (1) the voluntary choice of law by the parties

20 See also R. de Nova, 'Solution du conflit de lois et règlement satisfaisant du rapport international,' 37 *Revue Critique de Droit International Privé* (1948), p. 179.

in the contract itself, (2) the erection of a contractual *jus gentium*, and (3) the resort to the process of commercial arbitration.

If an international contract provides that it shall be governed by the law of some State and courts will recognise such an exercise of the 'autonomy of the parties,' then a substantial degree of legal certainty can be imported into the contract. Their freedom to select a law of the contract is itself subject to the rules of private international law which reflect varying degrees of liberality on this issue.[1]

Sometimes when private parties or one State have contracted with the national government of another, they have sought to erect their own system of law by providing that it shall be subject to the 'general principles of law of civilised nations,'[2] although it may be questioned whether such 'general principles' would furnish that certainty and predictability which international commerce requires.[3] It has also been suggested that a concession agreement from a State to a private corporation of another State may provide that it shall be governed by the rules of international law.[4]

When the established courts and their law fail to provide a satisfactory method for the handling of conflicts, the parties themselves may, by resorting to arbitration, create their own

[1] J. H. Beale; *op. cit.*, Vol. 2, p. 1174; G. C. Cheshire, *op. cit.*, pp. 200–210; A. V. Dicey, *A Digest of the Law of England with Reference to the Conflict of Laws*, 1932, pp. 667–668; A. Nussbaum, *Principles of Private International Law*, 1943, pp. 157–169; E. Rabel, *The Conflict of Laws: A Comparative Study*, Vol. 2, 1947, pp. 368–402; C. M. Schmitthoff, *A Textbook on the English Conflict of Laws*, 1945, p. 100; J. Westlake, *A Treatise on Private International Law*, 1925, p. 302; M. Wolff, *Private International Law*, 1950, pp. 415–420; F. A. Mann, 'The Proper Law of the Contract,' 3 *International Law Quarterly* (1950), p. 60; M. Wolff, 'Some Observations on the Autonomy of Contracting Parties in the Conflict of Laws,' 35 *Transactions of the Grotius Society* (1950), p. 143; H. E. Yntema, 'Autonomy in Choice of Law,' 1 *American Journal of Comparative Law* (1952), p. 341.

[2] See F. A. Mann, 'The Law Governing State Contracts,' 31 *British Year Book of International Law* (1944), p. 11; *Anglo-Iranian Oil Co. Case* (Jurisdiction), United Kingdom *v.* Iran, *I.C.J. Reports 1952*, pp. 93, 112–113 (Judgment of July 22, 1951); *Arbitration between Petroleum Development (Trucial Coast) Ltd. and the Sheikh of Abu Dhabi*, 1 *International and Comparative Law Quarterly* (1952), pp. 247, 250–251. The quoted phrase is derived from Article 38, paragraph 1 (c) of the Statute of the International Court of Justice.

[3] M. Wolff, 'Some Observations on the Autonomy of the Parties in the Conflict of Laws,' 35 *Transactions of the Grotius Society* (1950), pp. 143, 150–154. The power of parties to select such a system of law is questioned in M. Wolff, *Private International Law*, 1950, pp. 146–147.

[4] P. C. Jessup, *A Modern Law of Nations*, 1948, pp. 139–140.

tribunals which will deal directly with the facts of such disputes and thereby gradually build up systems of law of less than universal application. Particularly will this be true of arbitration in commodity exchanges and boards and in trade associations. For institutionalised behaviour will be found in the external relationships of corporate organisations engaged in international trade as well as elsewhere, and wherever we find institutionalised behaviour we will find the source of law.[5]

Public international law

It will be recalled that we made the dispute between Iran and the Anglo-Iranian Oil Company the starting point of our discussion describing how the various forms of law control the life of world society. With the creation and growth of that international corporate organisation, Iranians in large numbers as well as British technologists and executives found employment with the corporation. A vast corporate body became a part of the life of Iran as well as of world society. Within Iran conflicts arose as to whether Iranian employees were given equality of opportunity for employment at all levels compared with British employees. The Iranian native employees were afforded conditions of employment greatly superior to those otherwise available to them within the Iranian economy, thereby creating a native élite and consequent tensions. The presence of the alien British in a highly nationalistic culture created other tensions. There were also tensions in the Iranian nation itself, including the demands of a poverty-stricken, uneducated peasantry subjected to an outmoded land system, usury, and grinding taxation. If those demands could be diverted to the channels of nationalism, to hatred of the British foreigner, and to hope for national riches through expropriated oil, the day of reckoning and social reform at the expense of the landed proprietors could be postponed. These were the forces which were catalysed into action with a Mossadegh.

To indicate the social structure and forces in Iran in somewhat greater detail, it is a country in which tensions are created by a peasantry living at a subsistence level located on small holdings of land owned by absentee landlords, who spend their share

[5] See K. S. Carlston 'Theory of the Arbitration Process,' 17 *Law and Contemporary Problems* (1952), pp. 631, 649–651.

in the earnings elsewhere than on the improvement of the land; by division of the society into a small ruling class of wealthy families, a small and uninfluential middle class, and a large substratum of peasants, labourers and nomads; and by a lack of social mobility, social progress and social responsibility in that the surplus capital of the wealthy is not invested in corporate enterprises but largely in land, and that social responsibility is lacking for the payment of taxes and for the management of corporate enterprises whose capital is derived from the investments of others.[6]

Now let us examine how the relevant political and legal institutions intervened in the dispute. The legal, as distinguished from the social, creation of the corporation was found in its corporate charter; it was thereby made a British national and not even the later ownership of its stock by the British government changed its juristic personality. The Englishman looked at the corporate charter, at the tankers and marketing facilities of the Company, at the offices of its directing personnel, at the contractual ties involving the Iranian facilities, and said: 'Here is the Anglo-Iranian Oil Company, it is ours!' The Iranian looked at the towering oil refinery at Abadan and at the oil fields and said: 'Here is the Anglo-Iranian Oil Company, it is ours!' Yet the company was a world corporation, with offices and distribution facilities throughout the world. When the Iranian properties were appropriated by the Iranian government, the consequences were not, however, confined to Iran or Britain but had a world impact.

From the standpoint of international law, the dispute was a matter of 'State responsibility.' The basic social conflicts and tensions which engendered the dispute and of which the dispute was but a mere symptom were deemed irrelevant. Great Britain could obtain relief only if a denial of justice existed and if Iran conceded the legal correctness of her claim, or, at least, was willing to arbitrate the issue. From the standpoint of the International Court of Justice and its compulsory jurisdiction, the question was in part whether the dispute involved a treaty or merely a private contract. From the standpoint of the Security

[6] Overseas Consultants, Inc., *Report on the Seven Year Development Plan for the Plan Organisation of the Imperial Government of Iran,* Vol. 1, 1949; V. Sackville-West, *Passenger to Teheran,* 1940; R. Bullard, 'Behind the Oil Dispute in Iran,' 31 *Foreign Affairs* (1953), p. 461.

Council, the question was not the impairment of the power-balance but whether a threat to peace in fact existed and whether it was appropriate for the Council to intervene.[7]

Thus public international law, because of the limitations of its structure and rules, failed to provide any effective method for dealing with a world problem of the utmost importance.

Commercial treaties

Since, under the classic positivist conception of international law, only States were the subjects of international law, since the practice of States which was the source of international law was found in the patterns of practice of those governmental organs which were charged with the conduct of relations with the appropriate or corresponding governmental organs of other States, rather than in those continuing inter-State relationships carried on by the so-called private organisations of the State, as, for example, the international corporation, and since the patterns of practice of such governmental organs in the conduct of foreign relations only intermittently touched upon the rich and growing life of international trade and intercourse in what was termed the private sphere, the regulation of inter-State relations among corporations and individuals could not be reached by the laggard steps of customary international law. The international lawyer could not consistently with the precepts of his discipline, take cognisance of these growing relations of trade and intercourse because they were not 'State' relations. True, he had defined the State to include its subjects as well as its government, but State practice was conceived to be governmental practice and international law was held to be public rather than private law. Hence, the regulation of the developing inter-State relations of trade became the task of international legislation.

Prior to the First World War treaties of commerce included provisions of a general nature concerning protection and security of nationals and their property, ensured at least a limited access to the courts of each party, regulated maritime matters, consuls, detention, embargoes and, occasionally, included provisions

[7] *Anglo-Iranian Oil Co. Case* (Jurisdiction), United Kingdom *v.* Iran, Judgment of July 22nd, 1952, *I.C.J. Reports 1952*, p. 93; United Nations, Official Records of the Security Council, Sixth Year, No. 559, p. 26 (S/PV. 561); Alan W. Ford, *The Anglo-Iranian Oil Dispute of 1951–1952*, 1954.

relating to expropriation and compensation. Clauses were included providing for due process of law whenever the property of nationals of one party was taken by the government of the other party and incorporating by reference in this connection the customary and recognised international standards of protection.[8] Since the end of the Second World War, however, United States commercial treaties have evidenced an extraordinary degree of growth and development. Indeed, an examination of commercial treaties of other countries of the world as published in the *United Nations Treaty Series* pursuant to Article 102 of the Charter reveals that in no other country[9] has there developed a corresponding technique manifesting itself in provisions so comprehensive in character as those included in the treaties recently negotiated by the United States.

In general, these treaties are designed to ensure that the nationals of each party are accorded the right to enter the territories of the other, to travel therein and establish and carry on commercial enterprises and activities, and to enjoy the most constant protection and security. The treaties are distinguished by the comprehensiveness and precision of their detailed provisions. The scope of commercial enterprises permitted,[10] rights to employment and social insurance,[11] freedom of transit and the treatment of commercial travellers,[12] control of restrictive business practices,[13] treatment with regard to internal taxes and charges, and the regulation of double taxation,[14] the regulation of financial transactions, investment and withdrawal of funds, and exchange rates and controls,[15] judicial and administrative regula-

[8] R. R. Wilson, 'Property-Protection Provisions in United States Commercial Treaties,' 45 *American Journal of International Law* (1951), p. 83.

[9] *e.g.*, Norway-Yugoslavia Treaty of August 30, 1946, 30 United Nations Treaty Series, p. 188; India-Switzerland Treaty of August 14, 1948; 30 *ibid.*, p. 4; Philippines-Italy Treaty of July 9, 1947; 44 *ibid.*, p. 4.

[10] United States-Italy Treaty of February 2, 1948, Arts. 1 and 3; United States Treaties and other International Acts Series 1965.

[11] United States-Greece Treaty of August 3, 1951, Art. 11. Sen. Exec. Doc. J., 82d Cong., 2d Sess.

[12] United States-Ireland Treaty of January 21, 1950, Arts. 1 and 11. 1 United States Treaties and other International Agreements, pp. 785, 788, 794 (1950).

[13] United States-Denmark Treaty of October 1, 1951, Art. 18. Sen. Exec. Doc. I, 82d Cong., 2d Sess.

[14] United States-Uruguay Treaty of November 23, 1949, Art. 9, 23 *Department of State Bulletin* (1950), pp. 502, 504.

[15] *ibid.*, Art. 15.

tions,[16] and means for the pacific settlement of disputes[17] are some of the more important provisions included. Through these treaties, a code embodying standards of protection for foreign investment is in process of development.

Accompanying the growth of bilateral treaties of commerce there have been organised efforts by States to deal with common problems through multilateral agreements. In general, these have been directed to the control of trade barriers and unfair trade practices. Cartelisation, exchange controls, tax refunds, quota restrictions, tariff specialisations and State trading were devices which were not within the effective scope of customary international law as it had developed by 1945.[18] The League of Nations had made substantial steps in this direction through multilateral conventions, but these failed to halt trade policies which had significantly diverted and restricted trade. Trade barriers were later dealt with by such arrangements as Soviet state-trading, the United States reciprocal reduction of tariffs under the Trade Agreements Acts, the Benelux Customs Union and the Commonwealth Sterling Area. These arrangements were thereafter supplemented by multilateral arrangements such as the coffee and wheat agreements.[19] The interdependence of the Allies of the Second World War and their preparations for United Nations economic activities in such conferences as Bretton Woods and the International Monetary Fund Agreements created a basis for world wide acceptance of the multilateral conference as a device by which the great majority of trading nations could regulate commercial practice.

Although the most important of these, namely, the Havana Charter of 1948[20] has no far proved abortive, the interim agreement negotiated at Geneva known as the General Agreement on Tariffs and Trade or GATT[1] has come into effect and regulates nearly four-fifths of all world trade with thirty-four of the leading

[16] United States-Italy Treaty of February 2, 1948, Art. 15, n. 10, above.
[17] *ibid.*, Art. 26.
[18] For illustrative examples, see P. Einzig, *Bloodless Invasion*, 1939.
[19] See, generally, S. Enke and V. Salera, *International Economics*, 1951; C. P. Kindelberger, *International Economics*, 1953; H. G. Brainard, *International Economics and Public Policy*, 1954.
[20] Final Act of the United Nations Conference on Trade and Employment, March 24, 1948. Department of State, Publication 3117, Commercial Policy Series 113.
[1] General Agreement on Tariffs and Trade of October 30, 1947, 55 United Nations Treaty Series, p. 188.

trading nations as participants.[2] Because most results accomplished under the Reciprocal Trade Agreements Programme were embodied in GATT, thirteen of the twenty-seven bilateral trade agreements theretofore made by the United States have been suspended or terminated since 1947.[3] GATT rests upon a precarious foundation, for only sixty day notice of termination is required. Its major bulwark is the recognition by its participants that its benefits are available only to GATT members and not under the usual most-favoured-nation clauses.

Members of GATT agree to accord many important privileges. Unconditional and unrestricted most-favoured-nation treatment is granted. Quantitative restrictions, the chief source of interwar difficulties, are forbidden in principle and regulated under recognised exceptions. Reductions in tariffs are sought in a manner similar to the Reciprocal Trade Programme pattern of negotiation. Tariff specialisation is condoned, as permitting an area of compromise between difficult domestic pressures and the narrower area of importance to the foreign exporter. Because of political or geographical considerations, certain areas are accorded a status above that of most-favoured-nation treatment by GATT members. Thus United States concessions to the Philippines and Cuba, the British Imperial Preferential System, certain customs unions and free trade areas are permitted and their use encouraged where the effect is to foster international trade. Because a tariff may be 'padded' so that it can be reduced as a concession and still afford all the protection desired, GATT members are generally bound not to increase either their tariff rates or their administrative charges. Both GATT and the Havana Charter allow countervailing duties by members to meet predatory monopoly or bounty (subsidised) dumping practices.[4]

The success of GATT has led its members to agree to establish an Organisation for Trade Co-operation under the ægis of the United Nations to provide for continuous consultation and review of trade problems. This organisation is to consist of an executive committee, a secretariat and an assembly. Regular review of

2 Message of the President to Congress, April 14, 1955, 62 *Department of State Bulletin* (1955), p. 678.
3 Chamber of Commerce of the United States, *International Trade Policy Issues*, 1954.
4 See, generally, H. C. Hawkins, *Commercial Treaties and Agreements*, 1951; W. A. Brown, *The United States and the Restoration of International Trade*, 1950.

import restrictions of a quantitative nature and greater flexibility in modifying tariff rates are major objectives in establishing the Organisation for Trade Co-operation. If a government wishes to dispose of surplus or strategic stockpiles, it agrees to consult with other GATT members on the matter through this organisation.[5] It is 'a continuous mechanism for administration of trade rules and discussion of mutual trade problems.'[6]

The Growth of a Jus Gentium in World Society

The growth of a modern *jus gentium* applicable to individuals and corporate bodies in the international sphere will be gradual and by a process of accretion rather than revolutionary change, just as was the growth of the ancient *jus gentium* of Rome. Certain directions which such a growth might take are already apparent.

International trade tribunals

The process of international commercial arbitration has already developed tribunals which settle numerous cases involving international trade disputes. Nominally, they take place pursuant to a particular system of national law and their awards are sanctioned by its authority. In fact, they are the judicial organs of emerging systems of law arising out of trade conflicts involving international economic organisations and their awards are respected because of their effectiveness in solving the disputes and not merely because of the sanction of national power. Where such arbitral tribunals appear rather frequently in trade involving a particular commodity, for example, they might well be given a *de jure* status as international judicial bodies which would reflect their *de facto* status. An international trade tribunal has been proposed as a practical step towards integration.[7]

International claims tribunals

Suggestions have from time to time been advanced that the present system of *ad hoc* arbitration of international claims of

5 Agreement on Organisation for Trade Co-operation of March 10, 1955, 62 *Department of State Bulletin* (1955), p. 579.
6 Note 2, above.
7 See S. Timberg, 'An International Trade Tribunal—A Step Forward Short of Surrender of Sovereignty,' 33 *Georgetown Law Journal* (1945), p. 373.

individuals and corporate bodies against States be regularised through the establishment of duly constituted, permanent international tribunals to which aggrieved parties would have direct access. Most assuredly here is a step in the institutionalisation of international law for which established jurisprudence in numerous adjudicated international claims is already at hand.[8]

International tribunal for the protection of foreign private investment

In view of the importance of private foreign investment, both to industrially advanced nations as a means of sustaining a dynamic economy, and to less advanced nations as a means for economic progress and growth, a code and a court for the protection of foreign investment would seem to be an eventual necessity.[9] It is not enough merely to advocate the creation of such a tribunal to decide cases in accordance with the rules of international law in their existing state of development. The tribunal must be empowered to investigate the underlying sources of the dispute and not merely to determine and decide its formal legal aspects.

The corporation engaged in international trade must acknowledge responsibilities in the exercise of its power if it is to have protection in the continuance of its exercise of power under international law. International protection for the world corporation can be successfully accorded if agreed minimum principles are established governing the conditions under which it must function in each national society. For, if the world corporation is to achieve recognition and status as an approved legal personality under international law, it must become responsible under that law and accept obligations commensurate with those of the domestic corporation, namely, that it will satisfactorily discharge its functions in world society.

[8] *e.g.*, resolution of American Bar Association proposing a system of International Circuit Courts sitting in regular terms in the capital of each member State of an International Judicial System, 69 *Annual Report of the American Bar Association* (1944), pp. 165, 169; see M. B. Carroll, 'Postwar International Organisation and the Work of the Section of International and Comparative Law of the American Bar Association,' 39 *American Journal of International Law* (1945), pp. 20, 24; W. B. Cowles, 'Revision of the United Nations Charter and the Development of the Law,' 33 *Nebraska Law Review* (1953), p. 35.

[9] *e.g.*, Joint Report, Committee on Foreign Law and Committee on International Law, 'Protection Abroad of Private Investments,' 7 *Record of The Association of the Bar of the City of New York* (1952), p. 219.

The implications of this problem cannot be seen or worked out if we limit our observations to the use of such generalities as 'foreign capital,' 'foreign investment,' and the like. We must realise that when a large international corporation establishes a subsidiary, or commences operations in a particular country, this means that thousands upon thousands of specific human relations are introduced into the fabric of the community. Workers are employed, extensive new facilities and homes and schools built, and quantities of goods purchased and sold. New standards of living for local workers tend to create tensions within the local community. Unless there is a consensus in the community that the new enterprise means continually expanding opportunities for local workers, that the enterprise is making its fair contribution to the growth and progress of the country, that the foreign personnel and management of the enterprise understand, and are accommodating themselves to, the mores of the country, that the foreign personnel and management are refraining from influencing the conduct of the government and political institutions except by means appropriate for non-nationals, and that the enterprise is devoting its efforts to carrying out its primary corporate functions and is not engaged in such incidental and harmful activities as speculation, hoarding and the like, the international corporation will not rest on a sound social foundation. Law cannot be relied upon permanently to preserve a shaky social structure through the application of force. The management of the world corporation must not only see to it that the organisation efficiently carries out its corporate purpose, but also that it is successfully integrated in the social fabric and culture of each country in which it operates. This also means that the receiving State must give it an opportunity to do so.

Unless the foregoing principles are recognised by the management of the world corporation, it may become necessary through international agreement to establish the principle of equality of opportunity to the members of each national society in which the corporation operates to become employees of the corporation. It may also be necessary to recognise the principle that there must be free mobility within the corporation (*i.e.*, opportunity for advancement) for the individuals who are its employees, in accordance with their respective abilities and without regard to their race or nationality. It may further be necessary to establish the principles upon which the several States contributing to the strength of the world corporation shall share, according to their respective contributions, in its gains. Given these obligations on the part of the world corporation, a basis for its security and legal status under international law will be established and the way kept open for it to make its contributions to the welfare of the peoples involved. The corporation and the national government will thus each be subject to rights and obligations. The corporation will be assured that its property will not be arbitrarily expropriated and the government will be assured that the use of corporate property will be directed to public ends.

International law must eventually come to recognise that the problem of the control of the use of authority is not limited to the national State, but also arises in the life of transnational or world corporations. Inasmuch as these corporations are concerned with satisfying the needs of the individual in the modern interdependent world, we must establish rules of law which will, on the one hand, furnish them protection in the exercise of their functions and, on the other hand, impose a certain minimum of responsibilities upon the exercise by them of their authority.[10]

The establishment of standards of conduct and instruments of control in this sphere is not a matter for overnight legislation; it must be handled wisely and on a step-by-step basis. In calling attention to the social obligations of the international corporation, we must not overlook the obligations of the local governments to the corporation and to their citizenry. So long as the international corporation is carrying out its public purposes, it should be supported and encouraged by the several governments under which it functions. The tax and other gains realised from its activities should be devoted to the benefit of the entire country and citizenry and not be banked abroad or used in local projects having merely a prestige value.

Moreover, not all the obligations of which we have been

[10] See, generally, International Chamber of Commerce, *Fair Treatment for Foreign Investments: International Code* (Brochure 129); United Nations, *The International Flow of Private Capital 1946–1952* (Doc. E/2531, ST/ECA/22, 1953), *International Flow of Private Capital for the Economic Development of Under-Developed Countries* (Doc. E/2546, 19 Feb. 1953), *Report of the Ad Hoc Committee on Restrictive Business Practices* (Doc. E/2380, E/AC. 37/3, 30 Mar. 1953); S. Nakasian, 'The Security of Foreign Petroleum Resources,' 68 *Political Science Quarterly* (1953), pp. 181, 201–202.

speaking can be brought under the enforcement of courts of law. Many involve standards of conduct which cannot readily be measured and weighed by judicial tribunals. Whether such standards are being observed in good faith must at first be determined in a spirit of good will and in the absence of rancour by the parties themselves. The translation of such objectives of conduct into definite rules of conduct for judicial enforcement is a task which can be carried out only gradually.

The perspective and training of the international judge of the future

The growth of the *jus gentium* of Rome, the growth of the common law of England, was each the product of trained jurists deciding cases under the principle of free inquiry. That is to say, the law was always shaped by the social conduct in the light of the then existing structure of society and not because of the demands of sterile and outmoded precedent. The strength of Roman law lay in the spirit of the *jus aequum,* the strength of the English common law was preserved when Chancery and its system of equity helped bridge the change from a static and ritualistic law to a modern and flexible body of law in an industrial society.

International law in its turn must similarly be shaped by jurists faithful to the spirit of the law but not bound by particularist national viewpoints. The international jurist today is somewhat at the point of development as the lawyer in the national sphere at the beginning of the twentieth century. Justice Holmes said in 1897: 'For the rational study of the law the black-letter man may be the man of the present, but the man of the future is the man of statistics and the master of economics.'[11] His prediction has been carried out in the training of lawyers in the modern law schools, and law is today taught in the setting of the social sciences.

In international law we similarly need a new approach to the training of the international lawyer and the international jurist. He must be not alone the black-letter man of law and diplomacy. He must be conversant with the philosophy of law and ethics, comparative law, international economics, history, social

[11] O. W. Holmes, Jr., 'The Path of the Law,' 10 *Harvard Law Review* (1897), pp. 457, 469.

psychology and anthropology, among others. Given individuals so trained, individuals with all the technique and inherited traditions of the law, together with the insight and wisdom of a cultural education, we may finally be able to fashion international law into a true *jus gentium* and make it a real force in the lives of individuals and groups.

The Functional Approach to an International Order

The propositions central to the thesis of this study are: (1) Our social life is largely structured in organisations. Organisations are found to be the characteristic form of consciously co-ordinated human effort both within and without the government. For example, public administration and corporate and personnel management are, sociologically speaking, essentially concerned with similar human problems. (2) Such organisational activity is directed to specific services or goals, to the satisfaction of specific needs in society. (3) The hierarchy and structure of each organisation is a product of its environment and the manner in which its officials or persons in authority solve the problems faced in adjusting its behaviour patterns to the requirements of its environment so as to achieve its goals. (4) Out of the institutionalised patterns of behaviour thus developed, whether wholly between members of the organisation or whether between members and non-members, rules of law develop which are sanctioned sometimes by the organisation itself and sometimes by the general law of the State.

If this analysis of data be sound, then a most useful road which we can follow, to the end of expanding the international order and developing international law, is to channel international co-operation through the corporate organisation or agency. It does not matter so much whether the organisation be formally incorporated as a legal entity or whether it be termed an agency. What is important is that conduct be channelled through decisions by persons who are not officials of the State but officials of the organisation, responsible for achieving the goal of the organisation with a minimum of friction and a maximum of effect in the light of the energy and resources available for the task.

The transnational organisation as an instrument for international co-operation

The road to world peace will more likely be found through the economic and service organisations which unite it than through the national governments which divide it. Many phases of the technical assistance programmes could well be channelled through corporate structures established by joint governmental agreement and, within the ambit of their authority and role, relatively free from national direction. A report of the National Planning Association states that 'we will have to be concerned primarily with building a new set of working relationships and institutions among free peoples. . . . Such world-wide institutions will have to be more relevant to contemporary realities and have more authority than at present if they are to constitute the structural ties, economic and political, which will make possible much freer trade and payments, a much greater capital flow, and a much more satisfactory balance between raw material and industrial production among the major regions of the world.'[12]

An example of functionally directed international co-operation was that of the World Food Board proposals adopted by the Food and Agriculture Organisation of the United Nations at its Copenhagen Conference in 1946, which failed of adoption because of the lack of concurrence by the United States, Great Britain and the Soviet Union. These proposals would have created a World Food Board with power to purchase, store and sell stocks of agricultural commodities and to operate with its own funds contributed by participating states with a view, among other things, to assuring stable sources of supply within agreed price ranges.[13]

The Soviet Union is keenly aware of the advantages to be derived from the corporate organisation as a means of integrating its relations with countries desired to be brought within its orbit of power. The joint governmental corporation under the control of the Party is now a familiar feature of the economy of the satellite states of Eastern Europe. Following extensive Soviet-Iranian trade negotiations and increased Soviet trade and activity in Iran and Afghanistan, the Soviet Union chartered a foreign trade

[12] National Planning Association, *The Next Step of American Foreign Economic Policy* (December 4, 1951).

[13] A. De Russet, *Strengthening the Framework of Peace*, 1950, p. 56.

organisation, Vostokintorg (Oriental Foreign Trade), which was to have a monopoly of Soviet trade with Iran, Afghanistan, the Mongolian People's Republic and the Sinkiang Province of China. The organisation was granted almost a ninefold increase in funds over its predecessor and considerably wider powers. It was said that: 'The increased capital and broadened authority will give Vostokintorg great flexibility in the economic activity it attempts.'[14]

The Committee on Economic Questions of the Consultative Assembly of the Council of Europe has suggested the following as tasks which might usefully be turned over to governmental corporations established jointly by European governments:

> '(1) The hydro-electric development of the Alps. (2) The expansion of colonial production, particularly in Africa. (3) The production of synthetic gasoline, the refining of crude oil, and the distribution of oil and gasoline. (4) A European Bank for Investments. (5) Aviation transport. (6) The securing, for newly tapped sources of production, of a guaranteed market, along the lines of buffer stock agencies known to students of international commodity agreements. (7) The provision of technical assistance.'[15]

A study by Timberg points out that the international governmental corporation has numerous advantages over the process of negotiation and conference, in that it is functionally directed to specific services or goals, authority is delegated and defined, carried forward on an open, empirical basis without infinite formalities and red tape, staffed by an internationally-minded administrative and technical corps, with decisions being responsibly based on the necessary information.[16]

Legal status of the international corporation

The private corporation is, of course, a creature of the State of incorporation. It is established jurisprudence that only a 'State' can create the juristic person known as a 'corporation.' The constitutive charter of an international body may endow it

[14] *New York Times*, November 21, 1951, p. 4, col. 7.

[15] S. Timberg, 'The Corporation as a Technique of International Administration,' 19 *University of Chicago Law Review* (1952), pp. 739, 748 citing Council of Europe, Consultative Assembly, Documents 22 and 30, First Ordinary Sess. (1949).

[16] *ibid.*, pp. 750–751.

with legal personality for the purposes of the legal systems of the several States creating it.[17] The United Nations has been held by the International Court of Justice to be a juristic person.[18] The foreign private corporation is by comity entitled to sue in the courts of a State,[19] and this right may become safeguarded by treaty.[20]

The suggestion has been advanced that the legal status of 'economic international corporations' be regularised by means of a general International Convention, which would provide, among other things, for an International Corporation Register. An economic international corporation was defined as possessing the following characteristics: '(a) Sovereign States will be the founders of the corporation or will guarantee its corporate status; (b) the object of the corporation is to transact business extending over the territory of several countries; (c) the corporation is authorised to accept legal commitments and, in particular, to sue and be sued.'[1] A suitable branch of the United Nations could

17 Constitution of the Food and Agriculture Organisation, *Yearbook of the United Nations, 1946–1947*, 1947, p. 693 at p. 695: 'Art. 15. 1. The organisation shall have the capacity of a legal person to perform any legal act appropriate to its purpose which is not beyond the powers granted to it by this Constitution'; Articles of Agreement of the International Bank for Reconstruction and Development, *ibid.*, p. 754 at pp. 763–764: 'Art. 7, s. 2. The Bank shall possess full juridical personality, and, in particular, the capacity:
(i) to contract;
(ii) to acquire and dispose of immovable and movable property;
(iii) to institute legal proceedings.'
'Section 10. Each member shall take such action as is necessary in its own territories for the purpose of making effective in terms of its own law the principles set forth in this Article and shall inform the Bank of the detailed action which it has taken.' To similar effect see: Articles of Agreement of the International Monetary Fund, Art. 9, *ibid.* at pp. 772, 778.

18 International Court of Justice, *Reparation for Injuries suffered in the Service of the United Nations*, Advisory Opinion of April 11th, 1949: *I.C.J. Reports 1949*, p. 174 at p. 179: 'The Organisation is an international person . . . it is a subject of international law and capable of possessing international rights and duties, and that it has capacity to maintain its rights by bringing international claims'; U.N. Charter, Art. 104, 'The Organisation shall enjoy in the territory of each of its Members such legal capacity as may be necessary for the exercise of its functions and the fulfilment of its purposes.'

19 *Bank of Augusta* v. *Earle*, 13 Pet. 519 (1839); J. H. Beale, *op. cit.*, Vol. 2, pp. 768–769.

20 *e.g.*, Arts. 3 and 4, United States-China Treaty of Friendship, Commerce and Navigation signed November 4, 1946, entered into force November 30, 1948, 63 Stat. L., Part 2 (1949), p. 1299; U.S. Treaties and other International Acts Series 1871.

1 C. M. Schmitthoff, 'The International Corporation,' 30 *Transactions of the Grotius Society* (1944), pp. 165, 179; see generally C. H. Alexandrowicz, *International Economic Organisations*, 1952.

administer such a Register. A corporation so registered might be empowered to appear as a party before the International Court of Justice, and also in (a) the national courts of any signatory to the Convention and (b) any other national court whose rules of law permit.

Co-ordination of international economic activity: the Schuman Plan

Hitherto, the process of international legislation has largely found its expression in treaties which looked either to the political and legal institutions of the signatory parties for making their provisions effective in conduct, or to the creation of an international organisation or agency which functioned through delegates from national governments and relied on the power of such governments to implement its proposals. In other words, save only for such bodies as the International Bank for Reconstruction and Development, international legislation and international organisation moved largely through the instrumentality of the national State. The traditional methodology of international legislation was wholly ineffectual to deal with the international tensions centred in the coal-iron complex of the Ruhr-Lorraine basin and the iron and steel industry of western Europe.

These were some of the sources of the tensions: (1) The ore of Lorraine and the coke of the Ruhr were the natural bases of a steel industry which was artificially divided by the Franco-German borders. Further elements of natural cohesion were a highly developed transportation system of railways and waterways and skilled labour. The wedding of these elements in the steel industries of France and Germany, together with the industries of Belgium, the Netherlands, Luxembourg and Italy, represented a centre of industrial power which, among other things, was responsible for two-thirds of the steel exports of the world. (2) Productive energy only exists to the extent that there is a market, and the market was hemmed in and choked by national policies of self-sufficiency, protectionism, subsidies and export levies. (3) Inefficient and marginal producers were not only sheltered by national legislation, but also by cartel agreements and restrictive business policies. (4) Pre-war trade patterns had been rent asunder by the Sovietisation of Eastern Europe and the risk existed that in the search for markets, without which no industry can exist, Western German steel production would find its outlet in trade with the Soviet Union and thus *pro tanto* be drawn into the Soviet power system.

These divisive forces demanded co-ordination and the European Coal and Steel Community became the means for co-ordination. Where the World Food Board and its attendant executive powers had earlier failed to come into being, now a vastly stronger supra-national system of institutions with executive, legislative and judicial powers affecting vital sectors of the trade and industry of the six participating States was created. 'Sovereignty' was relinquished to an extent hitherto unknown.

Basically, the objective was the creation of a healthy, vigorous, competitive steel industry in the participating nations in which the benefits of research and competition would be distributed among investors, labour and the consuming public. This required the establishment of a common market, including the elimination of political trade barriers, the prohibition of cartel and restrictive business practices, provision for financial assistance to enable research and technological improvements, and control over prices, production and wages in the interest of the Community and the public. To achieve these ends, a High Authority was created to legislate and administer the policies of a common market. The High Authority was the centre of authority within the Community. But it was not the exclusive repository of authority; the concurrence of the Council of Ministers was required in certain cases.

The structure and sources of authority in the Community require further explanation. There are, essentially, three sources of power in the Community: the participating private corporations, the participating States through their national governments, and the participating workers, consumers and citizens of the several States. Unification of such disparate elements can be achieved either at the top, at the centres of authority themselves, which is the method of Communist infiltration in the west and Communist Party control in the Soviet Union, or at the bottom, which is the method of unification chosen by the western democratic State. It has hitherto been our experience that where co-ordinating authority is drawn from the top, policy tends to be directed to the interest of the particular groups involved, rather than to the interests of the larger society. A notable example of this tendency is the drift to cartelism, arrested only by vigorous national policy.

In the European Coal and Steel Community a compromise is achieved. The direction which this compromise will eventually take remains to be seen. The system of authority is partially dispersed and partially subject to checks. Gradation of acts of the High Authority vary from decisions, through recommendations, to opinions. Some decisions require an absolute majority of the productive capacity of the member States, the formula for which requires the concurrence of both France and Germany. Others require a two-thirds majority, the formula for which does not necessarily require such concurrence. Others require unanimity. Still others require the concurrence of the Council of Ministers.

The High Authority is the principal organ of the Community yet the member States closely control the election of the nine members of the High Authority and each can exercise a veto on the election of any member of the High Authority. The Council of Ministers is a body composed of representatives of each of the six member States.

Thus the participating States act through persons whom they closely control, directly or indirectly. The question for the future is whether the persons thus delegated with authority will throttle the growth of the Community in the interest of preserving national power, or will foster the interest of the Community at the expense of public interest (*i.e.*, will become 'cartel-minded'),[2] or will act in the public interest. In view of the extent to which State control predominates, it would seem that State interest would tend to prevail in the long run in decisions made. Greater autonomy in decision-making, subject to responsibility, seems desirable through amendment procedure available under the treaty. Perhaps some influence upon decision-making and policy may be exerted by the Consultative Committee and the Common Assembly, which are lacking in power but are drawn from a broader base. The latter particularly is envisaged as representative of the various peoples or their parliaments.

Law eventuates not only from the decisions of the High Authority but also from a Court of Justice, which functions as a tribunal for review and annulment of official acts and as a tri-

[2] As to the risks of cartelism in the Schuman Plan, see W. Diebold, 'Imponderables of the Schuman Scheme,' 29 *Foreign Affairs* (1950), p. 114.

bunal for awarding damages for official acts and defective administration. Somehow the Court must work out a formula whereby it can avoid the trap of 'conflicts of laws' as a means for decision, which would create a jurisprudence varying in content according to the situs of the operative facts of the cases, and instead a system of general and uniform jurisprudence.[3]

The European Coal and Steel Community is a revolutionary experiment in international co-operation. If it succeeds, we can look to further similar experiments, for the demand for international order and peace is one of the most insistent political demands of the day. To succeed, however, it must find a common basis for the co-ordination of the hitherto highly divisive interests of the national States, corporate and investing groups, and labour and consumer groups. This will demand statesmanship of the highest order not only by the High Authority, but by all interested groups.

An illuminating suggestion for a functional and regional administration of European inland waterways was made by Louis B. Wehle in 1946.[4] A plan of organisation for the Rhine system of waterways, by way of example, was described as follows:

> 'The Rhine system of the future . . . ought to be based on a common ownership by all river nations of all shore and channel facilities. Each nation would put into the pool the facilities owned by it or by its nationals and would get bonds for them. The common agency of the member nations would take over the facilities, issue the bonds, and operate the system. The agency would be made up of representatives of the river nations and of some outside shipping nations, just as was the pre-war Rhine régime. All vessels would have to be licensed by the agency, whose revenues would come from fees for licences, transshipment, warehousing, and other services . . .
>
> 'Under such a post-war Rhine agency system there

[3] Perhaps the best single study yet to appear on the Schuman Plan from the political and legal standpoint is G. Bebr, 'The European Coal and Steel Community: A Political and Legal Innovation,' 63 *Yale Law Journal* (1953), p. 1. See also J. A. McKesson, 'The Schuman Plan,' 67 *Political Science Quarterly* (1952), p. 18; R. Vernon, 'The Schuman Plan,' 47 *American Journal of International Law* (1953), p. 183.

[4] L. B. Wehle, 'International Administration of European Inland Waterways,' 40 *ibid.* (1946), p. 100.

> would be more need than ever for a Rhine commission to perform impartially the functions of rate and traffic regulation, of preventing monopolistic practices, of policing the channels and of safeguarding the import duty interests of the riparian nations. The decisions of such a commission ought to be subject to court review. The Rhine system would be regional. There would be similar regional agencies and commissions covering other river basins. For finally deciding conflicts between river basin regions, the International Court of the United Nations should be available.'[5]

The suggestion adopted the following basic principles: (1) that the controlling authority be regional, with co-ordination being effected either through the United Nations or some other central authority; (2) that personnel be selected on a representative basis; (3) that a regional authority be empowered to acquire and hold the necessary facilities and properties; (4) that a regional authority have the residual power and responsibility for the accomplishment of its tasks, to the extent that the central authority failed to act; (5) that provision be made for adjusting conflicts of jurisdiction between two or more regional authorities; (6) that a system of arbitral bodies, with eventual appeal to the International Court of Justice, be established for deciding justiciable controversies; and (7) that eventually there may be established 'an inter-continental authority for seas and internal waterways, on which will rest the responsibility for harmonising the principles and practices among the Authorities administering the continental internal waterway systems of the globe.'[6]

Some Current Fallacies and Illusions

Solution by command

We have already seen the relational aspect of authority, namely, that it involves a decision or command communicated by a superior to a subordinate and accepted by the latter in conduct, without independent re-examination and decision. We

[5] L. B. Wehle, *Hidden Threads of History: Wilson through Roosevelt*, 1953, pp. 278–279.

[6] L. B. Wehle, *loc. cit.*, pp. 116–120. See generally in connection with this section, D. Mitrany, *A Working Peace System*, 1944; D. Mitrany, 'The Functional Approach to World Organisation,' 24 *International Affairs* (1948), p. 353.

have seen how cohesion and order in the State exists because of the influence on conduct exerted by commands emanating from the government. With the over-recurrent tendency of human thought to seize upon *one* cause and say here is *the* cause of our difficulty, various individual components or elements going to make up the whole authority relationship have from time to time been seized upon, separately and apart from their context, to point the road to progress in the growth of an international order. In noting the fallacies inherent in any such assumptions, we should not, as we shall take occasion later to make explicit, in turn fall into the fallacy that each is not important in the growth of an international order. We only insist upon the necessity of realising that each of these varying schools of thought is but one mansion in a house of many mansions.

Perhaps the most elementary of fallacies is found in the proposition that if rules be formulated and ensconced in an international treaty, the rules will be manifested in conduct without regard to the explicitness of their formulation, the means of their enforcement, and the readiness of those to whom they are addressed to accept them in conduct. One such example is the current movement from the Universal Declaration of Human Rights, which stands as a symbol for the aspirations of men and, as such, itself exerts an influence in the policy of governments, to the Covenant of Human Rights and enforcement. The 'rights' of the Declaration or of the Covenant cannot represent law unless all the elements and conditions of the authority structure exist, governing the emergence of law through custom or though political and legal institutions accepted by the governed as legitimate. The Declaration and the Covenant may represent a pressure towards the eventual establishment of law, but not legal 'rights.'[7]

Sanctions make law

Few are as unsophisticated as the preceding paragraph might imply. The more frequent proposals for the growth of a world order centre on the theme that if a proposed new rule be sanctioned it will then become law. The current proposals to implement the Nuremberg Rules are in this category. So long as military power remains in this world, so long as such military

[7] See P. E. Corbett, *The Individual and World Society*, 1953, particularly at pp. 16–17.

power is centred in national States, so long as any such significant repository of military force evidences by its conduct that it is not likely to place the value of keeping its commitment to a treaty above the value of serving its national interests through the use of force, neither the Nuremberg Rules nor their implementation in an international criminal court are likely to bring about predictable human behaviour of abstention from war by governments.[8]

A more refined statement of this viewpoint is that if we had an international legislature, judiciary and police force, we would then have an international order.[9] The assertion ignores the fact that power is centred in States, that the government of each State represents an equilibrium among the social forces of the State in question, that priorities in social values vary among the cultures of the several States, that acceptance of governmental authority within each State is a balance of force and of interest, and that the officials of each State who are charged with the conduct of its foreign relations are the captives of the strategy or general formulation of policy brought about by their particular internal culture and political balance, on the one hand, and the necessities of their external environment, including access to the bases of their national power found outside their borders, on the other.[10]

All would concede that, in the final analysis, the ultimate bases of the authority system of any State are justice and force. Few would rest the authority of any world government upon a system of force affecting more than a relatively small minority. This, in turn, means that the policies and laws adopted by any world government must be responsive to the priorities in values and perceptions of the very large proportion of the peoples to whom they are addressed, that, somehow, a common denominator of identification and interest must be found among such peoples. The fear of destruction through atomic warfare has

[8] For a penetrating analysis of the legal problem whether the Nuremburg decisions constitute a 'precedent,' see H. Kelsen, 'Will the Judgment in the Nuremberg Trial Constitute a Precedent in International Law?' 1 *International Law Quarterly* (1947), p. 153.

[9] A summary of such proposals will be found in A. De Russet, *Strengthening the Framework of Peace*, 1950, Chap. 4. See generally R. W. Van Wagenen, *Research in the International Field, Some Notes on a Possible Focus* (Centre for Research on World Political Institutions, Pub. No. 1, Princeton), 1952.

[10] H. J. Morgenthau, *Politics Among Nations*, 1948.

not as yet created a priority in the value of survival upon which any such consensus could rest. Thus the creation of a world government would still leave us with the same problems which we had before and which led us to our present impasse, such problems, for example, as (a) the sharing, in a world of scarcity, of resources and access to specific institutions and organisations, including economic organisations, or (b) the control of power to achieve specific goals in specific ways upon which a consensus of the persons and groups involved exists or can be brought about.

Substitution of internationalism for nationalism

Since identification with the relevant group is always a factor in group cohesion, since the solidarity of the clan, community and State is, in part, a factor of the degree of such identification, the problem of establishing a world community, and hence a world order, is sometimes thought to be a problem of establishing the requisite degree of world loyalty through world symbols and the like.

The extension of Roman citizenship to the several parts of the Empire was, as was seen in Chapter 2, a necessary step to the creation of the Roman State, but the integration of that State was not solely a product of that step. The introduction of Roman law in the Hellenised East met the resistance of the acceptance of Greek law in the civilisation of the East. As Sohm puts it, the 'Romanising of the Hellenes proved to be the very process by which the Hellenisation of the Roman Empire and of Roman law was most effectually promoted. . . . Whatever the formal validity of Roman law might be, the mass of the people continued in actual practice to adhere to the habits of Greek national law. And not only did the movement towards Pan-Romanism, which sought to bring the entire Hellenic East under the sway of Roman law, fail in its object, but it actually opened the doors to Greek legal ideas, and gave them free scope to react, in their turn, on the further development of Roman law.'[11] Although identification with the world society is a necessary condition for the establishment of the world community, this is not the whole of the task that lies before us.[12]

[11] R. Sohm, *The Institutes*, 1907, pp. 115–116.

[12] A discussion of the problems incident to establishing world identification will be found in H. D. Lasswell, 'World Loyalty,' in Q. Wright (Ed.), *The World Community*, 1948, p. 200.

The propagation of universal values

We have seen that rules or norms governing conduct emerge as a consequence of conduct, that they must always be seen as a part of the particular social order in which they are found, and that the introduction of new patterns of behaviour among existing patterns of conduct is a delicate task involving the co-operation of numerous institutions. Attempts to formulate a system of values of universal appeal necessarily result in such abstractions as power, wealth, enlightenment, and the like, so as to enable any social system to be subsumed under them. If these values are to be translated into rules of law governing the day-to-day life of individuals composing the several States, inevitably there arises the obstacle that these values find different priorities and different modes of expression in the institutional life and culture of different peoples. The values may ultimately be the same as concepts or abstractions, but the meaning and priorities of such values as exemplified in human behaviour varies with the different cultures. The net result of any such attempts merely becomes an intellectual *tour-de-force*. The basic problem is rather one of so shaping international legislation as to accommodate the content thereof to the existing tolerances of the several cultures to which such legislation is to apply. In view of the disparities among those cultures and their respective value-orientations, the likelihood of any universal approach having a uniform content becoming the means to world unification is slight.

The value of 'wealth,' for example, has a different context and involves different relations with other values, such as the acquisition of skills, in an underdeveloped country from an industrially advanced country. For, basically, the resources and energy available to any one State are limited. Its power must be channelled among its various possible uses so that there is a reasonably stable social equilibrium in the particular society. To allocate the funds available for Korean rehabilitation and development to high speed highways and modern hotels, to allocate the funds available for Iranian development at this stage to a steel mill, as has been proposed, is but to lengthen the social distance between classes and to fail to place national growth upon a firm foundation—that of an awareness by the lower as well as the higher classes that there is a constant progress toward the goal of wealth and an accompanying preservation of those values upon which the particular order rests.

The creation of wealth demands skill and experience as well as capital. Some of the principles which must control the process of social growth were brilliantly and concisely stated in the *Report on Seven Year Development Plan for Iran* prepared by Overseas Consultants, Inc.:

> 'We have emphasised our belief that a rising national prosperity can rest only upon continuously improving conditions among those who furnish the labour for national production and become, at the same time, the consumers of the multiplying goods and services. To bring about those changed conditions, and to take full advantage of the resultant continuing opportunity for advancement, we emphasised that new skills must be developed or engaged in order that capital may be used effectively in producing new wealth for distribution among those contributing to its production.
>
> 'The number of factors that are involved in applying these two principles is great. Characteristically, these factors are not independent of each other but are closely related, a change in one affecting many others. Production in almost any field is affected by the health, skill and interest of the workers. The value of increased production depends upon the uses to which it is put, its availability when and where there is a demand for it, and the price at which it is bought and sold. These things depend upon the availability of money for investment and trade which, in turn, are affected by laws, tax systems, and established customs. Each of these aspects of national life and many more affect and are affected by each of the others. . . .'
>
> 'Co-ordination, as we mean it, requires a high sensitivity to the effects which will be produced by any substantial change in the vital social or economic conditions of the country. This includes the changes which must be undergone by the people themselves, particularly when long-established customs are involved, and the rate at which such changes which might result from unbalancing the supply of money in relation to the supply of goods and services available for exchange. It includes the effects of new demands for labour, and of migrations induced by

> regional developments. In the field of physical operations in connection with new works, both public and private, it includes attention to the balancing of requirements and availability of labour, of all classes, national and foreign funds and transport facilities.'[13]

When we seek to establish an international order we can do so only piecemeal and interstitially. The strategy and consequences of each step must be weighed as against alternative possible steps. There is no general formula for peace and order. Peace is but an equilibrium among many forces and these must each be handled carefully and wisely. Values, formulæ, plans, must all be translated ultimately into human action and, unless they are seen in the light of specific human problems and human conduct, their formulation serves but little practical purpose.

The panacea of scientific analysis

It is not enough merely to describe and analyse the problem of achieving world order in even the most sophisticated of terms. It is not enough to describe, as we have sought here to describe and others have sought elsewhere to describe, the various elements involved in the problem of achieving world order. It is not enough to assert that we need, on the one hand, a 'high degree of concentration of power' so as to bring 'coercion to bear to maintain security, freedom from violence and aggression,' for concentration of power always raises the problem of abuse of power and totalitarianism. Nor is it enough to counter this proposition with its opposite, which is equally true, that: 'A very wide dispersal of power, including a very wide sharing in control over the concentrated world security organisation, will be required.'[14]

Power exists wherever co-ordination of human energy exists. Co-ordination flows from leadership and authority. Leadership and authority, in turn, primarily rest upon acceptance by their followers, though also upon the force which they can bring to bear. Leadership and authority emerge when there is a successful moving equilibrium or balance between force and consent.

[13] Overseas Consultants, Inc., *Report on Seven Year Development Plan for the Plan Organisation of the Imperial Government of Iran*, 1949, Vol. 1, pp. 10–11.

[14] M. S. McDougal, 'The Role of Law in World Politics,' 20 *Mississippi Law Journal* (1949), pp. 253, 277, 278.

A 'high degree of concentration of power' will come into being only when the successful formula for the integration of the bases of power is found. That 'concentration of power' may or may not rest on 'a very wide dispersal of power' in the sense of democratic participation in decision making. Whether it will so rest will depend upon the historical factors involved at the time and place, and the requirements of the environment and the goal. Merely to assert that it *must* so rest is merely to state a desirable, though not always a possible, procedure (*viz.*, the authority system of the army). Policy must always be successively broken down into intermediate and final formulations until it ultimately emerges in specific human behaviour. Each of these steps involves procuring consensus among the peoples involved upon the priorities in the values involved, in habituating those peoples to a particular ordering of authority and acceptance of that authority as legitimate, of finding the cleavages in interest and value-orientation upon which a compromise solution and acceptance of some formula of majority-decision can rest; in short, of continuing to travel the long road towards political and social order which western civilisation has been pursuing for centuries. Questions of policy demanding solution here and now, or at any time, cannot be dismissed as 'details' which 'will of course depend upon the context of time and the compromises necessary to secure action.'[15]

World order by legislation

While the forms of political democracy have been introduced in most nations of the world, including Soviet Russia, each State has its own real structure of authority and distribution of power. Each State varies in the extent of its industrialisation, competitive patterns of behaviour, division of labour, mobility of the individual within the social structure, social distance between individuals, dynamism of change, and energy. The problem of changing the pattern of a particular culture is the most massive

[15] *ibid.*, p. 278. It is felt that Professor McDougal would be essentially in agreement with the foregoing, for his remarks should not be considered out of context, that is to say, the general approach of their maker. Professor McDougal has clarified and expanded his thesis in his 1953 lectures at the Hague and they should be read in this connection. M. S. McDougal, 'International Law, Power and Policy: A Contemporary Conception,' 82 *Academie de Droit International, Recueil des Cours* (1953), p. 137.

of all social problems. For as we move from autocracy to democracy in a social system, we create new stresses elsewhere in the system. The expansion in participation in decision-making in political institutions and economic organisations involves, among other things, changes in leadership techniques in training in primary groups such as the home, in education and in the media of communication. It involves the substitution of universalistic for particularistic values. It involves not only a transformation of the centralised and institutionalised controls of a society but also of all those indirect influences and standards which pattern conduct in a host of situations. Democracy, in short, is the product of a culture. An individual transplanted from one culture to another can in most instances be rather rapidly 'enculturated' or assimilated in his new environment. A democratic order of society, however, is not a product of manipulation or of export, though conscious manipulation will indeed hasten the process of democratisation. A democratic society is a product of deeply grooved patterns of behaviour and a highly complex integration of institutions and value-systems developed through centuries of growth. Thus the democratisation of Germany, for example, involves changing authority patterns in the home, in the school and in the factory; the substitution of new national legends and myths; changing habits of submission and deference; creating a sense of the inviolability of the person from the child through adulthood (for example, the German child is apparently not immune from demonstrations of affections from strangers), it involves, in short, a shift in political power, leadership techniques in all forms of social action, and in the values pervading the myriad of situations involved in day-to-day life.[16]

Role of international institutions

In establishing a world order, we must travel not merely one but many roads. History has woven this world into a pattern of many national societies, each with its own values and goals.

[16] See K. Lewin, *Resolving Social Conflicts*, 1948; K. Mannheim, *Man and Society in an Age of Reconstruction*, 1940; R. B. Cattell, 'The Principal Culture Patterns Discoverable in the Syntal Dimensions of Existing Nations,' 30 *Journal of Social Psychology* (1950), p. 1; R. B. Cattell, 'The Investigation of Cultural Dynamics: Concept and Methods,' in J. E. Hulett, Jr. and R. Stagner (Eds.), *Problems in Social Psychology*, 1952, p. 171.

When the pursuit of those values or goals is thought to be threatened by another national society, there is as yet no concensus that force may not be used to preserve them. That the killing of one's neighbour is lawful if done at the command of one's government still remains a proposition accepted by all national societies. To bring those societies to a participation in an effective world order in which there is a concensus that force is not possible as a relation between states is a task which will require all the above approaches to be utilised.

For the present, the organs and specialised agencies of the United Nations, including particularly the deliberations and resolutions of the Assembly, are a real force in the shaping of national policy.[17] Perhaps they are not as strong a force as many would wish them to be in the interests of world peace, but a force they nevertheless remain in determining the conduct of members.

In addition to international organisation and law as roads to peace, there is the road of diplomacy and agreement. Here the task is to establish an equilibrium of force and interest upon which an agreement can be based, seeking ever to supplant interest as the equilibriating element in place of force. As Sir Winston Churchill once said, 'It is idle to reason or argue with the Communists,' but 'they will keep their bargains as long as it is in their interest to do so.'[18]

17 See L. B. Sohn, *Cases and Other Materials on World Law*, 1950.

18 446 Parliamentary Debates (*Hansard*). House of Commons (No. 48, 1948), p. 562.

Chapter 7

CONTROL OF THE POWER OF THE ECONOMIC ORGANISATION

Control of the Power of the Economic Organisation

It has been shown that the first problem faced by the citizenry of the national State—a problem which they must continually face and attempt to solve in the course of national history—is that of political liberty. The citizenry faces the eternal dilemma: How can the area of national freedom implicit in the concept of sovereignty be reconciled with the necessity of limiting the 'constitutional' authority of government? The problem of the uncontrolled exercise of power by the group over the individual first arose in modern society in the relationship of the political institution to the members of the State. By the close of the eighteenth century, however, the philosophical foundation and the legal framework for the limitation of the power of the political institution *vis-à-vis* its members or subjects had been formulated.

The industrialisation of the United States in the nineteenth century, however, posed a new problem in power for the commonwealth to solve. Though industrialisation had grown rapidly, the United States was still predominantly an agricultural nation prior to the Civil War. Its principal imports were manufactures and its principal exports were agricultural products. The corporate enterprise was an important part of the national scene, but its possession of power had not yet become a national problem. Its status under the law was that of an autonomous body essentially free from any legal controls other than those applicable to any private person. It was required to keep its promises, to make good its torts and to obey the criminal law. Liberty of contract assured it freedom to pursue its ends and enabled it to bring all the power of the State to bear in maintaining the relationships thus established with others. The right to property assured it freedom and power to control whatever capital equipment it might find necessary to achieve its purposes. The exercise of these powers was subject only to the limitation that they should not be used in unlawful or criminal enterprises. Efforts to control their exercise beyond this point were struck down as an impairment of contract. The possession of these powers in all their freedom posed no particular problem for the body politic in the first half of the nineteenth century. Corporate groups were not then the repositories of economic power that they became when their autonomy from the State, coupled with their endowment of legal authority by the State under the concepts of freedom of contract and right of property, made unregulated corporate decisions a new problem in power. For the corporate groups of the later nineteenth century were vastly greater and more complex in their structure than those of the early nineteenth century. The pace of industrialisation after the Civil War in itself posed difficult problems of social adjustment, including all the problems incident to rapid urbanisation, overcrowding, slums, and the subjection of the individual to the massive impersonal currents of an industrial civilisation. Of greater significance was the fact that there were new giants in the land—combinations, trusts, monopolies and great corporate enterprises.

Legislative efforts to control these giants had to run the gauntlet of judicial review under the invigorated concept of due process. The concentration of the vast new wealth into the hands of these new giants posed, in a new form, the problem of power which the preceding century had solved through the Bill of Rights and a federal government of checks and balances. Both the major political parties in the campaign of 1888 proposed the regulation of combinations and trusts in an effort to capture the vote of those who had denounced the concentration of capital. The Sherman Act of 1890 was the final outcome of the struggle of the nineteenth century to bring the new and vast repositories of economic power under the control of law. The public issue in the enactment of the Sherman Act was not solely or even primarily economic. It was merely one outcome of a vast transformation of society. No longer did the American frontier exist where man could find refuge from the vicissitudes of an industrial civilisation. No longer did the self-sustaining farm provide a measure of security for the majority of the citizenry. Men were city dwellers. They were caught by the factory, caught by the office building. They were helpless units, each exercising his particular function in the corporate enterprise and each bargaining alone against that enterprise, whether as employee or consumer. In short, man sought a new bill of rights in the nineteenth century and found it in the promised abolition of trusts and combinations.

Twenty-one years later in the *Standard Oil Case*[1] the judicial interpretation of the Act became of age. Where previously all contracts in restraint of trade fell under the condemnation of the Act,[2] now the door became open through the general concept of reasonableness to the recognition of a variety of values. In place of rigorous inflexibility, flexibility and possibility of compromise were introduced. The spotlight of judicial interpretation shifted from the words of the statute to the realities of economic life, in which there is no ultimate truth, no best of all possible worlds, but only a balancing of interests and objectives. No longer was the basic concept abolition but, instead, regulation.

Two decades more and a new problem in the control of economic power arose. The problem of the nineteenth century involved a relationship between the individual and the great corporate institution endowed with the powers of contract and property and the freedom to exercise these solely in the corporate interest under the constitutional protections of liberty of contract and due process. The vulnerability of the individual in this relation resulted in the political demand that found its expression in the Sherman Act. The American culture, a product of the frontier, resisted centralisation of authority whether found in the political institution or in the economic organisation. But the worldwide depression of the 'thirties focused a new attitude toward law. The power implicit in law was no longer *per se* an evil. Law, in the view of Jhering and the body politic of the twentieth century, was a means to an end. The sensitive, complex organisation of modern industrial society, the failure of an unregulated competitive system to minimise the vicissitudes of the business cycle, the external stresses of war and threat of war, demanded a powerful centralised government. Hence an increasingly active intervention by the political institution in the functioning of the competitive system. The government sup-

1 *Standard Oil Co. of New Jersey* v. *United States*, 221 U.S. 1 (1911).
2 *United States* v. *Trans-Missouri Freight Ass'n*, 166 U.S. 290, 331–332 (1897).

planted or supported, as the case may be, the private corporate enterprise.[3] This development carried to its logical conclusion brought into being the totalitarian State, which could brook no rivals to its possession of power. The corporation either became the servant of the government in the execution of its policies, as in Nazi Germany, or it became a part of the government, as in Communist Russia.[4]

THE SHERMAN ACT AND LEGISLATIVE TECHNIQUE

The validity of the *laissez faire* assumption that voluntary, uncontrolled corporate activity would serve the needs of the State had, by 1888, become a violent political issue. Instead of expressing the idea of social purpose in its functioning, the giant business organisation of the nineteenth century had allowed its own values to come to the fore. It was no longer primarily a means for serving public purpose. Under the shelter of its autonomy from the State, the corporate enterprise inevitably shaped its relations to the market as a means for the satisfaction of private, group ends rather than for public service. This deviation from desired norms of conduct accordingly became a new problem in law. The common law on restraint of trade and monopoly, which was the only then existent system of legal rules then existing to control the problem, was the product of a simpler and primarily agricultural society. The practices of the late nineteenth century industrial market-place were infinitely more complex and subtle in their restraints upon competition than those of the early eighteenth century when *Mitchel* v. *Reynolds*[5] set the framework for the common law control of restraint of trade. Consequently, the clamour of labour, farm and other groups for control of the abuse of power by the business organisation as manifested in the market-place turned to the legislative process as the appropriate means for control. New patterns of conduct were to be imposed upon the business organisation through law and only the legislature could determine these.

Yet the classic phrases of the common law, 'restraint of trade

[3] R. Pound, 'Law in The Service State: Freedom versus Equality,' 36 *American Bar Association Journal* (1950), p. 977.
[4] V. Gsovski, *The Law of the Soviet State*, Vol. 1, 1948, p. 403; J. N. Hazard, 'Socialism, Abuse of Power, and Soviet Law,' 50 *Columbia Law Review* (1950), p. 448 at p. 449.
[5] 1 P. Wms. 181, 24 Eng. Rep. 347 (1711).

or commerce' and 'monopolise,' were the phrases selected in the Sherman Act to indicate the kind of conduct which would become unlawful. Section 1 of the Act merely condemned 'Every contract, combination in the form of trust or otherwise, or conspiracy, in restraint of trade or commerce,' while Section 2 ordered persons not to 'monopolise, or attempt to monopolise, or combine or conspire with any other person or persons, to monopolise any part of the trade or commerce among the several States, or with foreign nations.'[6]

As with all legislation, the Sherman Act was a compromise. The insistent demand of labour, farm and consumer groups was at least *pro forma* satisfied by a federal statute. Yet the words of the Statute were chosen so as to disrupt existing patterns of conduct in the least possible degree. Words of the common law were resorted to in order to describe the conduct to be prohibited and it could be safely assumed that the courts, with the respect for precedent characteristic of the judicial process in the nineteenth century, would limit themselves to established common law doctrine in applying the Statute. The net effect would be merely to make acts involving restraint of trade monopolising, as they were known at common law, subject to federal jurisdiction.[7] This assumption proved for twenty-one years to be the basic assumption underlying the enforcement of the Act by the courts.[8] The basic evil was not necessarily exorcised, but the legislature had served its function of resolving group conflicts and group demands. Words had been found in a statute on which an uneasy treaty of peace between the conflicting interests might be founded.

When the *Standard Oil*[9] and *American Tobacco*[10] cases introduced the qualification that the Sherman Act prohibited

[6] 26 Stat. 209 (1890); 15 U.S.C.A., ss. 1 and 2.

[7] Senator Hoar, a member of the Judiciary Committee which had reported the bill which became the Sherman Act, stated that the Committee have 'affirmed the old doctrine of the common law in regard to all inter-State and international commercial transactions, and have clothed the United States Courts with authority to enforce that doctrine by injunction.' 21 Cong. Rec. 3146. Senator Edmunds, another member of the Committee, said that it had decided to 'make its definition out of terms that were well known to the law already,' *ibid.*, p. 3148.

[8] *United States* v. *Trans-Missouri Freight Ass'n*, 166 U.S. 290 (1897); *United States* v. *Addyston Pipe & Steel Co.*, 85 Fed. 271 (6th Cir. 1898), *mod.* and *affd.* 175 U.S. 211 (1899).

[9] *Standard Oil Co. of New Jersey* v. *United States*, 221 U.S. 1 (1911).

[10] *United States* v. *American Tobacco Co.*, 221 U.S. 106 (1911).

only such restraints of trade as were unreasonable,[11] the role of the courts shifted essentially to that of an administrative regulative body. For with the word 'reasonable' glossed in the language of the Statute the field of inquiry shifted from the interpretation and application of judicial precedent to the realities of the economic world outside the courtroom doors.

The courts were thus finally driven to assume the task shirked by the legislature in 1890 and to define with some precision and detail the conduct of the business organisation which was to be brought under the rule of law. The economic life of society in the twentieth century possessed a richness of variety of structure and conduct which could not be strait-jacketed into a statute which had not moved beyond the common law of the nineteenth century. Other criteria beside precedent must be brought into court and weighed in the decision of the economic issues presented in anti-trust cases, if decision were to be based in life instead of logic. The formula of 'reasonableness' became the vehicle for the introduction of economic data in a process that would otherwise have been carried forward in the remote world of precedent. For reason in the abstract is a whimsical augur of results; it furnishes no workable guide upon which to predict judicial behaviour. In the language of the early common law judge, it must be 'right reason,' that is to say, it must be the judicial process at work in its procedures of fact determination, fact analysis, fact classification, weighing of competing values and search for workable rules of conduct which will smoothly and efficiently fit into the functioning of society.

Up to this point the history of the application of the Sherman Act has been presented as one of retreat instead of expansion. The genus 'restraint of trade' has been seen to be limited, under the judicial interpretation of the Act, to the species 'unreasonable' restraints of trade. The expansion in the application of the Act, which has in fact taken place, nevertheless, has come from, among others, the following sources: (1) the broadened concept of conspiracy to include 'unanimity of action' or 'concert of

[11] 'In thus grounding the "rule of reason" upon the analogy of the common law doctrines applicable to illegal restraints of trade the Court gave a content and meaning to the statute in harmony with its history and plainly indicated by its legislative purpose. Labour cases apart . . . this Court has not departed from the conception of the Sherman Act as

action'[12] or participation with 'awareness of the general scope and purpose of the undertaking,'[13] when such action or undertaking tends to uniformity of pricing behaviour in the market; (2) the application of the category 'restraint of trade' to complex market relationships tending to control prices, including the rule of illegality *per se* of joint conduct tending to affect prices[14]; (3) the rule that 'it is unreasonable, *per se*, to foreclose competitors from any substantial market'[15]; (4) the inclusion of 'monopoly' under 'monopolise'[16]; and (5) the prohibition of restraint by a patentee when acting outside the strict scope of his patent.[17] The broadened concept of conspiracy has in particular been enormously useful in expanding the area of control of the business organisation while still paying due observance to the other formal requirements of the Statute.

The Sherman Act is thus, on the one hand, a typical example of the functioning of the legislative process, in that at the time of its passage an acceptable formula was found on which the group interests involved might agree, and, on the other hand, a clear instance of a failure of the legislative process to discharge its role in society. For the rules of the common law had proved inadequate to deal with the emergent problems of a complex, industrial society, leading to the demand for change. Yet the legislature made no change and had not advanced an inch beyond the landmarks of the common law. It was inevitable either that the courts would expand the application of the Act or that the legislature would enact additional legislation. In fact, the legal control of business conduct has since expanded through both routes.

affording a remedy, public and private, for the public wrongs which flow from restraints of trade in the common law sense of restriction or suppression of commercial competition.' *Apex Hosiery Co.* v. *Leader*, 310 U.S. 469, 500 (1940).

12 *Interstate Circuit, Inc.* v. *United States*, 306 U.S. 208, 223 (1939).

13 *United States* v. *Masonite Corp.*, 316 U.S. 265, 275 (1942).

14 *United States* v. *Socony-Vacuum Oil Co.*, 310 U.S. 150 (1940): *Kiefer-Stewart Co.* v. *Joseph E. Seagram & Sons, Inc.*, 340 U.S. 211 (1951): *United States* v. *Trenton Potteries Co.*, 273 U.S. 392 (1927).

15 *International Salt Co.* v. *United States*, 332 U.S. 392, 396 (1947); *United States* v. *Yellow Cab Co.*, 332 U.S. 218 (1947); *United States* v. *Columbia Steel Co.*, 334 U.S. 495 (1948).

16 *United States* v. *Aluminum Co. of America*, 148 F. 2d 416 (2d Cir. 1945); *American Tobacco Co.* v. *United States*, 328 U.S. 781 (1946).

17 The increasing limitations upon the exercise of the power of patents by patentees and their licensees appear to stem from Judge Brandeis' decision in *Carbice Corp.* v. *American Patents Development Corp.*, 283 U.S. 27 (1931).

So long as the Statute spoke in the words of the common law, no particular constitutional problem was presented when the sanction for the prohibited conduct was penal. '[T]he common law as to restraint of trade thus taken up by the Statute' provided a sufficient degree of certainty, which was not rendered 'so vague as to be inoperative on its criminal side' by virtue of the fact that the criminality of the prohibited conduct was dependent on whether the jury considered it reasonable or unreasonable.[18] But as the role of the courts has moved from the essentially judicial one which characterised their application of the Statute during its first two decades to the regulative one which now largely characterise their application of the Statue, as the simple legal concepts applied by the courts in the first two decades of the Statute have been overlaid by a thicket of precedent that makes the Act possibly the most esoteric and unpredictable field of law that we have today, the fact that every violation of the Act is subject to a criminal penalty presents a new problem. The criminal law was not designed as a means of control for conduct whose deviation from desired norms was so doubtful and marginal. Its purpose is to control conduct commonly accepted to be anti-social to a serious degree, conduct which can, moreover, be objectively defined with reasonable certitude, so that the preventive and retributive functions of the criminal law can be carried out.

While there is a stratum of anti-trust law to which the criminal law can, in justice, be applied, it is usually not such conduct which reaches the courts today. Modern anti-trust cases present the courts with complicated factual situations, whose roots stretch into the distant past, presenting problems of social control ever in new form; the variety of our economic life and the values to be served, the conduct to be permitted or prohibited, are such as to escape legislative or judicial foresight. To use the criminal law as a means of control of such situations is not only to pervert the criminal law, it is to place the political institution in a position of power *vis-à-vis* the economic organisation which is impermissible in a democratically organised State.

Under the original conception of the Sherman Act, in clear categories of black and white instead of the infinite shadings of

[18] *Nash* v. *United States*, 229 U.S. 373, 376–377 (1913).

fact involved in present day judicial doctrine, it was a matter of indifference whether civil or criminal penalties were imposed. Now, however, there is almost no field of law as esoteric, replete with conflicting authorities and lines of authority, posing as difficult problems of public policy and as complex fact situations as anti-trust law. In these circumstances, is it consistent with the rule of *nulla poena sine lege* ('no punishment without law') to subject those charged with the management of business to the risk of criminal punishment for decisions responsive to the stimuli of the market? In the making of management decisions an extraordinary amount of market, cost and other data are examined and weighed. Counsel are consulted and the current status of anti-trust decisions considered. Past decisions are re-evaluated in the light of new trends in the law.[19] Yet such decisions always raise questions of public control and, when these questions are of sufficient public interest, they demand examination by the courts. It is always possible that a criminal prosecution may be invoked for the purpose of such examination, with the consequent trial taking place under expanded concepts of conspiracy which, so far, the criminal courts themselves have shrunk from applying in the historical categories of crime. In the *Tobacco Case*[20] counsel for Liggett & Myers argued that 'the common practices of the tobacco industry are in many instances usual features of business life today, and in all instances practices which business men guided by . . . self-interest, acting reasonably and in the absence of agreement, might adopt.'[1] Counsel for Reynolds pointed out:

> '. . . [T]he significance of these convictions extends far beyond the immediate consequences to petitioners and the tobacco industry. . . . For, if these convictions be lawful, the pattern of prosecution is applicable—with the result of almost certain and repeated conviction—to every other executive and corporation in a mass production industry . . . in which, as a matter of common knowledge, economic forces have produced identities or close similarities in manu-

[19] J. G. Van Cise, 'Practical Planning,' Commerce Clearing House, *Anti-trust Law Symposium*, 1951, p. 103.
[20] *American Tobacco Co.* v. *United States*, n. 16, above.
[1] Brief for Appellants, p. 234, *Liggett & Myers* v. *United States*, 147 F. 2d 93 (6th Cir. 1944).

facturing, packaging, pricing, advertising, marketing and even raw material acquisition.'[2]

What is needed is a workable anti-trust law as well as workable competition. That law should be formulated so as to foster and not to inhibit dynamic enterprise, risk-taking and imaginative business decisions. Vigorous business policy should not be constantly subject to the inhibitory threat of criminal prosecutions; instead, only those acts or business decisions which can clearly be said in advance to entail public injury should be made criminal. For the business leader's loyalty is to his enterprise, and when doubt exists his decision will always tend to be cast on the side of advancing the interests of his organisation. A modification of our twofold legal system of civil and criminal controls is accordingly needed, the system of civil remedies, *i.e.*, injunctive relief, should be applied to novel cases raising questions whether new forms of business behaviour must be controlled, and the criminal procedure should be limited to cases involving reasonably objective categories of conduct. With such a distinction established, courts would be much more able to develop the law in the civil cases, knowing that their decisions would not have unfair or undesirable implications from the standpoint of the system of criminal law; more dynamic business behaviour would be fostered, and it would be possible in all justice to make more severe the penalties of the criminal law as deterrents to violation of the anti-trust laws. In short, it is proposed that injunctive relief be available for any violation of the Sherman Act as now provided, that actions for damages be available to any person injured by violations of the Sherman Act, that the prohibitions of the Act remain unchanged so as not in any manner to disrupt its jurisprudence, but that criminal penalties be limited to specified categories of conduct.

The heart of the task which lies before us is the fact that the law tends to concern itself with the abuse of power rather than the problem of power itself. Criminals are punished by reason of their overt conduct and not because of their predisposition to crime. Yet if the corporate institution be conceived of not as an entity or personality but as a system of relationships, the

2 Petition for Writ of Certiorari, p. 14, *Reynolds* v. *United States*, No. 840, U.S. Supreme Court, Oct. Term, 1944.

problem of power itself can be handled by the law and the law can expand beyond the domain of abuse of power to which it hitherto has been principally confined.[3] If the approach herein suggested be adopted, the law can then grapple directly with the problem of power itself. The basic difficulty is to formulate an approach that will be sound from the standpoint both of judicial administration and of economics. If the approach be free from static concepts, from concepts of an absolute or mechanistic nature, and each problem of power be viewed in its particular setting and as a problem involving the relations of the particular system of power to its particular market or markets, then the way will be open for a new approach to the application of the anti-trust laws.

Even the market philosophy itself must always be open to question, for the basic problem is not the preservation of the market as such but the establishment of those conditions which will best conduce to desired performance of those functions necessary to the life of society.

The Sherman Act and the Judicial Process

In the *Standard Oil* decision the courts assumed a task that it was impossible for them satisfactorily to discharge. It may well be that in that case the decision to face economic realities, to move from the domain of statutory interpretation into the domain of the functioning of the economic system, had even then been too long deferred. It may also well be that there is no equally satisfactory alternative means of control of the activity of the business institution as under the Sherman Act so construed. Once, however, the courts admitted to judicial inquiry the question of the reasonableness of the activities of business organisations, they moved into a realm where economists, even today, tread lightly and with unsure foot. For, as Justice Peckham pointed out in 1897,[4] issues of reasonableness in the economic sphere are extremely difficult to handle from the standpoint of judicial administration. Law is fundamentally concerned with norms for conduct. Criminal law, in particular, is concerned

[3] Cf. E. V. Rostow, 'Monopoly Under the Sherman Act: Power or Purpose?,' 43 *Illinois Law Review* (1948), p. 745 at p. 763; Note, 'Vertical Integration in Aluminium: A Bar to "Effective Competition,"' 60 *Yale Law Journal* (1951), p. 294 at p. 296, n. 16 (1951).

[4] *United States* v. *Trans-Missouri Freight Ass'n*, 166 U.S. 290 (1897).

with definite, objective norms the violation of which entails penalty. (And it must be remembered in this connection that there are no degrees of turpitude involved in violations of the Sherman Act; it is a matter of indifference under the law if a violation exists whether it is to be subjected to the civil or the criminal procedures of the statute.) The judicial process proceeds case by case, precedent by precedent, to build up rules or norms of general application. These are to be applied in subsequent similar cases in all the inexorability and majesty of established principles of law. But objective standards of *reasonableness* are at best, even in relatively simple factual situations, difficult to establish in advance. Circumstances vary from case to case and what is reasonable in the circumstances varies from case to case. When the issue is what restraints are reasonable in a situation involving business conduct or the structure of business organisation, the precise questions of fact will rarely be similar and usually they will be quite complex.

To illustrate, in a particularly flagrant case of a price-fixing agreement in the *Trenton Potteries Case*,[5] the Supreme Court laid down the rule that such an agreement 'by those controlling in any substantial manner a trade or a business in inter-State commerce' was illegal *per se*. The certainty of the rule thus laid down proved illusory in the subsequent *Appalachian Coals Case*,[6] only to be restored to favour in the *Socony-Vacuum Case*.[7]

The administrative factor in the judicial process, the search for rules of general application which will relieve the court of the trial burdens incident to a case-by-case approach, and will provide business institutions with definite rules of guidance, had a curious application from the standpoint of the economist in the *Standard of California* decision. In a series of decisions beginning with the *Dry Ice Case*[8] the court had laid down the rule that it was illegal to extend the lawful monopoly of a patent to control any unpatented materials used in connection with the patent. This was reaffirmed in the *International Salt Case*, when the court took occasion to say: '[I]t is unreasonable, *per se*, to foreclose competitors from any substantial market.'[9]

[5] *United States* v. *Trenton Potteries Co.*, 273 U.S. 392 (1927).
[6] *Appalachian Coals, Inc.* v. *United States*, 288 U.S. 344 (1933).
[7] *United States* v. *Socony-Vacuum Oil Co.*, 310 U.S. 150 (1914).
[8] *Carbice Corp.* v. *American Patents Development Corp.*, 283 U.S. 27 (1931).
[9] *International Salt Co.* v. *United States*, 332 U.S. 392, 396 (1947).

In the subsequent *Standard of California Case* these words were seized upon in a proceeding under section 3 of the Clayton Act, which prohibited tying clauses having a substantial tendency to limit competition, in order to limit the judicial inquiry into the question of the reasonableness of requirements contracts between a petroleum supplier and gasoline dealers to the sole issue whether such contracts involved 'a substantial share of the line of commerce affected.'[10] It may parenthetically be noted that the troublesome problem of determining when a substantial injury to competition had occurred had in the meantime also become simplified from the administrative standpoint by the substitution of 'reasonable possibility'[11] for 'reasonable probability'[12] of such an injury. Considerations as to the economic advantages of requirements contracts not negotiated under the duress of a patent monopoly or as to whether Standard of California had a dominant position in the market concerned (only 6.7 per cent of the total market in the area was affected by the contracts in question) accordingly became irrelevant and the judicial task enormously simplified. Evidence as to the effects on competition of the practice attacked was, in the view of Justice Frankfurter, 'most ill-suited for ascertainment by courts.'[13] In commenting on the practical effect of this decision one of the most acute attorneys, then in the Anti-trust Division, made the following remarks, which may occasion some surprise to the economist or business man:

> 'In restricting the court's economic scrutiny to the single criterion of substantiality of industrial coverage, the case eliminates the need for canvassing the complex economic considerations usually advanced as supporting the reasonableness of exclusive distributorships. Thus, the courts need no longer ponder or evaluate allegations that competition in the industry had not in fact been adversely affected; that costs to the seller or buyer had been reduced; that the buyer is assured of his supply and protected against price increases;

10 *Standard Oil Co. of California* v. *United States*, 337 U.S. 293, 314 (1949). The complaint also alleged a violation of Section 1 of the Sherman Act but the Court found it unnecessary to rule on this point in view of the finding of a violation of Section 3 of the Clayton Act.

11 *F.T.C.* v. *Morton Salt Co.*, 334 U.S. 37, 46 (1948).

12 *Corn Products Refining Co.* v. *F.T.C.*, 324 U.S. 726, 739 (1945).

13 *Standard Oil Co. of California* v. *United States*, 337 U.S. 293, 310 (1949).

> that the seller does not dominate the industry. These are issues which tend to inflate, rather than to illuminate, this kind of anti-trust record, and the best way to economise an anti-trust proceeding is still the obvious one of cutting down the number of issues in dispute.[14]

The tendency of the legal mind to classify essentially dissimilar factual situations into the same legal pigeon-hole may come something as a surprise to the mind of the economist. Thus, as noted in the preceding paragraph, a rule developed in a case involving an abuse of patent rights was transplanted to a situation involving the use by a business enterprise of requirements contracts as a means of achieving a loose integration into a retail market. In each, the incident of the exclusion of competing suppliers from the segment of the market affected by the questioned action is made a turning point for the decision. In the first case the incident is viewed in its context, but in the second it is viewed isolated from its context. Whether from the standpoint of economics or public policy a sound result is reached in the second case is accordingly a matter of chance. All such considerations are excluded as 'ill-suited for ascertainment by courts.'

In the *Yellow Cab Case*[15] the court was confronted with the incident of exclusion of competing suppliers from an appreciable segment of the market, this time also in a context of vertical integration of a business organisation. A manufacturer of taxi-cabs had found the answer to its sales manager's prayer by buying itself into control of local monopolies of the taxi-cab business. To bring customers for taxi-cabs thus shielded from competition into the corporate fold of the manufacturer was to assure an impregnable outlet for a considerable volume of sales of taxi-cabs. The court held that a complaint under sections 1 and 2 of the Sherman Act stated a prima facie case of a conspiracy 'to monopolise or restrain . . . an appreciable segment of inter-state cab sales.'[16] In other words, the case turned not on the questionable economic soundness of a vertical integration of this character (query as to its soundness from the profit standpoint), but on the loss of sales by competing taxi-cab manufacturers as the result of the integration.

14 S. Timberg, 'The Rights of Customer-Seller Selection,' Commerce Clearing House, *Antitrust Law Symposium*, 1951, pp. 151, 153–154.
15 *United States* v. *Yellow Cab Co.*, 332 U.S. 218 (1947).
16 *ibid.*, p. 226.

Whether and in what circumstances the law should show solicitude for competitors thus excluded by a vertical integration was directly posed in the *Standard of California Case* discussed above but, inasmuch as that case was disposed of on the basis of section 3 of the Clayton Act, the prior *Yellow Cab Case* arising solely under the Sherman Act became irrelevant. Consequently not until the *Columbia Steel Case*[17] was this issue again directly presented to the courts. Here the issue was faced in the context of a vertical corporate integration by United States Steel with Consolidated Steel into the fabricated steel market in the western States. A market analysis of the relative position of the two concerns in their respective fields was made, and the decision was reached that the integration was valid notwithstanding the consequent loss to competing suppliers of the segment of the market represented by Consolidated's purchases. The *Yellow Cab Case* was considered and found not to support the conclusion that 'all exclusive dealing arrangements are illegal *per se*.'[18] Yet, at its succeeding term the court came close indeed to that very conclusion in the *Standard of California Case*. And in the *National City Lines Case*,[19] involving exclusive dealing arrangements between transit equipment suppliers and bus transportation companies, the *Yellow Cab* situation was again presented to the lower courts and the *Yellow Cab* rule again applied against the defendant suppliers. Finally, after trial of the *Yellow Cab Case* itself upon remand from the Supreme Court, judgment for the taxi-cab manufacturer was sustained in the Supreme Court in view of the ruling of the trial judge that the integration was due not to an illegal intent to restrain trade but to other business factors.[20]

The problem of joint activities of business organisations tending to affect the free determination of prices in the market has been viewed in the common law tradition that any such tampering with the market is *per se* an evil. Occasionally, as in the *Appalachian Coals Case* and the earlier *Chicago Board of Trade Case*,[1] other aspects of the basic economic problems involved

[17] *United States* v. *Columbia Steel Co.*, 334 U.S. 495 (1948).

[18] *ibid.*, p. 523.

[19] *United States* v. *National City Lines, Inc.*, 186 F. 2d 562 (7th Cir. 1951).

[20] *United States* v. *Yellow Cab Co.*, 338 U.S. 338 (1949). The *Standard Oil* decision was reaffirmed by the Supreme Court in *Richfield Oil Corp.* v. *United States*, 343 U.S. 922 (1952).

[1] *Board of Trade of the City of Chicago* v. *United States*, 246 U.S. 231 (1918).

break through and demand judicial scrutiny. Usually, however, the force of this line of precedent and authority confines the judicial investigation to the sole question whether there has been concerted action by competitors. Thus, in the *American Column & Lumber Case*[2] the formal legal issue was whether some 400 manufacturers of hardwood, producing about one-third of the total United States production, could disseminate price information among themselves through a trade association. The Court held this to be 'abnormal conduct' involving undue co-operation among the competitors. Justice Brandeis in a dissent called attention to the basic economic consequences of the decision:

> 'The refusal to permit a multitude of small rivals to co-operate, as they have done here, in order to protect themselves and the public from the chaos and havoc wrought in their trade by ignorance, may result in suppressing competition in the hardwood industry. These keen business rivals, who sought through co-operative exchange of trade information to create conditions under which alone rational competition is possible, produce in the aggregate about one-third of the hardwood lumber of the country. This court held in *United States* v. *United States Steel Corporation*, 251 U.S. 417, that it was not unlawful to vest in a single corporation control of 50 per cent of the steel industry of the country; and in *United States* v. *United Shoe Machinery Co.*, 247 U.S. 32, the court held that it was not unlawful to vest in a single corporation control of practically the whole shoe machinery industry. May not these hardwood lumber concerns, frustrated in their efforts to rationalise competition, be led to enter the inviting field of consolidation? And if they do, may not another huge trust with highly centralised control over vast resources, natural, manufacturing and financial, become so powerful as to dominate competitors, wholesalers, retailers, consumers, employees and, in large measure, the community?'[3]

With the doors thus closed to trade association activities as a weapon of small business against their giant competitors, the inevitable economic consequences of the decision were, first, an additional stimulus towards size (*i.e.*, the integrated single business

[2] *American Column & Lumber Co.* v. *United States*, 257 U.S. 377 (1921).
[3] *ibid.*, pp. 418–419.

unit) as prophesied by Brandeis, and, second, a strengthening of the reaction by small business against size itself which is now evident.

The public acceptance of the anti-trust laws, and faith in the rationality and justice of the judicial process, has enabled the courts to enter upon highly controversial domains of public policy which are closed to the more open legislative process. Legislation is always a compromise among conflicting interests and sometimes that compromise can only be achieved through elusive language. In other words, the courts may perhaps more easily rush in where the legislature fears to tread. The problem of the chain store can be dealt with legislatively by a Robinson-Patman Act but not the dissolution of the A. & P. grocery chain itself.

A more apt illustration may be found in the history of the public control of basing-point practices, that is, pricing practices which involve the common use by an industry of one or more localities or points of production at which prices are uniformly quoted by all sellers to buyers, whether or not such sellers may have plants located in all such localities. In condemning under section 2 of the Clayton Act a basing-point system adopted by Corn Products Refining Company, the court acknowledged that Congress in enacting the Robinson-Patman amendment to this section did not intend to prohibit multiple basing-point systems.[4] Yet, on the authority of section 2 of the Clayton Act, as amended by the Robinson-Patman Act, and section 5 of the Federal Trade Commission Act, the court three years later condemned a multiple basing-point system.[5] Efforts by Congress to clarify the legal status of basing-point practices presented by the last decision resulted in bitter debate, a compromise bill worded with considerable vagueness, and a presidential veto.

The foregoing analysis is believed to furnish at least some persuasive support for the conclusion that the mind and training of the lawyer do not necessarily approach the solution of the problem of what business activities are in the public interest in the same manner as the mind and training of the economist. The lawyer seeks as a basis for decision analogous precedents, in which the element unifying the precedent with the situation at hand may well be derived from wholly dissimilar contexts. The

4 *Corn Products Refining Co.* v. *F.T.C.*, 324 U.S. 726, 737 (1945).
5 *F.T.C.* v. *Cement Institute*, 333 U.S. 683 (1948).

precedent then becomes the rule for decision. Whether the basic economic problems are grappled with in any one case accordingly tends to be fortuitous. The approach of the advocate is always to cite cases and to try to bring the new case within established precedents and rules of law. All the artifices of logic and semantics are utilised to this end. The courts are 'ill-suited' to weigh and evaluate economic criteria; even when such criteria are considered by the courts, it is always within the framework of issues of previously established case-law. This reliance on legal precedent, in other words, tends to exclude from consideration those economic criteria which must be considered if any sound decision is to be reached. The basic assumption of the lawyer is that a case is rightly decided if due regard to precedent is given within the rules of his craft. The basic assumption of the economist is that a solution of any problem demands the investigation, weighing and analysis of all relevant data and criteria.

It must be acknowledged that there is a small group of anti-trust specialists among advocates and a small group of judges to whom the foregoing strictures are not applicable. They have risen to an impressive maturity in their sensitiveness to the intricate problems involved in the regulation of the business organisation under the present system of anti-trust laws. One of the basic problems of the law schools and the legal profession is to expand that area of competence. Perhaps the heart of the problem lies in the trial, for when judges can match counsel in their 'know-how' of the field, sound results are usually achieved. But the courts have few Learned Hands and few Brandeis's.[6]

An analogous situation exists in the patent field. It is believed that any patent lawyer could give instances in which the most extraordinary, fanciful and flimsy theories were solemnly proferred to judges in an effort to validate or invalidate patents. Such practices are an inevitable consequence of the hurly-burly tactics of the trial, of the litigious equation. It is for the judge to weigh and evaluate, not for trial counsel. Correspondingly in the *A. & P. Case*,[7] involving the legality of practices of a chain

[6] An interesting development in this connection was the appointment of an economist, Carl Kaysen, to be law clerk to Federal Judge Wyzanski to assist in *United States* v. *United Shoe Machinery Corp.*, 110 F. Supp. 295 (D. Mass., 1953).

[7] *United States* v. *New York Great Atlantic & Pacific Tea Co.*, 67 F. Supp. 626 (E.D. Ill. 1946), *affd.* 173 F. 2d 79 (7th Cir. 1949).

grocery system, economies resulting from integration were successfully contended by the prosecution to be 'subsidies,' whereby the non-integrated retailers were unlawfully driven from the market in price competition, a theory which essentially involves the fallacy of 'begging the question' from the economist's point of view. In law, however, when the savings of integration were passed on to the consumer, a violation of the anti-trust laws were held to have occurred. If the court is to make a choice between the interest of protecting competitors from the rigours of aggressive price competition and the interest of preserving the system of price competition itself, let it at least be a knowing choice.

A second conclusion, which recent comment of the profession would support, is that even when the basic economic problem is faced, subject to the limitations of legal technique just noted, the very massiveness of many anti-trust problems renders it impossible for the court to consider all relevant evidence proferred. The problem of the record, the problem of the trial of an anti-trust case today, is so prodigious that some winnowing, organising and evaluating of evidence must be done by the parties or directed by the judge if the trial is not to become a career for advocates and judge.[8] As Judge Medina said in the trial of the *Investment Bankers Case,* 'Pretty soon I'm going to make some ruling so we won't be here the rest of our lives.'[9] While a skilled organisation of the evidence would considerably simplify the judicial task,[10] the final conclusions reached by the court may be at best only an approximation of the truth.

The source of the problem of the size of the record in the trial of an anti-trust suit lies in the fact that many such suits do not, as is the case with most litigation, deal with relatively narrow sequences of facts closely connected in time and space. They arise from grooves of business conduct worn deep with time and

[8] G. H. Dession, 'The Trial of Economic and Technological Issues of Fact,' 58 *Yale Law Journal* (1949), pp. 1019, 1242; B. McAllister, 'The Big Case: Procedural Problems in Antitrust Litigation,' 64 *Harvard Law Review* (1950), p. 27; B. McAllister, 'Stating the Issues,' Commerce Clearing House, *Antitrust Law Symposium,* 1951, p. 13; H. Baldridge, 'Simplifying and Expediting Cases,' *ibid.*, p. 23; A. N. Hand, 'Trial Efficiency,' *ibid.*, p. 31; M. Handler, 'Anti-trust—New Frontiers and New Perplexities,' 6 *The Record of the Association of the Bar of the City of New York* (1951), pp. 59, 81.

[9] *New York Times*, March 17, 1951, p. 22, col. 4.

[10] Consider Judge Prettyman's suggestions, including the card indexing of evidence, in E. B. Prettyman, 'Six Suggestions for Improvement,' Commerce Clearing House, *Antitrust Law Symposium*, 1951, p. 34.

involving intricate and vast systems of relationships. The questions for decision posited by the general concept of reasonableness in such a context are more legislative than they are judicial in nature, in that the question faced is whether the norms developed through voluntary private, channels shall be replaced by those determined by a political institution. No simple question of an adjudication of 'rights' is faced by an anti-trust court, but rather the question of what general system of rules for an industry will, under the prevailing philosophy of freedom of competition, best serve the interests of society. Questions of priority among values and the channelling of conduct to attain such values are the preoccupation of an anti-trust court as they are of a legislature. In place of the system of norms developed by the business organisation in its legal autonomy there is substituted a system of norms determined by judicial decrees.

THE DEFINITION OF NORMS OF CONDUCT FOR THE ECONOMIC ORGANISATION

As with all legal problems, the problem of anti-trust laws involves both questions of policy and techniques of control. In the preceding section it was seen that the formal, logical approach of the legal method often closed the door to inquiry into many of the relevant aspects of economic and public policy presented in the cases brought to the courts for decision. The point was further made that the legal technique itself was 'ill-suited' to the sound handling of the complex economic issues and data involved in such cases. These criticisms should not be construed to imply that the courts have failed totally or even largely in their task. Given the limitations under which they work, it has certainly been the consensus that theirs has been a creditable performance and one that has served the public interest well in the past six decades.

The issues now confronting the courts, however, are so weighty, are so fraught with possible incalculable harm to our economic society, that we must face the question whether we can continue to rely exclusively on the courts and our existing structure of anti-trust laws to take care of the public interest in controlling the business institution. It is essential for the future of the United States that we proceed wisely and carefully and subject to no illusions or predetermined conclusions in the determination of anti-trust issues.

It will be observed that throughout this chapter the basic problem has been stated to be that of the control of the conduct of the business organisation rather than a problem of preserving 'competition.' The hypothesis of pure competition as the perfect regulator of the economy was essentially an outgrowth of the naturalist *laissez-faire* philosophy, utilised at the close of the eighteenth century and the beginning of the nineteenth to establish the independence and power of the new mercantile interests and class as against the landed interests. Today, the problem is one of establishing a rational system of control of the business institution, rather than the attainment of the blissful Nirvana of perfect competition. If economists are agreed upon anything today it is the inevitability of imperfect competition in our economic life.

The reason for this emphasis upon the business organisation as the focal point of our inquiry has, in part, been indicated in the remarks at the outset of this chapter on the emergence of the modern corporate organisation as presenting a problem in the distribution of power. The issue of the possession of power by the corporate organisation is the one central issue in the meaning of the terms 'freedom' and 'competition,' the necessity of keeping the door open to alternatives of action by the individual, to an effective choice among the groups in which he may participate. When that door is closed through slums and overcrowding, through lack of educational opportunity, or through denial of human rights, participation in criminal and anti-social activities results. For in such circumstances this is the only effective choice of the submerged individuals seeking to break out of their environment. When that door is open, however, the organisation becomes the source of great productive energy, an energy derived through the forces of reward, loyalty, and co-operation rather than through arbitrary compulsion. Corporate management has developed an extraordinary technique in maximising the human energy of the participants in the corporate organisation and the physical energy of its capital equipment. Means of communication within the group, progressive rewards for contributions to the group, internal norms of conduct and sanctions therefor, all of these must be effectively organised if the organisation is to survive in the constantly rising plane of competition. For as the *choice* of workers or the *choice* of customers to participate in the functioning of a particular business organisation becomes less attractive as compared with the opportunities proffered by competing organisations, in that measure the organisation lags in its growth or finally dies. When the door to freedom of choice is closed to the extent that it is in the Soviet system, and reliance on fear and force instead becomes the dominant means for achieving the ends of the social system, then the energy potential of the organisational life of the society is correspondingly sluggish. So long as a real choice among the organisations in which the individual shall participate is kept alive, then, on the one hand, the directing personnel of those organisations will be subject to the constraint of relying upon inducement to action rather than compulsion and, on the other hand, the members of the organisations will find that their lives have that freedom of action which is the essential characteristic of the democratic State. The business organisation thus possesses a source of energy that the political institution can only very imperfectly and infrequently realise. Law in the western democratic State does not primarily rely on fear and force, and seeks to accommodate its structure of force to the accustomed habits and mores of its citizens. Nevertheless, only imperfectly and in times of great national emergency is the political institution able to induce rather than compel action. The economic organisation, however, is one in which participation is voluntary. While man must work and man must buy in our society if he is to live, his freedom to select and choose the organisation in which he shall work and from whom he shall buy should be preserved. From that fact flows the energy of western civilisation.

As we have seen, the purposes of society and of the business organisation are not necessarily identical. For it is the blind tendency of all organisations to expand, and a basic directing force of the activity of the modern economic organisation is the profit motive. The manner of the expression of that motive varies from industry to industry, and fluctuates with the fluctuations of the business cycle itself. A gadget manufacturer is infinitely more venturesome in risk-taking than, for example, a manufacturer of locomotives. A manufacturer will tend to integrate forward into the retail market in a deflationary economy and to integrate backward to assure continued sources of supply in an inflationary expanding economy when consumer demand is ample. Consequently, behaviours of the business organisation vary from industry to industry and from period to period. Behaviours of business organisation will also be determined to some extent by the psychology of their managers (compare the post-war history of Sewell Avery and Montgomery Ward with General Wood and Sears, Roebuck). Deviations of corporate behaviour and structure brought about by factors such as these lead to the question: When shall the organised force of the political institution be brought to bear to prevent or punish the behaviour of the economic organisation?

This is not the question which the economist considers in his investigations. There may be business conduct that is unsound economically or there may be corporate structures that are fantastic from the long-range economic point of view (as distinguished from the profit point of view of the *entrepeneur* himself). The question with which we are faced when we say 'there ought to be a law' is a different and a narrower question. It is instead: 'When is the behaviour under consideration sufficiently injurious to the interests of the community to justify the interposition of its organised procedure of force?'

In order to answer that question we must first endeavour to determine our basic objectives. If we are seeking to preserve the free organisational activity that is the central characteristic of the American economic system, we must at the least ensure that each economic organisation (1) is afforded access to the market both for purchases of materials and sales of its products, subject to no restraint imposed by any other economic organisation and (2) is enabled to select such type of internal structure or system of co-ordination as it may determine, again subject to no restraints directly imposed by other economic organisations, so as to provide means of experimental growth for each such organisation and a stimulus to the dynamic expression of its fundamental purpose or purposes in our economic life. For we must always seek to maintain those conditions which will bring about the optimum performance of the economic organisation of its particular social functions. Current economic thought is shifting from a preoccupation with the mechanical aspects of market structure, *i.e.*, the size, both relative and absolute, of the various organisations comprising the industry in question, to a concern with the manner of the performance of the several functions of the economic organisation. The rivalry of competition is but an assumed condition of satisfactory performance. Sometimes, as in the case of public utilities, satisfactory performance must be sought by means other than the competitive struggle. Performance and structure are complementary instead of self-exclusive criteria. The current emphasis in economic thought on performance must be viewed as an attempt to add to the relevant criteria for investigation rather than to subtract.[11]

Function of the Market

The ultimate co-ordinator of human effort, the ultimate determinant of distributive justice, is the market. It is to the market that each of us brings his wares and his services. It is the market which determines how the resources of society, physical and human, shall be allocated. It is the market which determines one's share of the national income. It is in its relation to the market that the business organisation finds its purpose. The market is its source of life and energy; upon the success of its adjustment to the market depends its size, its strength and the rewards to its members. Its growth is described in terms of its relation to the market. Horizontal integration involves the growth of a business organisation within a single market. Vertical integration involves the supersession of a market by the performance of the function of the market within the organisation.

Yet, law is also a co-ordinator of human effort, intervening to preserve the social equilibrium and to minimise friction. No longer does our citizenry accept the automatic, mysterious functioning of the market system as the sole means for ordering our economic society and the sole determinant of distributive justice. No longer is it our philosophy that a market based on free consumer choice, in which the sole criterion for choice is price, will always be in any and all circumstances the best or the only method for inducing desired economic behaviour. Price competition may not always bring about those uses of our resources which best serve the public interest. Governmental intervention

[11] J. M. Clark, 'Toward a Concept of Workable Competition,' 30 *American Economic Review* (1940), p. 241; M. Adelman, 'Effective Competition and the Antitrust Laws,' 61 *Harvard Law Review* (1948), p. 1289; E. S. Mason, 'The Current Status of the Monopoly Problem in the United States,' 62 *ibid.* (1949), p. 1265; E. G. Nourse, *Price Making in a Democracy,* 1944; but cf. C. D. Edwards, *Maintaining Competition,* 1949.

will in such circumstances be necessary to establish those conditions which will direct business performance to desired ends.[12] As a minimum, however, the law can permit no conduct which impairs the foundations of the market system. These foundations include the following propositions: (1) The market shall be dynamic, that is to say, sufficient energy, *i.e.*, price competition, must be manifested by the organisations participating in the market to capture the market that the advances of technology will be constantly passed on to buyers. Here lies the driving force behind the concept of conspiracy in cases of rigid price behaviour.[13] Here also lies the explanation of cases permitting restraints essential for the preservation of a dynamic market.[14] (2) Any market upon which an appreciable network of organisational activity depends must not be subject to violent disruption, with consequent impairment of regularised performance.[15] (3) The elements of bargaining in the market shall be limited to price, in which price is to be considered as a function of product quality, attendant services and stated monetary value.[16] (4) Price behaviour shall be uniform, that is to say, variances in price at any one time to different buyers shall be permissible only to the extent that they reflect the performance of non-customary marketing services by either buyer or seller.[17] (5) No one

[12] Cf. D. W. Smythe, 'Facing Facts About the Broadcast Business,' 20 *University of Chicago Law Review* (1952), p. 96, particularly at pp. 104 106; L. Fuller, 'Some Reflections on Legal and Economic Freedoms—A Review of Robert L. Hale's "Freedom Through Law,"' 54 *Columbia Law Review* (1954), p. 70.

[13] Cf. notes 12, 13, above, p. 196; cf. *F.T.C.* v. *Cement Institute*, 333 U.S. 683, 713, 716 (1948); *Triangle Conduit & Cable Co.* v. *F.T.C.*, 168 F. 2d 175 (7th Cir. 1948), *affd. sub. nom. Clayton Mark & Co.* v. *F.T.C.*, 336 U.S. 956 (1949).

[14] *Board of Trade of the City of Chicago* v. *United States*, 246 U.S. 231 (1918); *Appalachian Coals, Inc.* v. *United States*, 288 U.S. 344 (1933).

[15] *United States* v. *Patten*, 226 U.S. 525 (1913).

[16] *United States* v. *Paramount Pictures, Inc.*, 334 U.S. 131, 160 (1948); *Paramount Famous Lasky Corp.* v. *United States*, 282 U.S. 30 (1930); *United Shoe Machinery Corp.* v. *United States*, 258 U.S. 451 (1922); *International Business Machines Corp.* v. *United States*, 298 U.S. 131 (1936); *International Salt Co.* v. *United States*, 332 U.S. 392 (1947); see the dissent of Justice Brandeis in *F.T.C.* v. *Gratz*, 253 U.S. 421, 429 (1920). That price is a function of attendant services as well as of product quality is only imperfectly recognised in the law, see note 17, below.

[17] This rule, as above stated, is only partially realised in the law. Robinson-Patman Act, 49 Stat. L. 1526 (1936), 15 U.S.C.A., ss. 12–27; *United States* v. *New York Great Atlantic & Pacific Tea Co.*, 173 F. (2d) 79 (7th Cir. 1949) and *Standard Oil Co. of California* v. *United States*, 337

organisation shall pre-empt such a volume of a market for any product which markedly differs from other substitute products[18] as to enable the organisation in question to exact collateral demands[19] and to control, for the benefit of itself rather than for society, the functioning of the market.[20] Nor may the lawful monopoly of a patent be used to coerce buyers of products outside the scope of the patent.[1] (6) No one organisation[2] or aggregate of organisations[3] shall deny access to the market to other organisations in any appreciable degree. This principle, however, should not be perverted so as to condemn the withholding of patronage by buyers as a means of price pressure.[4]

The Problem of Monopoly Power

The "power" of a business organisation, in the sense of its energy potential or productive capacity, its ability to modify or affect the environment in which it functions, is neither good nor bad. It is merely a quantum of energy.

The fact that the power or productive capacity of different business organisations varies likewise has no value significance in and of itself. If the fact that a billion dollar business is bigger than a million dollar business is to have value significance, it must be weighed from the standpoint of whether the bigger

U.S. 293 (1949), as discussed in M. Adelman, 'Integration and Antitrust Policy,' 63 *Harvard Law Review* (1949), p. 27 at p. 53 *et seq.*; M. Adelman, 'The A & P Case: A Study in Applied Economic Theory,' 43 *Quarterly Journal of Economics* (1949), p. 238; M. Adelman, 'Effective Competition and the Antitrust Laws,' 61 *Harvard Law Review* (1948), p. 1289 at pp. 1334–1347 (1948); Note, 'Trouble Begins in the "New" Sherman Act: The Perplexing Story of the A & P Case,' 58 *Yale Law Journal* (1949), p. 969.

18 *United States* v. *E. I. Du Pont de Nemours and Co.*, 118 F. Supp. 41 (D. Del. 1953); E. H. Chamberlin, 'Product Heterogeneity and Public Policy,' 40 *Proceedings of the American Economics Association* (1950), p. 85 at p. 86.

19 *International Business Machines Corp.* v. *United States*, 298 U.S. 131 (1936).

20 See note 16, above, p. 196.

1 *International Salt Co.* v. *United States*, 332 U.S. 392 (1947); Note, 'Patent Abuses and Antitrust: The Per Se Rule,' 64 *Harvard Law Review* (1951), p. 626.

2 *Associated Press* v. *United States*, 326 U.S. 1 (1945); *Lorain Journal Co.* v. *United States*, 342 U.S. 143 (1951); *United States* v. *Aluminum Co. of America*, 148 F. 2d 416, 425–426 (2d Cir. 1945).

3 *Fashion Originators' Guild of America, Inc.* v. *F.T.C.*, 312 U.S. 457 (1941).

4 *Contra United States* v. *New York Great Atlantic & Pacific Tea Co.*, 67 F. Supp. 626 (E. D. Ill. 1946), *affd.* 173 F. 2d 79 (7th Cir. 1949).

concern is more or less likely to achieve the particular purpose to be served.

From the standpoint of values in the economic sphere, the concern may be judged on the following bases: (1) Its productive efficiency, the extent to which physical resources and human energy will be conserved in the production of the goods and services in question; (2) its marketing efficiency, the extent to which physical resources and human energy will be conserved in the transfer of time, place and possession utilities; and (3) its marketing behaviour, the extent to which it uses procedures other than that of pure price competition to capture its markets.

The problem of monopoly is not the problem of the big firm. The problem of the big firm is a problem of whether 10 is bigger than 1, whether 10 is more efficient than 1, or whether 10 is more detestable than 1 (that is, detestable from the standpoint of individual values expressed in political demands). The problem of monopoly, however, is a problem which must be stated in terms of relations other than merely a comparison based on quantity. For a monopoly to exist, in the view of the economist, we must have a product 'significantly different from others on the infinite chain of substitutes,' the facilities for the production of which are 'under a single control.'[5] A product is 'significantly different from others' if buyers so regard it—hence we become concerned with the nature of the product as viewed by the market. A 'single control' will exist when authority for the decision-making process as to conditions under which the supply of the product will move to the market is highly centralised, that is to say, when it is exercised in effect as a single decision, whether the maker of that decision be a single entity or a group.

The determination of monopoly for purposes of legal control raises further additional factors. The question whether we have business conduct justifying legal control will depend partly upon the nature of the conduct and partly upon the nature of the regulation. A much lesser degree of monopoly power may justify regulations controlling the exercise of that power than monopoly power which will justify the extreme remedy of dissolution. We have seen that the first fallacy involved in current anti-trust debate is that of confusing the problem of the big concern with

[5] E. H. Chamberlin, 'Product Heterogeneity and Public Policy,' *loc. cit.*

the problem of monopoly. We now see the second fallacy, namely, that a finding of monopoly power must necessarily and exclusively lead to the conclusion that the sole legal remedy is the elimination of that power, *viz.*, dissolution. In the *Corn Products* decision of Judge Hand in 1916, after deciding that the defendants had violated the Sherman Act, whether the Act be viewed as condemning 'the mere possession of an economic power' or 'the exercise of the power,' dissolution was apparently viewed as the necessary remedy 'if power alone be forbidden by the Statute.' Only if 'the exercise of the power is what the Statute touches,' could the court consider the question of remedies, 'What is practically necessary to prevent a repetition of those unfair means?'[6] Nearly thirty years later in the *Alcoa Case*, after holding that the ability to produce over 90 per cent of a product centred in a single control was in and of itself a monopoly condemned by section 2 of the Sherman Act, Judge Hand said: 'Dissolution is not a penalty but a remedy; if the industry will not need it for its protection, it will be a disservice to break up an aggregation which has for so long demonstrated its efficiency.'[7] In the recent *United Shoe Machinery Case*, control of '75 to 95 per cent of the total current demand for shoe machinery' coupled with 'other factors,' including a relationship with the market comprising 'a network of long-term, complicated leases with over 90 per cent of the shoe factories,' did not lead inevitably to dissolution. 'A petition for dissolution,' said the court, 'should reflect greater attention to practical problems and should involve supporting economic data and prophesies such as are presented in corporate reorganisation and public utility dissolution cases.'[8] The significance of the *Alcoa* decision is *not* that it has established

6 *United States* v. *Corn Products Refining Co.*, 234 Fed. 964, 1012, 1015 (S.D.N.Y. 1916).

7 *United States* v. *Aluminum Co. of America*, 148 F. 2d 416, 446 (2d Cir. 1945). Upon remand, despite the facts that Alcoa's market position in 1947 and 1948 was 76.7% and 84.7% of sales of pig and ingot production, respectively, and that its percentage of sales of primary aluminum by domestic integrated producers to non-integrated fabricators was 88% and 85%, respectively, in the same years, Judge Knox refrained from ordering the dissolution of Alcoa and instead ordered the divestiture of Aluminium Limited of Canada. *United States* v. *Aluminum Co. of America*, 91 F. Supp. 333, 356, 362, 418–419 (S.D.N.Y. 1950).

8 *United States* v. *United Shoe Machinery Corp.*, 110 F. Supp. 295, 307, 343, 348 (D. Mass., 1953), *affd.* 347 U.S. 521 (1954).

a new theory of control,[9] but that it has simply enlarged the area of jurisdiction of the courts for purposes of control. To the classical categories of conspiracy in restraint of trade and monopoly illegally gained or exercised there is now added a new class of defendants, namely, business firms merely possessing monopoly power.[10] The significance of the *Alcoa* decision may not go even this far; it may simply involve a reduction in the difficulties of proof of violation in 'monopolising' cases.

The preoccupation with the *rationale* of individual cases has blinded us to the realities of the process of the control of business conduct which has developed in the field of anti-trust law. Sir Henry Taylor wrote in the last century that 'in the affairs of life the reason may pervert the judgment. The straightforward view of things may be lost by considering them too closely and too curiously. . . . The fault of law-bred mind lies commonly in seeing too much of the question, not seeing its parts in their due proportions, and not knowing how much of material to throw overboard in order to bring a subject within the compass of human judgment.'[11] The decree, not the opinion, is the heart of an anti-trust case. We have in the language of the Sherman Act a statute which does not legislate, that is, legislate in sense of defining new norms for conduct theretofore privileged. The Sherman Act merely conferred jurisdiction upon the federal courts over cases involving restraints of trade and monopolising. The common law had defined the meaning of these terms, and their further elaboration and definition was a task for the courts. The enormously complicated and highly unique situations of fact presented to the courts in this field demonstrated, first, that no one factual situation could, by the selection of a few salient elements, be classified as similar to another previously disposed of[12]—hence,

[9] E. V. Rostow, 'Monopoly under the Sherman Act: Power or Purpose?,' 43 *Illinois Law Review* (1948), p. 745; W. S. Bowman 'Toward Less Monopoly,' 101 *University of Pennsylvania Law Review* (1953), p. 577; Note, 'Vertical Integration in Aluminum: A Bar to "Effective Competition."' 60 *Yale Law Journal* (1951), p. 294 at p. 296, n. 16.

[10] E. H. Levi, 'A Two Level Anti-Monopoly,' 47 *Northwestern University Law Review* (1952), p. 567.

[11] H. Taylor, *Notes from Life, The Statesman*, 1878, pp. 384–385.

[12] Cf. the unsuccessful attempt of the Government to analogise primary and secondary aluminum to first and second run movies, and thereby bring *Alcoa* under the rule of the *Paramount Pictures* case [*United States* v. *Paramount Pictures, Inc.* 334 U.S. 131, 172–173 (1948)] in *United States* v. *Aluminum Co. of America*, 91 F. Supp. 333, 358 (S.D.N.Y. 1950).

the rule of reason[13]—and, second, attempts to lay down rules of illegality *per se* were not always successful[14] and were always subject to criticism, even by those who most loudly clamoured for certainty.

The essence of the problem lay in the fact that neither the legislature nor the courts could lay down rules of universal application,[15] that some means must be found to legislate or regulate on a case-by-case basis, that no corporation would voluntarily consent to put itself in a class different from others,[16] that the classic symbol of 'monopolising' had not kept pace with the expanding doctrine of 'conspiracy' as a means for subjecting corporations to a process of special legislation or regulation,[17] that while 'conspiracy' had brought many defendants to their knees, it had been at the cost of enormously protracted and expensive trials,[18] and that so long as the Sherman Act was considered as a criminal instead of a regulative statute, the trial problems of proving intent and abuse of power would tend to frustrate control and limit the sphere of application of the statute. Hence some new and simpler means must be found for obtaining jurisdiction

13 *Standard Oil Co. of New Jersey* v. *United States*, 221 U.S. 1 (1911).

14 See pp. 201–205, above.

15 'Legislation has nearly confessed its inability to keep pace with the activity of man in discovery, in invention, and in the manipulation of accumulated wealth,' H. S. Maine, *Ancient Law*, 1907, p. 320.

16 'United emphasises the point that if a decree requires United to offer for sale all machine types which it leases, the decree will discriminate against United, because its competitors will be subject to no parallel injunction. United says that this discrimination violates United's legal rights. In support of this contention, United relies upon the language in *Hartford Empire Company* v. *United States*, 323 U.S. 386, 409–410, 65 S. Ct. 373, 385, 89 L. Ed. 322, in which a judicial decree was modified, because it placed a defendant for the future, "in a different class than other people."' *United States* v. *United Shoe Machinery Corp.*, 110 F. Supp. 295, 350 (D. Mass., 1953), *affd.* 347 U.S. 521 (1954).

17 J. A. Rahl, 'Conspiracy and the Anti-trust Laws,' 44 *Illinois Law Review* (1950), p. 743; *Theatre Enterprises, Inc.* v. *Paramount Film Distributing Corp.*, 346 U.S. 537 (1954).

18 G. H. Dession, 'The Trial of Economic and Technological Issues of Fact,' 58 *Yale Law Journal* (1949), pp. 1019, 1242; B. McAllister, 'The Big Case: Procedural Problems in Antitrust Litigation,' 64 *Harvard Law Review* (1950), p. 27. After the lapse of over two years, Judge Medina said in the trial of the *Investment Bankers* case, 'Pretty soon I'm going to make some ruling to curtail the proof so we won't be here the rest of our lives,' *New York Times*, March 17, 1951, p. 22, col. 4. At one point in the proceedings 17 children and 3 grandchildren had been born to the families of the 64 lawyers participating in the case and 4 marriages had taken place, *New York Times*, May 23, 1953, p. 21, cols. 2 and 3.

over the defendant for purposes of regulating his business conduct in the decree.

The real significance of the Sherman Act is that, by 1950, there were more than 250 consent decrees entered since 1906, 150 of which were entered since 1938. The latter group covered a far greater number of companies than the earlier group.[19] If to the consent decrees we add the decrees entered in the usual fashion, it will be seen that we have a vast body of corporate and industry regulations established through the anti-trust laws. We must, moreover, realise that each decree affects not only the defendant in question but also all those who do business with it. If they are to do business with it, they too must do so on the terms laid down in the decree. The big subpœna,[20] the trial of the case, are all a ritualistic prelude to the real task of deciding the exact respects in which the defendant is the 'bad man' referred to by Justice Holmes and setting forth the conduct which he must cease.

Courts continually law down dichotomies for purposes of decision. For Justice Peckham cases were to be distinguished on the basis of whether the restraint was direct or collateral,[1] for Chief Justice White the basis of distinction was whether the restraint was reasonable or unreasonable,[2] while for Justice McKenna the lawfulness of monopoly power was dependent upon whether it was accompanied by acts evidencing an abuse of power.[3] Judge Hand in the *Alcoa Case* did not summarily condemn all monopolists. A seller might possess the power to control the market price of a commodity yet have found himself involuntarily in this position, that is to say, he may have had monopoly thrust upon him. When sellers have eliminated all competitors solely by virtue of the skill and excellence of their competitive behaviour—their 'superior skill, foresight and

19 J. T. Chadwell and R. W. McLaren, 'The Current Status of the Anti-trust Laws,' 1950, *Illinois Law Forum*, p. 491 at p. 512, note 99.

20 W. N. Seymour, 'The Big Subpoena: Proceedings to Quash or Limit: Compliance,' Commerce Clearing House, *Antitrust Law Symposium*, 1953, p. 32.

1 *United States* v. *Joint Traffic Ass'n.*, 171 U.S. 505, 568 (1898).

2 *Standard Oil Co. of New Jersey* v. *United States*, 221 U.S. 1 (1911).

3 '[T]he law does not make mere size an offence, or the existence of unexerted power an offence. It, we repeat, requires overt acts, and trusts to its prohibition of them and its power to repress or punish them. It does not compel competition nor require all that is possible,' *United States* v. *United States Steel Corp.*, 251 U.S. 417, 451 (1920).

industry,' they are not necessarily to be condemned. Such a monopolist is the 'passive beneficiary of a monopoly, following upon an involuntary elimination of competitors by [approved] automatically operative economic forces.'[4] For example, market demand might be so small that only a single large plant could economically supply it. Changes in market demand might drive out all but one producer. Such monopolies were excusable.

However, the definition of membership in the second category of monopolists, which was to be within the condemnations of section 2 of the Sherman Act, was a marvellously subtle exercise of logic. The major and minor premises of the syllogism first laid down by Judge Hand for this purpose may be set forth as follows: '[A]ll contracts fixing prices are unconditionally prohibited,' 'a monopoly necessarily involves an equal . . . power [equal to that possessed by the group acting in concert] to fix prices,'[5] from which the conclusion should follow that any person is a monopolist who possesses a degree of power to fix prices in a market which would be prohibited were it derived from contract between two or more persons. Now, if price fixing agreements are illegal *per se* without regard to the market power exercised by the parties so agreeing,[6] then the conclusion just stated would in turn logically mean that any group of business firms fixing prices might find themselves classed as monopolists. But Judge Hand shrank from this *reductio ad absurdum*. Instead he subtly shifted to another and undisclosed major premise: All persons fixing prices in a market in any manner violate the Sherman Act. For the price fixing cases the syllogism would be completed with the reasoning that defendants had fixed prices by agreement from which the conclusion would follow that they therefore violated the act. Judge Hand, however, skipped over the price fixing cases to the monopoly cases and for these cases set forth the minor premise that persons possessing a degree of market power which, if exercised, would fix prices, *do* fix prices when they exercise that power. The 'distinction is . . . purely formal; . . . it would disappear as soon as the monopoly began to operate; for when it did—that is, as soon as it began to sell at all—it must sell at some price and the only price at which

[4] *United States* v. *Aluminum Co. of America*, 148 F. 2d 416, 430 (2d Cir. 1945).
[5] *ibid.*, at 427-428.
[6] *United States* v. *Socony-Vacuum Oil Co.*, 310 U.S. 150 (1940).

it could sell is a price which it itself fixed. Thereafter the power and its exercise must needs coalesce.'[7] The possession and the exercise of the power to fix prices violates the act. With the second syllogism elaborated, Judge Hand is in a position to shift back to his first syllogism and modify its terms. The final step in the course of reasoning becomes: Contracts fixing prices 'are really partial monopolies,'[8] that is to say, a group of persons acting in concert to fix prices must be conclusively presumed to have the market power to fix prices, any person having *in fact* a market power to fix prices must under the Act be treated on the same basis as the group acting in concert, and both must consequently be deemed to violate the Act when their power is exercised. Note the change in equivalents: the monopolistic equivalent of the group acting in concert does not arise from an identity in the power possessed by the group but in the possession of an amount of market power which would enable the monopolist to achieve the same benefits through control of price as the group would achieve through agreement. The determination of what that amount of market power should be is a study in probabilities. It raises the questions: (1) What is the evil to be regulated? Is the law to be concerned with persons who only have sufficient market power to *affect* prices in certain circumstances? Or is it to be confined to persons who have such a degree of market power that they can in large measure *fix* prices? (2) How high a degree of probability of control of price shall we require from the evidential standpoint? What percentage of control shall we require? What other factors, if any, shall we take into consideration? (3) What is our market? Is it for any product whatever? What elements shall we take into consideration for the purpose of differentiating products? Is a highly advertised cigarette significantly different from one not so advertised? Is the market for the same movie on its first run significantly different from its second run market? Is the $400 gas range significantly different from the $79 gas range? In addition to the problem of the differentiation of products for purposes of market definition, we have the problem of defining market areas—what is the geographical market? When, for

[7] *United States* v. *Aluminum Co. of America*, 148 F. 2d 416, 428 (2d Cir. 1945).
[8] *ibid.*

the purposes of legal control, shall we define a market not on the basis of product or of area but on the basis of class of buyers? Is it proper to take not a particular shoe machine as the product for purposes of market definition but a group of buyers, for example, the shoe manufacturers, or the shoe industry, as the market?

Judge Hand answered these questions in the *Alcoa Case* on the basis that the crucial product was 'virgin' aluminium, the market for that product was national in scope, and the percentage of control of the market necessary to justify intervention by the courts was certainly ninety per cent, but that 'it is doubtful whether sixty or sixty-four per cent is enough to constitute a monopoly; and certainly thirty-three per cent is not.'[9]

The *Alcoa* doctrine is an open-end doctrine, capable of enormous expansion. Its philosophy is that the basic evil to be controlled is the possession and exercise of the power to fix prices in the market. In any one case, in order to find the evil to exist, it is necessary to determine first the person or persons possessing and exercising the power, second, the necessary amount of power and, third, the relevant market. With the thrust of the anti-trust law constantly towards expansion of its domain of control, we may expect each of these elements to be refined, elaborated and expanded.

The possibilities of control of the conduct of the business institution through section 1 of the Sherman Act have now been largely exhausted. The internal or intra-enterprise conspiracy doctrine[10] is the analogue of the *Alcoa* doctrine. While, through the legal fiction of a 'bathtub conspiracy' among affiliated corporations, it permits control to be exercised over what is in fact a single business enterprise, it still remains necessary to prove conspiracy and restraint of trade. In other words, the requirement still remains that evidence of collusion be produced. There was for a time a distinct trend towards the acceptance of uniformity of competitive behaviour as conspiracy,[11] but the

[9] *ibid.* at 424.

[10] *United States* v. *Yellow Cab Co.*, 332 U.S. 218, 227 (1947); *Keifer-Stewart Co.* v. *Joseph E. Seagram & Sons, Inc.*, 340 U.S. 211 (1951); *Timken Roller Bearing Co.* v. *United States*, 341 U.S. 593 (1951).

[11] *viz.*, participation with 'awareness of the general scope and purpose of the undertaking.' *United States* v. *Masonite Corp.*, 316 U.S. 265, 275 (1942).

uniformity of action condemned in the *Cement Case*[12] and the doctrine of conscious parallel action sustained by a divided court in the *Rigid Steel Conduit Case*[13] have apparently closed this door to further expansion of the conspiracy doctrine under section 1 and transferred jurisdiction of cases involving conscious parallelism from the Department of Justice to the Federal Trade Commission.[14]

Control of the business enterprise under section 2 of the Sherman Act had, until the *Alcoa* doctrine, to run the gauntlet of specific intent for attempts to monopolise,[15] while the monopoly cases required evidence of abuse of monopoly power before judicial intervention could be obtained.[16] The simplicity of the *Alcoa* doctrine makes possible an even greater expansion of the Sherman Act than that heretofore achieved through the conspiracy doctrine.

We noted above that the first question to be answered under the test of the *Alcoa Case* is the determination of the person or persons possessing and exercising the prohibited degree of market power. Under the facts of that case, the determination was simple—it was a single business enterprise. But consider this possibility: Suppose a group of several firms possessed the prohibited degree of market power. The *Tobacco Case*[17] would require proof of conspiracy to bring each of them within the scope of the *Alcoa* doctrine. However, suppose that each member of the group pursues 'manœuvres not honestly industrial'[18]

12 *F.T.C.* v. *Cement Institute,* 333 U.S. 683 (1948).

13 *Triangle Conduit & Cable Co.* v. *F.T.C.,* 168 F. 2d 175 (7th Cir. 1948). *affd.* by divided court *sub. nom. Clayton Mark & Co.* v. *F.T.C.,* 336 U.S. 956 (1949).

14 J. A. Rahl, 'Conspiracy and the Anti-trust Laws,' 44 *Illinois Law Review* (1950), p. 743 at p. 761; *Theatre Enterprises, Inc.* v. *Paramount Film Distributing Corp.,* 346 U.S. 537 (1954).

15 'For this reason conduct falling short of monopoly is not illegal unless it is part of a plan to monopolise, or to gain such other control of a market as is equally forbidden. To make it so, the plaintiff must prove what in the criminal law is known as a "specific intent"; an intent which goes beyond the mere intent to do the act. By far the greatest part of the fabulous record piled up in the case at bar, was concerned with proving such an intent,' *United States* v. *Aluminum Co. of America,* 148 F. 2d 416, 431–432 (2d Cir. 1945).

16 E. R. Johnston and J. P. Stevens, 'Monopoly or Monopolisation—A Reply to Professor Rostow,' 44 *Illinois Law Review* (1949), p. 269; E. H. Levi, 'A Two Level Anti-Monopoly Law,' 47 *Northwestern University Law Review* (1952), p. 567.

17 *American Tobacco Co.* v. *United States,* 328 U.S. 781 (1946).

18 *United States* v. *Aluminum Co. of America,* 148 F. 2d 416, 431 (2d Cir. 1945).

or 'not economically inevitable.'[19] In other words, suppose it had taken action not in response to competition but designed to prevent competition. In such a case, might not each be said to enjoy monopoly power, since that power had been achieved by market behaviour 'not honestly industrial'?

The United Shoe Machinery Corporation was found to possess '75 plus percentage of the shoe machinery market which United serves.' This fact, together with 'other factors,' was held to result in a violation of section 2. The 'other factors' were the circumstances that United had pursued 'practices not economically inevitable,' not 'honestly industrial,' or not 'excusable.'[20] United had not achieved its power by *illegal* means; its structure and practices under review had been sustained by the Supreme Court three times.[1] If a single enterprise which had acquired the prohibited degree of market power by means not illegal but nevertheless 'not honestly industrial' is to be condemned, may not each member of a group of enterprises similarly situated be likewise condemned? It would not be the first time the courts have reasoned by analogy.

The second component element of the basic test in the *Alcoa* decision is the determination of the power to fix prices. This is subject to expansion in at least two ways. The courts may include within the power to *fix* prices the power to *affect* prices. They did so in the *Socony-Vacuum Case* involving a group of competitors acting in agreement.[2] They could under the logic of *Alcoa* take a similar step in a monopoly case. And it must be remembered that the percentage of the gasoline market involved in the *Socony-Vacuum Case* was but five.[3] Or, second, the courts may make the controlling percentage to be the source of a presumption, leaving to the plaintiff, the government, the establishment of the existence of the prohibited percentage and placing upon the defendant in such case 'the burden of proving that its share of the market was attributable to its ability, natural advan-

19 *United States* v. *United Shoe Machinery Corp.*, 110 F. Supp. 295, 345 (D. Mass. 1953), *affd.* 347 U.S. 521 (1954).

20 *ibid.*, at 343–345.

1 *ibid.*, at 348, citing *United States* v. *Winslow*, 227 U.S. 202 (1913); *United States* v. *United Shoe Machinery Company of N.J.*, 247 U.S. 32 (1918), and *United Shoe Machinery Corp.* v. *United States*, 258 U.S. 451 (1922).

2 *United States* v. *Socony-Vacuum Oil Co.*, 310 U.S. 150 (1940).

3 *ibid.*, at 170.

tage, legal licence, or, perhaps, to others' lack of interest in entering the market.'[4]

The third component element in the test of the *Alcoa Case* is the determination of the relevant market. From the standpoint of the economist, the market to be investigated is the market for a product, with such product being 'significantly different from others on the infinite chain of substitutes.'[5] But the market may be a class of buyers or an industry, as in the *United Shoe Machinery* case. Under one tabulation in that case, the percentage of use by shoe manufacturers of the defendant's machines ranged from 48 to 100 per cent, depending on the kind of machine involved. In another tabulation, the percentage ranged from 41 to 100 per cent. Yet, somehow, an average of '75 plus percentage of the *shoe machinery* market which United serves' was arrived at by the court.[6] Offhand, the procedure would seem similar to finding that a defendant who had 40 per cent of the sales of corn and 100 per cent of the sales of wheat in a commodity market would have control of the corn-wheat market to the extent of 70 per cent, the average of the two. In any event, the remedies in the *United Shoe Machinery Case* were made applicable to the entire business of the defendant. The holding in the case must rest on either the proposition that the relevant market was a class of buyers, and that monopoly as to some of the products purchased by those buyers must be deemed to be equivalent to a monopoly as to all purchased from the party in question, or that an enterprise having a diversified line of products, in certain of which it has monopoly power as against its competitors, is to be deemed to have monopoly power as to all its products.

The relations of United Shoe Machinery Corporation to the

4 *United States* v. *United Shoe Machinery Corp.*, 110 F. Supp. 295, 343 (D. Mass. 1953) *affd.* 347 U.S. 521 (1954). Note the similar reasoning of Justice White in the *Standard Oil* case: 'Because the unification of power and control over petroleum and its products . . . aggregating so vast a capital, gives rise, in and of itself, in the absence of countervailing circumstances, to say the least to the prima facie presumption of intent and purpose,' *Standard Oil Co. of New Jersey* v. *United States*, 221 U.S. 1, 75 (1911). See also the remark of Justice Douglas: 'But size is of course an earmark of power,' *United States* v. *Griffith*, 334 U.S. 100, 107, n. 10 (1948).

5 E. H. Chamberlin, 'Product Heterogeneity and Public Policy,' *loc. cit.*, note 18, above, p. 215.

6 *United States* v. *United Shoe Machinery Corp.*, 110 F Supp. 295, 343 (D. Mass. 1953), *affd.* 347 U.S. 521 (1954) (italics added).

shoe manufacturing industry involved an interesting, if not unique, industrial structure. The Corporation, through its leasing of shoe machinery to the shoe manufacturing industry, saved the latter the heavy initial capital investment which the purchase of such machines would otherwise have entailed. The profits of the enterprise made possible a large research budget in the Corporation which the host of small producers could not individually have provided. The result was, on the one hand, the position of dominance of the Corporation *vis-à-vis* the shoe industry, and, on the other hand, a highly competitive shoe industry which would probably otherwise not have developed. The eventual outcome of the decision may well be to bring powerful forces to bear towards both vertical and horizontal integration in the shoe industry.

The term 'market' becomes subject to subtle manipulation to reach desired results, as the recent *Times-Picayune Case*[7] shows. The majority and minority of the Court there divided on the question whether the relevant newspaper market was to be measured by sales during the morning, or by sales during the entire day. In view of the importance of the utility of time in the newspaper field, the minority would appear to be on sounder ground in selecting the morning newspaper market as the relevant market. It is interesting that the distinction made in the *Paramount Pictures Case*[8] in the markets for first and second run movies, which would appear to be highly relevant on the law, was not mentioned by either the majority or the minority.

We have hitherto affirmed the proposition that a finding of monopoly is in essence a jurisdictional finding and that it does not necessarily lead to the logically applicable remedy of dissolution.[9] In the first place, for purposes of remedies, percentages of market power are not necessarily controlling.[10] More important is the fact that dissolution is the exception, rather than the rule. Not one of the monopoly cases in recent years has led to a dissolution, though a certain degree of divestiture has upon occasion been ordered.[11] This is not the place to discuss the wisdom of the

7 *Times-Picayune Publishing Co.* v. *United States,* 345 U.S. 594 (1953).
8 *United States* v. *Paramount Pictures, Inc.*, 334 U.S. 131 (1948).
9 See pp. 217–218, above.
10 'The relative effect of percentage command of a market varies with the setting in which that factor is placed,' *United States* v. *Columbia Steel Co.*, 334 U.S. 495, 528 (1948).
11 *e.g.*, the divestiture of Aluminium Limited of Canada in *United States*

reluctance of the courts to order dissolution, though it may perhaps be said that the economists have not as yet produced data (as distinguished from opinion) which is of such a substantial and convincing character as overwhelmingly to lead a court to the conclusion that concentration of economic power must be destroyed, whatever the costs in attendant economic dislocations. Nor does it appear that the public clamour for the dissolution of the large concern is at this time deafening in its impact.

It is submitted that a code of competitive behaviour for the business institution is now becoming apparent in the anti-trust cases. A. A. Berle has elsewhere called attention to the existence of 'the "inchoate law" of the system of industrial concentrates'[12] and the protection through constitutional law of personal rights from invasion by economic power.[13] We have elsewhere taken occasion to define the basic features of the code of competitive behaviour developed through the anti-trust law.[14]

Under the dichotomy of the *Alcoa* and *United Shoe Machinery Cases* a special rule of law is now emerging for the business concern possessing or sharing substantial economic power in the market. Such a concern is to be confined to practices 'honestly industrial.' Only 'superior skill, foresight and industry' will justify its market position. The use of the long-term lease and various other business practices are to be denied United Shoe Machinery because they do not encourage 'competition based on pure merit . . . they are unnatural; they unnecessarily exclude actual and potential competition; *they restrict a free market.*'[15] To such a firm the rule is applicable that the 'elements of bargaining in the market shall be limited to price, in which price is to be considered as a function of product quality,

v. *Aluminum Co. of America*, 148 F. 2d 416 (2d Cir. 1945) and 91 F. Supp. 333 (S.D.N.Y. 1950); the divestiture of certain supplies business from United Shoe Machinery Corp., *United States* v. *United Shoe Machinery Corp.*, 110 F. Supp. 295, 353 (D. Mass. 1953), *affd.* 347 U.S. 521 (1947); and the setting aside of the District court's findings on divestiture in *United States* v. *Paramount Pictures, Inc.*, 334 U.S. 131, 174 (1948).

12 A. A. Berle, 'The Developing Law of Corporate Concentration,' 19 *University of Chicago Law Review* (1952), p. 639 at p. 656.

13 A. A. Berle, 'Constitutional Limitations on Corporate Activity—Protection of Personal Rights from Invasion through Economic Power,' 100 *University of Pennsylvania Law Review* (1952), p. 933; see A. A. Berle, *The Twentieth Century Capitalist Revolution*, 1954.

14 See pp. 214–215, above.

15 *United States* v. *United Shoe Machinery Corp.*, 110 F. Supp. 295, 345 (D. Mass. 1953), *affd.* 347 U.S. 521 (1954) (italics added).

attendant services, and stated monetary value.'[16] Thus the businesses in the *Tobacco Case,* which in part achieved their market dominance by the differentiation of their premium price product through advertising, may at some later date be ordered to reduce their advertising budgets.

The escape hatch of the *Alcoa-United Shoe* doctrine will prohibit the large concern 'progressively to embrace each new opportunity as it opened'[17]—conduct which might otherwise seem to be the end purpose of the competitive drive. The ideal norm will be the norm of pure price competition, but the definition of that norm in the concrete case will be a highly elusive process, in which judicial logic will clash with practical business necessities. A firm selling a diversified line of products on a standard mark-up pricing basis may now possibly be condemned because it has in specific cases cut its mark-up in the face of competition.[18] It now seems that research and patent policy must not be too closely shaped by existing and potential competition.[19] At every point, the firm's competitive behaviour will be carefully scrutinised as to its conformity with the ideal of what the judge conceives to be pure price competition. Competitive behaviour privileged where the small firm is concerned may be denied the big firm.

To recapitulate, on the one hand there is the vista of a constantly expanding area of judicial intervention and control through the *Alcoa* formula. On the other hand, there is a possibility of relief for the defendant under an ideal of competitive behaviour which is, at this point, highly vague in content and consequently subject to highly unpredictable judicial administration. Not illegal practices, nor predatory practices, nor practices involving an abuse of economic power, but practices 'not honestly industrial' or not involving 'automatically operative economic forces' are now to be condemned.

RETROGRESSIVE TENDENCIES IN THE ANTI-TRUST LAWS

We shall always have in the judicial enforcement of the anti-trust

16 See p. 214, above.

17 *United States* v. *Aluminum Co. of America,* 110 F. Supp. 416, 431 (2d Cir. 1945).

18 *United States* v. *United Shoe Machinery Corp.,* 110 F. Supp. 295, 325–329 (D. Mass. 1953), *affd.* 347 U.S. 521 (1954).

19 *ibid.,* at 329–333.

laws the clash between *stare decisis* and the rule of reason—the clash between the certainty and administrative convenience of precedent in the operation of the judicial process and the need for flexibility and open-mindedness implicit in the rule of reason approach. Partly as a result of the tendency of courts to rely on precedent as a means for the decision of complicated cases for which courts find themselves to be 'ill-suited,' and partly as a result of legislation, certain retrogressive tendencies in the anti-trust laws are manifest:

The substitution of form for substance

Excessive power inevitably manifests itself in abuse of power. It is with the latter that the law usually concerns itself. Not until the *Alcoa* decision [20] did the anti-trust law come to grips with the basic problem of the mere possession by an economic organisation of excessive power in a market, without regard to evidence establishing the abuse of such power.

One form in which a business organisation may take advantage of a dominant position in a market is through the exaction of tying clauses. Its position of power in one market is used as a club to compel buyers to purchase in another and freer market.[1] Such an abuse of power was condemned by section 3 of the Clayton Act [2] and in numerous cases.[3] But the injury resulting from the conduct was made the basis for decision in another line of cases affirming the doctrine that it is illegal *per se* to exclude competitors from any substantial market.[4] It is not only the result, but the conduct by which the result is brought about, that is the concern of law. For example, it is not only the existence of death but the manner in which death is produced that is the concern of law. It is conduct, more particularly, deviational conduct, which creates problems in law. Without such conduct *damnum absque injuria*. The fundamental fallacy

20 *United States* v. *Aluminum Co. of America*, 148 F. 2d 416 (2d Cir. 1945).

1 Note, 'Section 3 of the Clayton Act—Coexisting Standards of Legality?' 49 *Columbia Law Review* (1949), p. 241.

2 38 Stat. L. 731 (1941), 15 U.S.C.A., s. 14.

3 *United Shoe Machinery Corp.* v. *United States*, 258 U.S. 451 (1922); *International Business Machines Corp.* v. *United States*, 298 U.S. 131 (1936); *International Salt Co.* v. *United States*, 332 U.S. 392 (1947).

4 *United States* v. *Yellow Cab Co.*, 332 U.S. 218 (1947); *Standard Oil Co. of California* v. *United States*, 337 U.S. 293 (1949); *United States* v. *National City Lines, Inc.*, 186 F. 2d 562 (7th Cir. 1951).

here involved lies in a subtle substitution for the term 'market' as commonly used, *i.e.*, the process of exchange of a commodity as between all the sellers and buyers, of the terms 'substantial market' or 'appreciable segment' of the market. These latter terms are used to refer to that portion of the market represented by the purchases of one or more specific buyers whose dollar volume of buying is not *de minimus*. If more precise and accurate terminology were here employed, it would be seen that the courts are not concerned with the basic problem of the exclusion of sellers from access to *the* market by unlawful restraints but with the vastly different question of the exclusion of sellers from selling to a *particular* buyer or buyers. It is the very essence of the marketing process that each sale excludes other competitors. The circumstance that the sale takes the form of an exclusive dealing contract or a requirements contract should be of no consequence to the law, unless such an agreement be consummated by a seller using not the contemplated transfer of his product but his position of power in the market as a basis for bargaining. When such a position of power exists, its control in law should not turn on the fact that a contract of sale of a commodity rather than a purchase of a business was the vehicle chosen for its exercise. Of more importance, however, is the fact that the solicitude thus manifested by the courts for competitors and their protection from the operation of the competitive process strikes at the very heart of the free market system upon which our society relies as the guarantor of a vigorous, healthy economy.

The foregoing doctrine that competitors are not to be excluded from markets in any substantial degree, with the term 'substantial' being determined on a purely quantitative, arithmetical basis instead of on the relative basis of the effect of the exclusion upon the market, and with the source of the exclusion (*i.e.*, whether it is an abuse of power in the market by an economic institution) a matter of no legal consequence, may possibly be resorted to by the courts as a criterion for decision of revitalised section 7 of the Clayton Act.[5] However, there is evidence that neither the courts nor the Federal Trade Commission will adopt such a formalistic approach in the construction of section 7.[6]

[5] 38 Stat. L. 731 (1914), 15 U.S.C.A. Sec. 18, as amended 64 Stat. L. 1125 (1950); R. P. Hernacki, 'Mergerism and Section 7 of the Clayton Act,' 20 *George Washington Law Review* (1952), p. 659.

[6] *Transamerica Corp.* v. *Board of Governors of Federal Reserve System*,

The substitution of criteria of form for those of substance reappeared in the doctrine of the *Timken Case*,[7] that a business enterprise characterised by common ownership and control of its properties and operations is to be put into a separate class for purposes of anti-trust control when it conducts its operations through legally separate entities of parent and subsidiary corporations, instead of through separate departments or divisions of a single corporation.[8] Instead of viewing the market relations of such a business organisation as a single whole and determining whether in any respect its external relations are socially injurious, the courts here adopted the purely formal approach that by virtue of its separate incorporation in law each subsidiary (or parent) corporation is to be treated as a separate entity in fact. The result is accordingly reached that violations of the anti-trust laws can occur *within* a business enterprise. In other words, conduct permissible to a business organisation whose corporate *legal* structure conforms to its social reality becomes impermissible to a business institution which channels its authority through the legal instrumentality of stock control, instead of an agency or master and servant relationship.[9] Little social purpose can be seen in making such purely formal distinctions.

Norms destructive of price competition

We have pointed out above the significance of the market as a stimulus for vigorous organisational activity and growth, and a means for both stimulating, and passing on to society the benefits of, technological advance. That conduct of the business organisation which is most to be fostered is vigorous price competition.

Yet group pressures, including those of competitors who have been unable to achieve the economies of more vertically integra-

206 F. 2d 163 (3d Cir. 1953); F.T.C. *v.* Pillsbury Mills, Inc., 3 Commerce Clearing House, *Trade Regulation Service*, 1953, par. 11,582; cf. *F.T.C.* v. *The Maico Company, Inc.*, *ibid.*, at par. 11,577.

7 *Timken Roller Bearing Co.* v. *United States*, 341 U.S. 593, 598 (1951).

8 Counsel for the Government contended: 'Parent and subsidiary corporations must accept the consequences of maintaining separate corporate entities.' The Chief Justice inquired: 'Your theory is that if you have a separate corporation, that makes a difference?' 'Yes.' 19 *U.S. Law Week* (1950), p. 3291 at pp. 3292, 3294.

9 Accord: *United States* v. *Yellow Cab Co.*, 332 U.S. 218, 227 (1947); *Kiefer-Stewart Co.* v. *Joseph E. Seagram & Sons, Inc.*, 340 U.S. 211, 215 (1951).

ted competitors, have been able to bring enough pressure to bear upon the legislature to secure enactment of the Robinson-Patman Act.[10] To the extent that a uniform price for a product is required, the Act serves to support one of the principal foundations of the market system (proposition '4' at page 214 above) and is therefore to be commended. To the extent, however, that the Act fails to permit variances in price which reflect the performance of non-customary marketing functions by either buyer or seller, it is a clog on price competition.[11] And to the extent that it permits price competition to be limited to merely matching prices, instead of cutting prices, and requires economic justification for even such a limited form of price competition, it closes the door to one of the methods most likely to result in generally lowered prices. For erosion in a price structure is more likely to be gradual than sudden.[12]

Price regulation by private interests

An approved shelter from pure price competition is found in the trade mark. As a hallmark of origin it seeks to retain the custom of the satisfied buyer and to attract new buyers. And satisfaction and attraction may flow from advertising as well as from product quality.

So long as the basic foundations of the market system remained unimpaired the use of trade marks created no problem in law, other than prohibiting other institutions from capturing buyers through trade mark deception instead of by price competition or by different, non-infringing trade marks. But in the Miller-Tydings Act of 1937[13] and now in the McGuire Federal Fair Trade Law,[14] contract assumes the extraordinary role of creating third party *obligations* when at common law it could only create third party rights or benefits. Contract thus becomes the vehicle for private legislation. The conduct prohibited by such legislation is price competition. And when the principal sources of products in the market are each identified by trade marks, a system of private law is created which destroys the

10 See note 17, above, p. 214.
11 See M. Adelman 'Integration and Antitrust Policy,' 63 *Harvard Law Review* (1949), p. 27.
12 M. Adelman, 'Effective Competition and the Antitrust Laws,' 61 *ibid.* (1948), p. 1289 at pp. 1327–1330.
13 50 Stat. L. 693 (1937).
14 66 Stat. L. 631, 632 (1952).

social role of the market, other than as a means for the transfer of ownership. Where, elsewhere in the law, the highly tenuous, all-inclusive concept of conspiracy is used by the courts to frustrate rigid price behaviour, here private legislation is allowed to strike at the heart of the market process, free price competition, and to establish shelters for organisational stagnation.

Legal shelters for competitors

Cartels are commonly condemned for their restraints on price competition, in which such devices as production quotas and price fixing are employed to protect inefficient, obsolescent or marginal enterprises from extinction. The several tendencies summarised above together indicate that perhaps no society is prepared to accept the full logic of rigorous price competition. The wind is tempered to the weak, overtly in one society and covertly in another. Yet preservation of any ideal requires a constant struggle against opposing forces. To indicate the above trends in our legislation and judicial decision may perhaps arrest their further course. The weak should be strengthened as well as protected. Access to the technologies of production, marketing and distribution, the ensuring of adequate credit, the making available of marketing consultant services, government sponsored research, are the avenues for the preservation of small business which the law should foster.

International Control of Restrictive Business Practices

When we entitled this chapter 'Control of the Power of the Economic Organisation,' we quietly dropped our customary use of 'power' as an equivalent of energy and instead used it to point to the problems of authority, dominance, market control and relationships, and the use and abuse of the rights of contract and property, which have flowed from the grant of legal personality to the private corporation. We have in this chapter been concerned with problems stemming from relations, rather than power, such as the relation of the economic organisation to the market, including other producers, as well as buyers, in the market.

The experiment of De Forest led to the invention of the audion, or three element radio tube. From this invention the radio industry developed and the eventual production of some fifty billion dollars' worth of radio and electronic products. The power of the radio industry, its gigantic flow of products, created no problem in law, but the relative size of the organisations producing those products and their use of the right to make contracts, to withhold access to their production except on their terms, and the types of relations which they established with one another and with the many markets which they served created many problems in law.

The Sherman Act imposed upon the courts of the United States the task of preserving a free competitive system in which no individual *entrepreneur* could be permitted to authorise others to make his market decisions for him and in which there was always to be rivalry among producers for the market. The Rule of Reason of the *Standard Oil Case* enabled a pragmatic approach to be taken by the courts in the solution of anti-trust controversy but only subject to the basic assumption that the ideal of free competition must be maintained. For it is to be remembered that the Statute interdicted *every* restraint of trade and *all* monopolising.

In the United States, the postulates of public control of business were: (1) Freedom of contract and right to property in the corporate organisation were not to prevail as the underlying assumption but rather the economic ideal of free competition, (2) the government, through the legislature, should use its authority to preserve that ideal as a social fact, (3) the day-to-day task of preserving free competition should be entrusted to the courts, even though in many aspects it might be considered a task more legislative than judicial in nature, (4) the courts should have relatively little latitude to permit departures from the competitive ideal in practice, and (5) the principle of *stare decisis* should prevail in judicial administration, even though in some cases a decision that a given practice was illegal *per se* might not *in that case* be in the public interest.

In other countries, however, different assumptions prevailed. In the United Kingdom the ideal of *laisser-faire* and the principle of freedom of contract took precedence. Industry functioned relatively free from governmental direction. Though the very words restraint of trade and monopoly are English, though contracts in restraint of trade were void at common law,[15] though

[15] *Mitchel* v. *Reynolds* (1711) 1 P.Wms. 181.

the Statute of Monopolies of 1624 prohibited the grant of legal monopoly franchises by the Crown,[16] the fundamental assumption in matters of business policy was that of *laisser-faire*. Contracts in general restraint of trade were enforceable if reasonable in the interests of the parties and the public, and not maliciously intended to harm competitors.[17] Restraints reasonable in the interests of the parties were, however, rarely, if ever, deemed injurious to the public.[18]

The principle of governmental non-intervention in matters of business judgment raised no public issue so long as British industry retained its technological excellence and was subject to the competition of the world itself under free trade. In the period between the two World Wars, governmental intervention in business became accepted but governmental policy was then directed towards rationalisation and stabilisation of destructive competition rather than to the attainment of the ideal of free competition.

Hence the Monopolies Act of 1948,[19] on the one hand, marked a turning point in public policy and, on the other hand, did not in its philosophy of control depart markedly from the existing underlying assumptions. Under the Act, restraints of trade and market dominance were to be subjects for investigation rather than condemnation. The investigation was to be by a commission rather than a court. The powers of the commission were limited, and parliamentary, rather than judicial, regulation was envisaged. Restrictive practices were not as such summarily condemned; their abolition depended upon the public interest in the circumstances.

The Act created a Monopolies and Restrictive Practices Commission, of from four to ten members, assisted by a staff of workers, functioning under the general supervision of the Board of Trade. The Commission investigates only matters referred to

[16] 21 Jac. 1, 1624, c. 3.

[17] *Nordenfeldt* v. *Maxim Nordenfeldt Guns and Ammunition Co.* [1894] A.C. 535; *Mogul Steamship Co.* v. *MacGregor, Gow and Co.* (1889) 23 Q.B.D. 598, *affd.* [1892] A.C. 25.

[18] See *Att.-Gen. of Australia* v. *Adelaide Steamship Co.* [1913] A.C. 781 at 795. As to the requirement of malice, see *Sorrell* v. *Smith* [1925] A.C. 700 at 712.

[19] 11 & 12 Geo. 6, 1948, c. 66. For an excellent analysis of this Act, contrasting it with the Sherman Act of the United States, see Note, 'The British Monopolies Act of 1948: A Contrast with American Policy and Practice,' 59 *Yale Law Journal* (1950), p. 899.

it by the Board of Trade. It may only report on the facts, unless the Board directs it to determine whether any of the conditions found to exist operate against the public interest. The hearing is not an adversary but rather an investigatory procedure; for example, there is no absolute right to cross-examination. There is no provision for judicial review.

In general, the conditions to which the Act is directed and against which the Commission may move are: (1) a business organisation or a group of inter-connected corporate organisations controlling one-third of the supply of a product, (2) agreements or arrangements between organisations controlling one-third of the supply of a product which prevent or restrict competition, or (3) agreements or arrangements which prevent the supply of a particular product. Only where the Board of Trade so directs may the Commission determine whether any specific practices operate against the public interest. The Commission's reports may be referred by the Board of Trade to each House of Parliament and must be so referred if the Commission were directed to make findings as to the public interest. There is a limited right for Ministers to issue orders subject to parliamentary control.

On the Continent, industrial firms tend largely to be organised into associations or federations, which to a considerable degree control production and marketing by their members. It is only in the post-war period that the problem of restrictive or cartel practices has become a public issue.[20]

The Treaty constituting the European Coal and Steel Community contains provisions designed to ensure a competitive market.[1] Article 65 of the Treaty prohibits agreements and concerted practices which prevent or restrict competition within the common market and which fix or influence prices, restrict or con-

[20] See Foreign Legislation Concerning Monopoly and Cartel Practices, Report of the Department of State to the Subcommittee on Monopoly of the Select Committee on Small Business, U.S. Senate, Subcommittee Print No. 5, 82d Cong., 2d Sess., 1952: United Nations, Economic and Social Council, Official Records, 16th Session, Restrictive Business Practices, Supplements Nos. 11A and 11B, U.N. Docs. E/2379 and E/2379/Add. 1, E/AC. 37/2 and E/AC. 37/2/Add. 1; E/2379/Add. 2, E/AC. 37/2/Add. 2; S. Timberg, 'Restrictive Business Practices,' 2 *American Journal of Comparative Law* (1953), p. 445.

[1] See particularly Arts. 3, 4, 5, 60 and 65 of the Treaty, printed U.N. Doc. E/2379/Add. 2, E/AC. 37/2/Add. 2, cited note 20, above; G. Bebr, 'The European Coal and Steel Community: A Political and Legal Innovation,' 63 *Yale Law Journal* (1953), pp. 1, 4–10.

trol production or allocate markets. Restrictive practices are permitted only when authorised by the High Authority as contributing to a substantial improvement in the production or marketing of the products in question. The approach of the Coal and Steel Community to the control of restrictive business practices seems more akin to that of the United States than that of the United Kingdom.

It was the purpose of Chapter 5 of the Havana Charter for an International Trade Organisation to establish principles and means for the control of harmful restrictive business practices.[2] Pursuant to resolution 375 (XIII) of September 13, 1951, of the Economic and Social Council, the principles of the Havana Charter have now been elaborated by the *Ad Hoc* Committee on Restrictive Business Practices into draft articles of agreement.[3] The Organisation or agency contemplated to be established by the proposed agreement is not necessarily the International Trade Organisation. The form which such Organisation or agency should take is expressly reserved by the *Ad Hoc* Committee pursuant to paragraph 6 of its constitutive resolution.[4]

The attempt of the Havana Charter to control restrictive business practices internationally was part of a comprehensive approach of the Charter to free international trade of governmental policies and other burdens which has choked and shaped its growth in the past. The proposed agreement of the *Ad Hoc* Committee was by way of contrast limited to the single problem of restrictive business practices. Neither adopted the principle of regional control of specific commodities upon which the European Coal and Steel Community is based. Both contemplated the establishment of agreed rules for the conduct of business organisations in the sphere of international trade and means for the application of such rules to the entire business community of the member nations or parties to the agreement.

The basic philosophy of the draft agreement may be summarised in the following propositions: (1) It is possible to adopt a broad approach to the solution of the problem of restrictive

[2] Final Act of the United Nations Conference on Trade and Employment, March 24, 1948. Dept. of State, Publication 3117, Commercial Policy Series 113.

[3] United Nations, Report of the *Ad Hoc* Committee on Restrictive Business Practices 12 (U.N. Doc. E/2380, E/AC. 37/3, 30 March, 1953).

[4] *ibid.*, pp. 3, 7 and 12.

business practices affecting international trade, even though only that segment of trade which is not conducted or regulated by governments is to be subjected to measures of control and even though no attempt is made to deal with governmental barriers to trade, as in the case of the International Trade Organisation; (2) the measures of control should be of the most flexible character, ranging from the making of technical studies to procedures essentially legislative and judicial in character; and (3) the Organisation should nevertheless be essentially powerless to make its decisions binding and effective, except in so far as the domestic law of any one member may permit, in order that each member shall retain for itself the freedom to determine what form and direction its economic life shall take.

The draft agreement in part very wisely adopts the approach of the International Labour Organisation of working with governments and of making studies and recommendations to members 'concerning such conventions, laws and procedures as are relevant to their obligations under this Agreement' and arranging for 'conferences of Members to discuss any matters relating to restrictive business practices affecting international trade.'[5] It is believed that the essential nature of the present problem is such that it can best be handled through the procedures of diplomatic negotiation and international legislation dealing with specific problems in respect of which a consensus or common agreement among the parties exists.

In going beyond this sphere of control, however, the draft agreement may be subject to criticism on the following grounds:

(1) The agreement created a system of obligations to prevent restrictive business practices which is binding upon member nations only to the extent each member permits them to be, thereby creating a system of obligations which has no real substance except as any one member may have so organised 'its constitution or system of law and economic organisation' as to result in a decision of the Organisation becoming an obligation binding it to performance. In other words, those nations which have developed a strong system of internal law controlling restrictive business practices, such as, notably, the United States, will have a direct duty to carry out their obligations under the agreement, while a nation which lacks such a system of law may plead

5 Art. 4, *ibid.*, at p. 14.

that very lack as an excuse for not carrying out the decisions of the Organisation. The system of obligations, therefore, rests with unequal force upon the subjects of the system. If it be answered that, even though the obligations created under the agreement may be moral rather than legal, they are better than nothing, the reply must be made that the procedures of negotiation and specific international legislation are preferable to a procedure in form that of adjudication, but which, in substance, lacks the requisites of the process of adjudication and which adds to the sources of dispute among nations while permitting each nation still to go its own way.

(2) In addition to creating the unequal system of obligations noted above, the agreement leaves untouched the sphere of governmental acts, statutes and regulations and the acts of intergovernmental organisations.[6] The consequence 'may be the sanctioning of a far-flung network of intergovernmental arrangements restricting the effectiveness of the market system.'[7] The future bargaining position of those nations devoted to the free-enterprise system and having effective internal systems for the control of restrictive business practices will be largely lost if they should adopt the agreement, for they will have then placed themselves under international control *vis-à-vis* their cartelistic neighbours but will not have corresponding rights and powers as against their neighbours. There will in such circumstances be little inducement for countries which have governmentally organised economies voluntarily to place themselves under an effective system of international control.

(3) Perhaps the basic difficulty in the agreement is that it does not appear to adopt a consistent philosophy of control, but rather is a mixture of British and American approaches. On the one hand, the agreement contemplates that members shall undertake certain obligations, that complaints of their breach may be filed, the facts thereof investigated, and decisions thereon made by the controlling body with which the members concerned are to comply. On the other hand, the nature of the procedure is more investigatory than it is adversary and the controlling body is more akin to a legislature than it is to a court.

The body by whom decisions are to be made is the Organisa-

[6] Art. 3, paragraph 4, *ibid.* at p. 13; see also *ibid.* at p. 4.
[7] M. A. Heilperin, *The Trade of Nations*, 1952 (2d Ed.), p. 202.

tion, composed of all the members, rather than a judicial tribunal. The Organisation is suitable for conference, discussion and legislative purposes but it is most unsuitable for acting as a judicial body. The representatives of the members, by whom decisions will be made, will tend to occupy political rather than judicial roles and probably will not possess a judicial background. A court must be separated from its constitutive legislature, staffed by persons who are qualified to act as judges and are limited in number, independent, impartial and subject to a developed body of law.[8]

The provisions of the draft agreement relating to the investigatory or quasi-judicial functioning of the Organisation reveal the difficulties of attempting to establish in international administration means of control analogous to those of the national State. The creation of a Permanent Court of International Justice and its successor, the International Court of Justice, was possible because a body of international law existed which could be applied by the Court, because a common technique of ascertaining and expounding that system of law had become a part of the training of a small group of advocates who practised before the Court; because the training of those advocates was entrusted to a responsible system of institutions—the great universities of the western world, which were in turn a product of centuries of growth; because the work of the Court was handled by still other institutions, such as the Registry; because the Court was governed by carefully devised and published rules of procedure; and because the eminence and training of its judges were, on the one hand, a guarantee to the States concerned of sound judgments responsibly arrived at and, on the other hand, a source of prestige and respect which brought about an acceptance of the Court's decisions by the peoples of such States.

In the instant case, it would not be enough merely to substitute a body having the outward characteristics of a court in place and stead of the Organisation for the purpose of making decisions. A court cannot exist without a body of law which has either developed through the life of a society or group or is

[8] Cf. the advisory opinion of the International Court of Justice sustaining the independence of the Administrative Tribunal of the United Nations as against its constitutive body, the General Assembly, *Effect of Awards of Compensation Made by the United Nations Administrative Tribunal, I.C.J. Reports 1954*, p. 47.

acceptable to the members of the society or group. A court cannot exist without all the accompanying institutions, traditions and standards which guarantee an effective social performance consonant with the values of the society or group. A court cannot dictate, it must declare the law.

We are concerned with the very life-blood of national societies —the economic organisations whose functioning determines the welfare of the people and creates the power of the State. The control of the conduct of such organisations through the anti-trust laws in the United States has been a product of over six decades of growth and experimentation. It is now rested in a corps of extraordinarily skilled lawyers, economists and judges. A most voluminous doctrine of texts, commentaries and judicial opinions has created a certain assurance that any tampering with the functioning of the free market-place will be with the scalpel and not with the sledge-hammer. The foundation principle of the 'Rule of Reason' is itself an assurance that rigid doctrine will not be used to the detriment of the public welfare.

The growth of an international system of judicial control of restrictive business practices will have to be a gradual growth, if it is to be effective and promote the common interest. It cannot be suddenly legislated into being. It will come into being when, step by step, all the institutions of a judicial system, including a body of living law, have grown into being. These institutions would include an advisory staff and a practising bar who would possess a common training comparable, in this field, to that of the international lawyer of today. Only through the development of a body of law and commonly accepted standards of training in that body of law and related fields of learning will it be possible to elevate those to whom the task of the international control of restrictive business practices is delegated above the basic assumptions and particular value systems of individual nations from which such persons are drawn.

The Economic and Social Council of the United Nations at its nineteenth session in 1955 considered the Report of the *Ad Hoc* Committee and the various comments relating thereto of governments and other public and private bodies. By its resolutions of May 26, 1955, the Council noted its continuing concern with the existence in international trade of restrictive business practices having harmful effects and urged governments to adopt laws with a view to counteracting such effects. Various steps were requested to be taken by the Secretary-General, but the draft agreement proposed by the *Ad Hoc* Committee was not approved.

In the meantime, the fact remains that there is a growing concern in a number of States over the problem of restrictive business practices in international trade, though a variety of points of view exists concerning the seriousness of the problem and the approach to be taken for its control. Pending the development of a greater consensus, the making of further studies by the Secretariat, as recommended by the Economic and Social Council in its resolution of May 26, 1955, seems desirable.[9]

[9] See generally M. Domke, 'The United Nations Draft Convention on Restrictive Business Practices,' 4 *International and Comparative Law Quarterly* (1955), p. 129; S. K. C. Kopper, 'The International Regulation of Cartels—Current Proposals,' 40 *Virginia Law Review* (1954), p. 1005.

Chapter 8

THE INDIVIDUAL WITHIN THE ORGANISATION

Organisational Order

In this work the organisation has been defined as a system of relationships. Order and system must exist within the organisation if it is to function successfully. Norms for conduct must be established and stabilised. Means must be established for controlling deviations from those norms.

The process of ordering the system of relationships comprised within an economic organisation is termed management; in a governmental organisation it is termed public administration. Behaviour of an increasingly concrete, fixed and repetitive character emerges as one moves from the area of management to the area of labour. Norms for behaviour in the performance of the various roles as they appear within the organisation must be accepted by those who perform such roles. The acceptance of the norm may be motivated by command, force and discipline, when the organisation is said to be authoritarian in character, or it may be motivated by attitudes of loyalty, self-interest and understanding. When established procedures involving participation in decision making exist towards accommodating the content of the norms of the organisation to the demands and expectations of those who are to be subject to such norms, the organisation is described as democratic in character. The resultant norms become *accepted* as well as *enforced* rules for conduct. In a democratically organised organisation, management, instead of being solely charged with the decision-making process, shares its function with those who will be affected by such decisions to the end that acceptance of command will be whole-hearted rather than constrained by force. Such a sharing of the decision-making function requires the establishment of channels of communication between the groups in question, both in the formulation of norms and in their enforcement.

As we move to the role of the worker, *i.e.*, those members of the organisation whose norms for conduct are highly concrete and specific, we find that such norms apply to many instead of few. To create and sanction these norms as law through contract becomes impossible as a matter of individual, person-by-person negotiation. There cannot be a multitude of disparate employee contracts, each having a different normative content, when workers all perform essentially similar functions, occupy similar relationships, and hence are all subject to essentially similar norms.

Representation of employees accordingly becomes necessary if channels of communication between management and labour in the formulation and enforcement of norms are to be established. The union of workers, a separate, autonomous organisation functioning partly within and partly without the economic organisation, accordingly emerges. The first channel of communication between management and union is in the negotiation of the collective bargaining agreement. Within its scope the management shares its decision-making function with others and ceases to have exclusive control of that function. The management must bargain collectively, *i.e.*, bargain with the designated majority representative of labour.[1] The worker as well as the management becomes bound by the norms of the resulting collective bargaining agreement. The workers thus bound include not only those who have voted with the majority and have thus given their consent to representation, but also those in the minority who have not so consented.[2] Hence the extraordinary situation in law of the creation through contract of third party *obligations*. For if the logic of the contract analogy were rigorously followed, no universal system of law for the organisation binding on all its members could be created. The circumstance that they may be in a minority, so far as union representation is concerned, is wholly irrelevant in considering their position in the functioning of the economic organisation. Union and non-union workers alike are common members of the organisation and must all be equally subject to its internal system of law.

The ends of the union, however, are not necessarily identical with those of the organisation within which it functions. The union is subject to different pressures. Its significance to its members and hence its existence as an organisation is dependent

[1] 29 U.S.C.A. Sec. 158 (a) (5) (Supp. 1955).
[2] 29 U.S.C.A. Sec. 159 (a) (Supp. 1955).

upon its continued success in producing more and more rewards from the economic organisations in which it represents, *i.e.*, acts for, its members. Attitudes of hostility and division are often fostered as a means to that end. Hence contract, in the form of the collective bargaining agreement, while serving the function of co-ordinating activity, at the same time often remains an uneasy and temporary treaty of peace between conflicting groups having different ends.[3] In any event, however, while it endures the normative content of the collective bargaining agreement becomes the internal administrative law of the economic organisation, dealing with such basic interests as who shall work, wages, shop rules and discipline, disability and pension.

To view the resultant norms as contractual and, therefore, rigid, fixed and with their breach subject to the penalty of damages,[4] is to lose sight of the fact that these norms are the living law of the organisation and must be flexibly administered in a constantly changing social milieu so as to achieve the ends of the organisation itself. So long as the collective bargaining agreement is viewed as a compromise between hostile, divided groups, termed management and labour, instead of a democratically formulated statement of the way in which the work-life of the organisation shall be ordered, so that the organisation shall make its highest contribution to the public interest and welfare, just so long will frustration instead of harmony characterise industrial relationships. For management and labour are not disparate groups, but members of a common organisation performing different functions toward the attainment of a common end.

Legislative and Judicial Aspects of the Administrative Law of the Economic Organisation

We have characterised the process of the negotiation of the collective bargaining agreement as the first important channel of

[3] A most penetrating analysis of the problem of contract with which we are here concerned will be found in W. C. Chamberlain, 'Collective Bargaining and the Concept of Contract,' 48 *Columbia Law Review* (1948), p. 829. For an illuminating discussion of the problems raised by relationships between a union and its members, see C. W. Summers, 'Union Powers and Workers' Rights,' 49 *Michigan Law Review* (1951), p. 805, also 'The Right to Join a Union,' 47 *Columbia Law Review* (1947), p. 33.

[4] 61 Stat. L. 156 (1947), 29 U.S.C.A. Sec. 185 (Supp. 1955).

communication between management and labour. Here groups having both common and separate interests confer and compromise, and adjust their claims and demands, to the end of reaching common agreement. If the consequences of that agreement were binding only upon the participants in the process, we would have the familiar category of contract. But we have seen that they extend beyond the participants to all workers similarly situated, and that non-union as well as union members become subject to the law of the agreement. Management and union representatives thereby become, in the negotiation of the collective bargaining agreement, the legislature for the enactment of the administrative law of the organisation.[5]

Following the formulation of the general norms contained in the agreement, the process of their concretisation begin. The content of the norms must be particularised as concrete instances of friction and grievance arise. Unfortunately, not all friction and grievance arising in the life of the shop can be brought within the compass of the current collective bargaining agreement. Hence, the legislative process must again be brought to bear in the negotiation of an amendment or even a new agreement. To the extent, however, that problems in the administration of the norms of the current collective bargaining agreement are presented, a need for additional channels of communication between management and labour arises. Grievances and disputes must also be resolved democratically. The grievance procedure accordingly becomes a means of effectuating communication between management and labour directed to the end of settling disputes through mutual adjustment. Significantly, the law here creates third party rights for non-union members, for the logic of contract must not be carried to the point of denying them recourse to the grievance procedure of the union's collective bargaining agreement.[6] If they are to be subject to the system of law

[5] 'Congress has seen fit to clothe the bargaining representation with powers comparable to those possessed by a legislative body both to create and restrict the rights of those whom it represents,' *Steele* v. *Louisville & Nashville R. Co.*, 323 U.S. 192, 202 (1944).

[6] 29 U.S.C.A. Sec. 159 (a) (Supp. 1951); *Hughes Tool Co.* v. *N.L.R.B.*, 56 N.L.R.B. 981 (1944), order modified and enforced, 147 F. 2d 69 (5th Cir. 1945). The Board of Inquiry established by the State of New York to make recommendations for peace on New York City's waterfront made the recommendation that individual union members be granted access to their own initiative to a permanent arbitrator. *Business Week*, February 2, 1952, p. 30.

created by the agreement, they must be accorded equal access to the means of recourse available under the contract. They cannot be denied the right to be heard on the ground of their non-membership in another organisation, the union, when union and non-union members are all equally members of the economic organisation and subjects of its system of law.

The grievance procedure alone cannot effectually resolve all disputes. There will always be cleavages which mutual, voluntary adjustment alone cannot bridge. The need is for a process of adjudication of disputes which will be keyed to the organisation, and arbitration, rather than the courts, satisfies that need. No rules of evidence hamper the scope of its investigation. Those rules, as an instrument of jury control, would be inappropriate here. No stranger to the realities of the particular organisational order acts as investigator and judge. The arbitrator is an appointee of the parties and is chosen for his skill and expertness in the field of inquiry. The facts with which the labour arbitrator must deal are facts concerning organisational life, and the ends which he must seek to serve are organisational ends. To the degree that he is skilled in the perception of such facts and appreciates the relevance of the particular relations with which he is confronted to the attainment of organisational ends, to that degree will his award be respected and accepted. For he is dealing with no temporally and spatially isolated incident viewed as a 'case,' but he is dealing with continuing relationships within the institution which are constantly changing, which the environment of the organisation is constantly affecting and which, in turn, in their performance, react upon the organisation. This explains why the place of precedent in labour arbitration is not the same as in the common law, which seeks a rule not only for the litigant parties but for all the citizenry.[7] This is not to say that there may not be a similarity in arbitral decisions dealing with common problems in organisational life. Absenteeism, altercations, dishonesty, drunkenness, incompetency, loafing and similar activities injurious to the organisational order cannot be countenanced in any organisation and usually only raise issues as to the appro-

[7] W. H. McPherson, 'Should Labour Arbitrators Play Follow-the-Leader?' 4 *Arbitration Journal* (N.S.) (1949), p. 163; K. S. Carlston, 'Arbitration: An Institutional Procedure,' *ibid.*, p. 248; Note, 'Case Law or Free Decision in Grievance Arbitration,' 62 *Harvard Law Review* (1948), p. 118.

priateness of the particular disciplinary measures applied.[8] However, even such decisions should not necessarily assume the status of binding or even persuasive precedent in another arbitration involving similar issues but arising in a different organisational context.

Thus institutionalised behaviour again creates a body of law. For law is the final instrument of social control, through it order and direction are given to social action. Authority must be exerted in regularised patterns, if order within the organisation is to prevail. Each member of the organisation, including those who possess as well as those who are under authority, must become subject to a fixed body of rules regulating the performance of his role within the organisation. In each organisation, as a consequence, rules emerge governing the administration of authority within the life of the organisation. Since such rules are rules of less than universal application, arbitration tribunals become the only bodies which can discharge the judicial function in such a system of law. Thus, labour arbitration is the judicial organ of the system of administrative law of the economic organisation.

We shall now proceed to an examination of certain systems of work life with a view to showing that there has emerged, in each such system, rules governing the administration of authority within the life of the organisation and that, coloured by its particular background, legal and otherwise, arbitration or some other form of judicial body has tended to emerge.

Civil Service in the United States

In the several jurisdictions within the United States there is no universally accepted set of principles stating either the rights of the civil servant or the means whereby such rights should be established or guaranteed. There is, of course, a consensus that government holds a unique position among employers as a result of the importance of the interests it represents. The classical premise has accordingly been that the government must in every instance exercise its sovereignty by a unilateral determination of the rights and obligations affecting its employees. In recent years, however, a number of exceptions have been attached to this premise.

[8] Note, 'Precedents in Labour Arbitrations,' *Washington University Law Quarterly* (1949), p. 71.

Thus, even under the influence of the authoritarian concept of government, the legislature, through civil service acts and regulations, established certain rights for the civil servant. In particular, the public employee was protected against some types of arbitrary acts on the part of his immediate administrative supervisor, and certain general provisions were instituted regarding conditions of employment, promotion, wages, and the like. Employees, through their lobbies, instigated much of this legislation and exercised a considerable control over it. Their success in so doing led some public service employees to view the classic legislative determination of the civil servant's position as entirely satisfactory.

The developments of the greatest theoretical and practical importance, however, reach beyond the system of statutory control of the public service and are related to the official recognition of unionism among public servants. Although courts and administrators do not everywhere look with equal equanimity upon union activities and aspirations in the public services, the federal government as early as 1912 permitted the organisation of its employees in labour unions. Public service union aims now range from a desire to avoid any issues, save those of security of tenure and economic advantages, to demands for a part in shaping general administrative personnel policy. Attitudes and responses of administrators similarly reflect such divergent views as the Navy Department's disfavour of even such mild union activity among its civilian employees as the joint presentation of grievances to the T.V.A.'s deliberate and initial intention of making the employee organisations a part of administration on a wide range of issues.[9]

It is widely agreed that there are certain limits to the privileges of the public servant. He cannot exercise the weapon of the strike except in certain rare and non-typical situations, and he is usually denied the extent of control over job-opportunities which the closed shop allows the employee in private industry. It is still often maintained that he cannot, through contract or otherwise, limit the sphere of administrative discretion. There is, however, evidence of a gradual revision of this latter assumption as it is increasingly realised that some form of collective bargain-

[9] M. R. Godine, *The Labour Problem in the Public Service, A Study in Political Pluralism*, 1951, Chaps. 3, 4, 6, 9 and 10.

ing is almost inevitable wherever labour has the right to organise; that the bargaining process can be so organised as not to compromise the required ultimate control by the government, and that the requisite 'sovereignty' can permit the government to pledge itself to observe certain types of agreement for limited periods of time and under normal circumstances.[10]

Apart from such activities as would or might qualify the necessary freedom of the public body, there is an increasingly vast area within which public servants, organised and unorganised, are playing an active role in determining the conditions and policies which affect them. As yet, public service unions have but rarely been granted the exclusive right to represent the labour force concerned. This has not, however, prevented the establishment of a great number of collective bargaining agreements. Many administrators frankly admit that the public service is noticeably improved by the existence of bilateral negotiation and joint consultation in many personnel policy matters such as disposition of grievances, process of discipline, determination of status and fixing of wages.

Civil Service in France

In France, the concept of authoritarianism was, by the early twentieth century, carried to the point of such extreme absolutism, with accompanying disregard of the welfare of the civil servant, that by way of reaction there developed an agitation for a radical syndicalism. The latter's concept of the fundamental autonomy of each public service would have left little place for the government as an ultimate unifying organ. To ameliorate the absolutism of the government, and to offset somewhat the danger of the threatening syndicalism of the civil servants, a system of statutes guaranteeing certain rights to functionaries was instituted in the early twentieth century. Such a compromise solution, however, satisfied neither the need for flexibility in administration nor the demands of democracy. It is understandable that in practice, therefore, the syndicates of functionaries continued to exist and to exert pressure. Although consistently decried by public officials, condemned by theorists, and declared illegal by the courts, the syndicates had achieved wide unofficial recognition by French administrators by the time of the outbreak of the

[10] *ibid.*, pp. 86–91, also Chap. 10.

Second World War.[11] Suppressed by the Vichy Government, the syndicates emerged full-blown after the liberation and were recognised by the law of October 19, 1946.[12]

By that law, the French functionary is declared to be in a situation determined by statute and regulation. Rarely, and perhaps never, does he have a typically contractual relation to the government.[13] But the law provides that functionaries participate through the intermediary of their syndicates in the reform of both the organisation and the methods of the public service. Three bodies establish channels of communication between the syndicates, as representatives of the functionaries, and the policy-making and administrative organs of government. Joint administrative commissions are permitted expression of opinion on each individual decision touching the career of a functionary. Joint technical committees discuss not only questions of method, but also general questions of the statute of functionaries and the organisation of the public service. Finally, a joint superior council of the public function acts as a supreme jurisdiction for administrative commissions and technical committees and as an advisory organ to the minister in charge of the public function. Through this council syndicates are guaranteed the opportunity to discuss, on a basis of equality with the administration, all problems vital to the service.[14]

It is not surprising that this revolutionary reorganisation of governmental policy, has, like the Preamble of the Constitution of 1946, been found in practice to be more an ideal than an actuality. A competent French observer has pointed out that the significant services of the syndicates remain, in part, what they were before the syndicates attained legal recognition, namely, the solution through personal contact with immediate supervisors of daily problems in applying generally accepted administrative rules. This does not usually involve the ponderous machinery of commissions, committees and councils. For the rest, and when it comes to matters of policy-making, administrators are still

[11] F. Gazier, 'Le syndicalisme dans la fonction public,' 11 *Droit Social* (1948), p. 274.

[12] D. and A. Dalloz, *Recueil Dalloz de Doctrine de Jurisprudence et de Législation,* 1946.

[13] M. Waline, *Traité Élémentaire de Droit Administratif,* 1950, pp. 304–308.

[14] F. Gazier, *loc. cit.*; J. Trouvé, 'The French Civil Service Office,' 11 *Public Administration Review* (1951), p. 180.

reluctant to admit that any but themselves have responsibility for this important task. The syndicates, in such a situation, rely upon their extra-legal but *de facto* authority of force evidenced in the strike.[15]

The task of the French civil service is to move from the establishment of channels of communication essentially of a consultative character limited to issues for the most part of a grievance nature, to the more maturely developed systems such as that of the United States in which negotiation, the public law contract and arbitration become the indicia of a system of administrative law of the public service organisation.

International Civil Service

International administrative law is principally a product of the years beginning with the founding of the Secretariat of the League of Nations, though of course a number of international institutions was already by then in existence. The initial assumption in the evolution of international administrative law was that public administration is hierarchical in structure. In the case of the League, moreover, the powers of the Secretary-General in matters of personnel policy were not formally defined or limited but were left to his administrative discretion. Such a condition, long since challenged and radically qualified in national administration, was understandable in the first few months of the League's history. The degree of legal independence the League would come to have, the tasks that would be given it and the organisation that would best suit its needs were not yet adequately envisaged. It was difficult to specify in detail the personnel policies it should adopt, and impossible to declare fully the legal status that would be conceded the international functionary. Nor did it seem especially important to proceed at once to a clarification of these matters. It was at the beginning considered neither likely nor desirable that any one should make a career of international public service and thus be vitally and personally affected by the absence of clarity regarding his rights.[16] The subsequent development of administrative law in the Secretariats of the League of Nations and of the United Nations has brought about a reversal of these views.

15 F. Gazier, *loc. cit.*, p. 277.

16 E. F. Ranshofen-Wertheimer, *The International Secretariat*, 1945, p. 300 *et seq.* (Washington, D.C., 1945).

Experience early made it clear that sound functioning of international public service requires, even more than does national public service, a delimitation of administrative prerogative in matters of personnel policy, and the establishment of conditions of employment, for at least a considerable number of employees, such as permanence of tenure, specified opportunities for promotion and a pension system. The League's Assembly did not establish the Provisional Statutes for the Staff of the International Secretariat until June, 1921, and the first definitive edition of the permanent Staff Regulations did not appear until January, 1932.[17] Utilising the experience of the League, the United Nations General Assembly was able to adopt a set of Provisional Staff Regulations during the first part of its first session when it also submitted for the consideration of the Secretary-General draft provisional staff rules.[18] Permanent Staff Regulations were adopted in final form on February 2, 1952, at the General Assembly's sixth session.[19]

Whether the international functionary has his legal status as functionary by virtue of a contract, in any usually accepted sense of the term contract, whether the contract if it exists is to be interpreted according to public or private law, whether the administrators can modify it unilaterally and whether such a contract gives rise to acquired rights are questions which have been much debated for the past quarter of a century.[20] Preponderant opinion seems to be that the letter of appointment constitutes a contract interpretable through public law, and principally in terms of the staff regulations and staff rules which are designated as forming part of the contract.[1] The United Nations Administrative Tribunal has said that a distinction should be made between the contractual elements and the statutory

[17] *ibid.*, p. 256.

[18] Resolutions adopted by the General Assembly, January 10 to February 14, 1946 (A/64) 15, IV, 10. For text of Provisional Staff Regulations, cf. *ibid.*, pp. 18–19.

[19] Resolution 590 (VI), February 2, 1952. General Assembly, Official Records: Sixth Session, Supp. No. 20 (A/2119). The Staff Regulations, as amended, in force as from January 1, 1955, were published January 5, 1955, embodying the amendments subsequently made by the General Assembly.

[20] S. Basdevant, *Les Fonctionnaires Internationaux*, 1931, pp. 63–107; E. F. Ranshofen-Wertheimer, *op. cit.*, pp. 257–259.

[1] Cf. H. Kelsen, *The Law of the United Nations*, 1951, p. 318; Lebeau, *Note on the Relations between the Staff and the Administration in the United Nations Secretariat* (U.N. Doc. 50/20342).

elements in the legal position of staff members. Those matters which affected his personal status, such as the nature of his contract and his salary grade, were deemed to be contractual, while matters affecting in general the organisation of the international civil service and the need for its proper functioning, such as general rules which have no limitation to particular persons, were deemed to be statutory. The Tribunal considered that the contractual elements could not be changed without the consent of both parties, while the statutory elements could be changed at any time though regulations established by the General Assembly.[2] Although the regulations specifically include the provision that they are subject to amendment, they state also that supplements and amendments shall not prejudice the acquired rights of staff members.[3]

The League of Nations found that the establishment of the Staff Regulations and Rules was only the first step in the creation of a system of administrative law. A judicial tribunal for enforcing the rights of employees under the rules thus established was needed. The Assembly of the League accordingly established an Administrative Tribunal to decide disputes involving breaches of the Staff Regulations and letters of appointment.[4] A similar tribunal was established by the United Nations with effect from January 1, 1950, under a statute adopted by the General Assembly November 24, 1949.[5] With respect to the need for such a tribunal, the International Court of Justicc pointed out that it would 'hardly be consistent with the expressed aim of the Charter to promote freedom and justice for individuals and with the constant preoccupation of the United Nations Organisation to promote this aim that it should afford no judicial or arbitral remedy to its own staff for the settlement of any disputes which may arise between it and them.' The Court said that it was 'inevitable that there would be disputes between the Organisation and staff members as to their rights and duties'

[2] *e.g.*, Administrative Tribunal, Judgments Nos. 19–25, 27, 53.

[3] *e.g.*, Art. XII, 12.1, Permanent Staff Regulations of the United Nations, p. 17.

[4] League of Nations Official Journal (Spec. Supp. No. 53), pp. 27–29 (1927). Resolutions and Recommendations adopted by the Assembly during its Eighth Ordinary Session.

[5] Fourth Session, Verbatim Record of the 255th Plenary Meeting (U.N. Doc. A/PV 255 24 Nov. 1949) 16–40. For text of statute, see Report of the Fifth Committee (U.N. Doc. No. A/1127 22 Nov. 1949).

under the Staff Regulations and Staff Rules.[6] The Court decided that the decisions of the Administrative Tribunal under consideration were final and binding on the General Assembly and not subject to review by it.[7]

The immunity of the international administration from suit in any national court whatsoever, and the absence of any international court designed to hear such issues as complaints of international functionaries against their administrative superiors, necessitated the institution of these tribunals separated from the active administration but fitted to hear cases related to it. They have demonstrated their utility and impartiality even in such difficult matters as the interpretation of the administration's right to modify the bearing of the Staff Regulations upon a given employee through express reservation in the contract of employment.[8]

Channels of communication between the staff and the Secretary-General, intended to give the staff a voice in matters such as personnel policies, disciplinary action and termination, were established in the League of Nations through the Staff Committee, Judicial Committee and Administrative Committee, but these proved of little practical importance.[9]

The Staff Organisation of the United Nations is, however, a most vigorous body, and its Staff Council zealously contends for an ever-increasing effectiveness of staff opinion in the several spheres where, under the Staff Regulations, they have a right to be heard. Article X of the Regulations permits the Secretary-General to establish administrative machinery with staff participation to advise him in disciplinary cases. Article XI provides specifically that the staff shall participate on the board that advises the Secretary-General with regard to appeals against disciplinary action or against administrative decisions alleged to violate staff rules or regulations or the terms of employment of any staff members. Finally, Article VIII permits the Staff Council to make proposals to the Secretary-General for improvements in working or living conditions of the staff and specifically provides

[6] *Effect of Awards of Compensation Made by the United Nations Administrative Tribunal*, Advisory Opinion of July 13th, 1954: *I.C.J. Reports 1954*, p. 47 at p. 57.
[7] *ibid.*
[8] S. Basdevant, *op. cit.*, p. 92.
[9] E. F. Ranshofen-Wertheimer, *op. cit.*, pp. 262–264.

for a channel through which the staff may make suggestions regarding personnel policy and amendments to the Staff Regulations or Rules. A Joint Advisory Board has accordingly been established 'to ensure that the Secretary-General receives regular advice regarding personnel policies and general questions of staff welfare.'[10] Problems of integrity, conduct and suitability of staff members, and in particular the problem of subversive activities of staff members, has occasioned a number of reports by the Secretary-General to the General Assembly, advice by a commission of jurists to the Secretary-General, revisions in the Staff Regulations, termination of services of certain staff members, as well as the advisory opinion of the International Court of Justice of July 13, 1954, referred to above.[11]

French Labour Law

The system of labour law found in the United States could perhaps be characterised as being, as yet, relatively free from governmental direction and intervention, although relying on governmental authority for much of its strength and vitality, but as consistently moving towards a system of administrative law as the hitherto governing contract analogy breaks down in practice. As a consequence of this trend from contract to general law, the autonomy of the legal system thus created is tending to diminish. In France, however, we find a system which is strongly authoritarian in character, with reliance on legislation rather than contract as the means of control, but in which the trend is toward increased organisational autonomy and resort to contract.

Several object lessons concerning the law of work-life are to be learned by observing some of the problems in French labour law and the various responses that have been made to them. That

10 United Nations, General Assembly, Official Records: Seventh Session. Annexes. Vol. II. From 14 October 1952 to 28 August 1953. Agenda item 75, p. 7.

11 Reports of the Secretary-General on Personnel Policy, U.N. Doc. A/2533, 2 November 1953, General Assembly: Eighth Session. Agenda item 51; Opinion of Commission of Jurists, 29 November 1952, U.N. Doc. A/INF/51 5 December 1952; S. M. Schwebel, 'The International Character of the Secretariat of the United Nations,' 30 *British Yearbook of International Law* (1953), p. 71; Note, 'National Ideologies and the International Public Function,' 81 *Journal du Droit International* (1954), p. 277; M. Cohen, 'The United Nations Secretariat—Some Constitutional and Administrative Developments,' 49 *American Journal of International Law* (1955), p. 295 (footnote 1, p. 295, thereof contains a bibliography).

law is now exceptionally expansive in its scope, extending to all 'subordinated work,' *i.e.*, to all work done by one person but legally under the direction of another.[12] We are here concerned, however, not so much with the extent of the law as with its import and nature.

With respect to the source of the law, a study of French experience in the labour field reveals that a given network of related organisations may simply lack the capacity for autonomy in establishing its fundamental organisational and functional principles. France has had great difficulty in establishing a labour law which would be at the same time genuinely indigenous to the organisations to which it would apply, sufficiently democratic, and workable in the larger legal framework into which it must fit. Three obvious obstacles have always been present to a greater or lesser extent. The Catholic labour unions, which, following the precepts of the Encyclical *Rerum Novarum,* usually tended to collaborate with employers wherever possible, were hardly representative of the typical union spirit.[13] Prior to the First World War French syndicalism was predominantly revolutionary in character, regarding as treasonable to the union movement any attempt to obligate itself through even the most reasonable collective bargaining agreements.[14] The nationalistic spirit engendered by the war eliminated this extremism on the part of labour, but the counterpart of it, the employers' stubborn resistance to all measures curbing their traditional control over conditions of work, is still a salient characteristic of the French scene. In spite of necessary qualifications of their control, especially those established during the difficult and frightening period of strikes in the mid-thirties, there has never been a predominating bona fide acceptance of the unions as a full partner in industry such as has fortunately characterised wide sectors of American industrial life. France has never developed the tradition of, and feel for, collective bargaining, conciliation and arbitration to the degree known in the United States.[15]

12 A. Rouast and P. Durand, *Précis de Législation Industrielle,* 1948, pp. 1–3.

13 V. R. Lorwin, 'France,' in W. Galenson (Ed.), *Comparative Labour Movements,* 1952, pp. 313, 338; see generally V. R. Lorwin, *The French Labour Movement,* 1954.

14 A. Sturmthal, 'Quelques réflexions sur les relations industrielles en France et aux États-Unis,' 14 *Droit Social* (1951), pp. 387, 388.

15 V. R. Lorwin, *loc. cit.*, p. 343; A. Sturmthal, 'Collective Bargaining in France,' 4 *Industrial and Labour Relations Review* (1951), pp. 236, 247.

Intransigence on the part of employers is coupled with a prevail-ink weakness in the labour movement as a whole deriving from an incredible apathy toward unionism on the part of many labourers, from a continual flux and shift in membership among those who are interested, and from eternal dissension within and among unions growing from philosophical and political issues which often have no bearing on the immediate strength of the movement.

The reactionary character of employer federations and the disunity within the labour ranks give ample play to another factor which has always tended to prevent optimum autonomy within French industrial life, namely, the tendency which still survives for the government to view itself as the only valid source of law. Until management and labour can consistently legislate for themselves the government *must,* and in this case gladly will. It did not help for the Vichy Government, in its Charter of Labour, to proclaim its interest in the development of 'professional law,' that is, law which is the product of harmonised industrial units legislating for themselves, when all freedom of unions, employer federations and collective bargaining was in fact outlawed until the liberation.[16]

The result, in any case, is that law and administration do in fact establish most of the relations between employer and employee,[17] and the degree to which they have done so has increased rather than decreased since 1936,[18] which marked a high point of the interest in collective bargaining save perhaps for 1950. The law of February 11, 1950,[19] however, represents a genuine attempt to establish significant collective bargaining practices.[20] Under this law the approval by the government of collective bargaining agreements,[1] required during the period 1946–1950, was eliminated.

A collective bargaining agreement, though established by labour and management in one sector of an industry, soon becomes relevant to other sectors of the same industry. In France,

[16] *ibid.*, p. 241.

[17] Sturmthal, *loc. cit.*, note 14, above, pp. 387–388.

[18] C. Savouillan, 'Pour l'étude de l'arbitrage obligatoire,' 14 *Droit Social* (1951). pp. 96, 97.

[19] *Journal Officiel,* 12 Feb. 1950, with corrections 22 Feb. and 14 Mar. 1950.

[20] A. Sturmthal, *loc. cit.*, note 15, above, p. 236.

[1] *ibid.*, p. 243.

collective bargaining is typically national or regional in scope.[2] The contracting parties may themselves represent such regions, or an agreement local in scope may be extended by the Minister of Labour to larger areas.[3] A provision in the law of 1946, not incorporated in the 1950 law, even established a hierarchy of agreements, from the national through the regional and local down to the plant agreement, and specified that all collective bargaining agreements below the national level must be made within the framework of agreements previously established on a higher level.[4] While this has unquestioned advantages in a country where labour is not strong enough in all quarters to defend itself, it also has the disadvantage of requiring conformity even when local conditions do not indicate its desirability.

Sometimes the interest of the government is essentially that of encouraging collective bargaining processes over which it has little or no influence, but which are not likely to prosper without some governmental intervention. In 1936, for example, the Minister of Labour could extend an agreement once made if he chose so to do, but he was not empowered to change the agreement.[5] Typically, however, the government has certain positive interests which cause it to limit the area of collective bargaining and to enact certain laws applicable to industry. Thus in 1946 the government withdrew wage levels from the sphere of matters to be freely determined and did so in the interest of a directed economy.[6] This restriction was removed in 1950,[7] except that the government still retained the power of restraining collective bargaining processes from establishing what it considers to be a prohibitively high minimum wage. Another example of governmental interest in labour law is found in the nationalised industries. These have governing councils, including representatives of the working personnel, which are supposed to establish wages and working conditions through a procedure akin to collective bargaining. In fact, however, the government's interests are so great and its power so vast that it leaves little resembling a free bargaining process.[8] It may be added, however, that law is often made through genuine labour participation.[9]

[2] A. Sturmthal, *loc. cit.*, note 14, above, p. 389.
[3] A. Sturmthal, *loc. cit.*, note 15, above, p. 243.
[4] *ibid.*, p. 242.
[5] *ibid.*, p. 238.
[6] *ibid.*, p. 241.
[7] *ibid.*, p. 243.
[8] *ibid.*, p. 247–248.
[9] A. Rouast and P. Durand, *op. cit.*, pp. 40–41.

It is true that an organisation must be founded upon principles which permit its linking with other organisations and particularly with the government. It is equally true that the strength and viability of an organisation will be weakened if it bases its functioning upon principles that relate to factors which are well beyond its control or are of little interest to a substantial part of its membership. The most powerful French unions today are controlled by Communists to the extent that their programmes of action frequently turn upon developments in Franco-Soviet political relations.[10] In these cases the labour organisations are expending their energies toward the accomplishment of the purposes of bodies of a different nature from themselves and often beyond their control. It is possible for an organisation such as a Communist labour union to be in effect extroverted, caring more for its effect upon other bodies than for its own wellbeing, though this is certainly not the usual pattern. It may well be that labour unions, in seeking to establish law for work-life, should go to the bottom of more political and philosophical problems than they do in America. Nevertheless, it still seems pertinent to observe that many unions have, in the pursuit of such principles, neglected several factors upon which their very strength for continued existence may prove to depend, such as the immediate welfare of numbers of their members who are little, if any, interested in Communism as such.

Collective bargaining agreements are the single most important evidence of the power of industrial and commercial organisations to legislate for themselves. It is not easy to arrive at a clear conception of the legal nature and status of such agreements. French law and juristic thought have been responsible for five major interpretations since 1919,[11] some features of which may now be observed.

In 1919 the collective bargaining agreement was subjected to a purely contractual analysis. The courts, rather than the Minister of Labour, were the principal governmental organs concerned with them. This analysis was only possible so long as such agreements could be considered as having no binding power over third persons. Almost immediately the public law jurists realised that such an analysis fell far short of the facts. But not

10 A. Sturmthal, *loc. cit.*, note 15, above, p. 247.
11 A. Sturmthal, *loc. cit.*, note 15, above.

until 1936 did the law recognise that collective bargaining aims at and achieves varying degrees of regulation of an entire profession and thus has the marks not of contract or consensus but of public regulation. Several factors are to be noted in this connection.

In the first place, the French collective bargaining agreement is not itself a contract of labour, but an instrument for determining the conditions of future individual contracts.[12] Secondly, the approval of the Minister of Labour, which has sometimes been but is not now required, would seem to mark such approved agreements as being regulative in character. The same is true to an even greater extent for labour law effective in areas to which it was extended by ministerial decree. In fact, however, the agreements are regulative even without benefit of this type of governmental concurrence. Their subject matter is itself in part dictated by statute, thereby linking them initially with public purposes as legislated. Also, collective bargaining agreements are binding upon third parties in two senses. The agreement affects members of the signatory organisations as well as the organisations themselves, and, with regard to those affected, the agreement imposes itself as a regulation in public law rather than a contractual relation, all contrary stipulations in individual contract being impossible.[13]

It would be a mistake, however, to lose sight of the considerable contractual element in the portion of labour law established by collective bargaining. The bargaining is often initiated by the parties rather than by the government, it involves an agreement arrived at by negotiation, and it creates contractual obligations as well as certain types of public law obligations.

Collective bargaining in France involves such an organisation of the 'profession' as results in procedures for joint commissions, conciliation and arbitration. The character of the arbitration procedure is an interesting index to the degree of good faith in the original collective bargaining. Thus, in the period 1936–1939, which commenced so hopefully and ended so bleakly, the government found that it could not assume that industry through free negotiation would establish, resort to and abide by, arbitration. Arbitration was accordingly made obligatory. In most

[12] A. Rouast and P. Durand, *op. cit.*, p. 224.
[13] *ibid.*, pp. 227–228.

cases the industry failed to establish arbitral bodies composed of arbitrators appointed by labour and management. Resort was typically made to a 'super-arbitrator' appointed by the government, thereby placing the source of the law outside the organisation structure.[14]

Compulsory arbitration was again provided for in the government's 1949 draft of the present labour law. Both labour and management opposed this provision, apparently fearing that in effect it would reinstate many of the government controls of labour relations which it was the purpose of the new law to eliminate.[15] As a result, the present law makes conciliation but not arbitration compulsory. Arbitration by the government can scarcely avoid a political cast and one which may often be distasteful to both employer and employee. For the French there is the added difficulty that to many compulsory arbitration seemed to imply renunciation of the strike. Moreover, failure to accept the ensuing award would involve a breach of the original contract of labour.[16] The importance to labour of the right to strike is recognised in the Preamble of the Constitution of 1946 which consecrates the right to strike, except where prohibited by statute. Since the strike is the ultimate weapon of labour, the workers did not intend to see formulae for obligatory arbitration interpreted as limitations upon that right. Nor can they afford to allow rupture of the labour contract, for that would involve loss of a series of basic guarantees and indemnities necessary to them within that economy.

Indeed, the term 'compulsory arbitration' is a misnomer. The structural elements of a procedure consensual in origin and nature, discharging the judicial function in a system of administrative law for an organisation or series of like organisations, are here borrowed to serve the function of making law for the parties when the necessary democratic conditions incident to the process of negotiation are, for one reason or another, ineffective. Compulsory arbitration is lacking in those procedures on which the strength of the collective bargaining process depends, and instead involves a delegation by the government to a non-legislative body of the power of legislation. The social problem in 'compulsory

14 V. R. Lorwin, *loc. cit.*, pp. 343–344.

15 A. Sturmthal, *loc. cit.*, note 15, above, p. 244.

16 C. Savouillan, *loc. cit.*, p. 97. See also note by C. Blondel, 14 *Droit Social* (1951), p. 172.

arbitration' is not the resolution of disputes as to rights under determined and accepted rules for conduct, but is the formulation of the rules themselves. This is a task for negotiation or legislation and not adjudication. Compulsory arbitration involves an attempt to mask these social realities and to bring about an acceptance by the parties of a novel procedure essentially legislative in character by cloaking it with an inappropriate and misleading symbol.[17]

To summarise, French experience in labour law reveals that industrial organisations strive to establish autonomous systems of law, for law imposed from without is often oriented around concepts and toward aims which are inconsistent with the demands of industrial life; that the meshing of the demands of organisations which must function together but which have conflicting systems of values is often unsuccessful and hence productive of tension; that individuals who simultaneously have roles in such conflicting organisations cannot always successfully adjust themselves to the requirements of their conflicting roles, with consequent organisational disintegration, for in the ultimate analysis the life of an organisation is dependent upon its significance to its members and its ability to satisfy in adequate measure their felt needs; and that the task of law, here as well as elsewhere, is to direct organisational activity toward public ends without at the same time exerting such pressures that frustration supplants significance in organisational life.

Authoritarianism and Democracy in Organisational Order

Authority, in the sense of identifying those from whom command emanates and in whom the function of decision-making rests, is essential for organisational order. But authority is not to be

17 'Attention is immediately directed to the fact that no dispute has arisen between the parties to the contract over the terms and provisions of the contract, or any difficulty arising thereunder. . . . The railroad company desires to make a new contract. It desires to reduce wages ten per cent and seeks arbitration under the Arbitration Law for the purpose of arriving at new terms and agreements as to the rate of wages. No power exists in the courts to make contracts for people. They must make their own contracts. The courts reach their limit of power when they enforce contracts which parties have made,' *Matter of Buffalo & Erie Ry. Co.*, 250 N.Y. 275, 278, 165 N.E. 291, 292 (1949). 'A power to decide *ex aequo et bono* is a power to abrogate or modify existing legal rights, and essentially that is a power to *legislate*,' J. L. Brierly, *The Law of Nations*, 1949, p. 269.

conceived of separately and apart from the subjects of authority. Authority is a relational concept involving action between at least two persons. The constantly changing conditions faced by an organisation require that some of its members be vested with the role of determining whether its existing system of relations should be changed in any respect, and whether new responses to the changed environment are necessary. In addition to this process of re-evaluating and recreating the existing organisational order, it is also necessary to determine whether the performance of the existing system of relationships comprised in the organisation is meeting desired standards of efficiency. Those persons whose task it is to make such determinations and to translate such determinations into the life of the organisation exercise the leadership function but are also said to be possessed of authority. Such persons have sometimes been termed the directing personnel. They are the members of the organisation who formulate and initiate new relations and ensure that the existing system of relations is satisfactorily performed.

As we have seen, authority becomes manifest when a communication is made by the directing personnel of an organisation to other members requiring the performance by them of some function within the organisation in accordance with a certain standard of excellence. The validity of authority rests neither in those who exercise it, *i.e.*, make the communication, nor those who are its subjects, *i.e.*, receive and carry out the communicated decision. Since authority is purposeful in character, its validity is to be measured by the degree of its effectiveness in bringing about the performance in a satisfactory, economical manner of those functions which will best accomplish the ends of the organisation. In the organisational order, authority is a relational concept, always involving a relation between the directing personnel and the other members of the organisation to whom the direction or communication in question is given. The communication may be made with or without accompanying procedures for the participation of those to whom it is addressed, with a view to determining the content of the communication. If such procedures are lacking, the organisation is said to be authoritarian in nature. The communication by the directing personnel then assumes the form of command. An organisation of such a character will, however, find in the social struggle for survival that the strength of its system of norms lies not only in force and discipline but in the acceptance of such system by the governed. For the internal strength of the organisation depends in the last analysis upon the measure of its significance to its members. A democratic participation in the formulation of the norms of the organisation (collective bargaining) and their enforcement (arbitration) is necessary if the full potentialities of the acceptance of norms by those subject to them are to be realised.

The two opposing forces of authoritarianism and democracy are found at work in any organisation. In the flux of society there is a constant shifting in the strength of these forces within each organisation. There is no one perfect combination of them, for human motivations and judgment are not perfect and, moreover, the environment of each organisation varies, requiring the utilisation of these forces in varying proportions in order to ensure its strength, growth and survival. Organisations should not be judged solely by whether they are of an authoritarian or democratic cast for neither of these can be the subject of absolute value judgments. It so happens that in a political world which has been moving from authoritarianism to democracy we have come to assign a negative value judgment to the former and a positive value judgment to the latter. Yet, under the menace of threatening aggression in the international scene, and the haunting fear of economic depression in the domestic scene the current political tendency has been towards the centralisation of authority rather than its decentralisation. We must remember that the problem of authority is a never-ceasing one in society, and that a solution of that problem valid under one set of circumstances is not necessarily valid under another. The structure of social action must not become static but must remain fluid if the ends of society are to be served to the highest possible degree.

To summarise, the exercise of authority is but another term for the process of decision-making and command. Organisational order requires direction of energy, the co-ordination of a multitude of tasks ranging from policy making to the most automatic of operations. Adjustment to external and internal variances in anticipated behaviour constantly demands new decisions and commands. The resultant impact of decision and command upon the individual within the organisation, its effect upon the performance of his organisational role, the necessity that the norms imposed shall be related to his needs and limitations, as an individual, all call forth the demand for a democratic sharing in the process of ordering the general norms of the organisation and for an impartial, regularised, judicial interpretation and application of these norms to particular instances of friction, grievance and dispute. The demand for a democratic sharing in the process of decision-making expands to the area of management itself as the individual worker realises his identification with the fortunes of corporate enterprise.[18]

The Security of the Individual within the Organisation

Just as our society has seen the emergence of a new value in the security of the organisation from the vicissitudes of the marketplace, so there has also emerged the value of the security of the individual within the organisation. The organisational structure of modern society has had two consequences for the individual. On the one hand, his membership in a particular economic organisation became his shelter against economic want. While within it, and through his wage reward, he was assured access to the market as consumer and participation in all the other roles, recreational and otherwise, which loom so large in the life of a society in which success and the enjoyment of creature comforts are primary values of the individual. Cast loose from the organisation he was without moorings—a displaced person. On the other hand, the price for such security was his subjection to the power of the organisation itself. From both these sources flowed the demand for individual security within the organisation, security from sudden or arbitrary discharge, security from unregularised decision-making and security through pension against personal obsolescence. The union became the focal point for the securing of these elements of security, and the collective bargaining agreement the source of their establishment as rules of law for the organisation. However, '[c]ollective bargaining does not alter the amount of power which is exercised over the individual. It only shifts its source.'[19] Hence, a new variant

18 Cf. W. H. McPherson, 'Codetermination: Germany's Move Toward a New Economy,' 5 *Industrial and Labour Relations Review* (1951), p. 20.
19 C. W. Summers, *loc. cit.*, note 3, p. 246, above, p. 816.

in the never-ending problem of power and authority in modern society arose, and the control of the modern trade union in turn emerged as a new problem in law. When the union expands beyond the business organisation to an entire industry, then it achieves a position of power beyond the framework of a particular organisation and derived from the strategic position of the industry in society itself. Monopoly manifests itself in a new form in the mining of coal and the making of steel when the strategic position of these industries in the economy becomes a source of power to the union controlling their functioning.[20]

Let us briefly trace the strategical consequences of the political decision in the Wagner National Labour Relations Act to permit the growth of trade union organisations as a countervailing measure against the power of industrial management. It furnished a release for the highly explosive forces of worker-demands but it also led to the creation of vast labour union organisations controlling labour supply in strategic industries. Decisions by labour leaders to withhold such labour supply from the market created a social force which in effect utilised the power of monopoly. Thus, to the systems of social power of government and of management was added another system of social power, that of labour. But whereas management, a group relatively small in number and generally habituated to accept governmental decisions, did not resist governmental authority, labour tended to recognise no authority other than its own, for the authority of the leaders rested upon a volatile and clamouring rank-and-file. The authority of government was unable to control through the use of force the vast bodies of workers organised in unions. The consequence is that such techniques of control as compulsory arbitration cannot be relied on to produce industrial peace, while the end of the road is the total breakdown of governmental authority, such as manifested itself in France in the early fall of 1953.

Power once grasped is not readily and willingly relinquished. A solution which is, therefore, not likely of achievement, is the limitation of each trade union to the confines of each economic organisation. So limited, the members of the union would tend to identify themselves with the organisation and its fortunes as an

20 An interesting study in this connection is F. Tannenbaum, *A Philosophy of Labour*, 1951.

organic whole. The problem of conflicting group memberships might be somewhat lessened and the problem of social power would be solved by dissolving the aggregates of power in the national industrial union into smaller centres.

The problem of distributive justice in modern economic society is presented in one form in the United States, another in Great Britain and yet another in Soviet Russia. The first two are characterised by three structures of power, government, management and labour, for the nationalisation of industry in Great Britain was found by the worker not to change the authority-system of the factory nor to alter his economic position. The last is characterised by a single and pyramidal structure of power, the Party controlling the government and the mass organisations of industry and labour.

The philosophy of the western democratic State at this stage in its history is, therefore, one which accepts each of these three systems of power and attempts to utilise the power of government to co-ordinate, in one way or another, the power of labour and management. In their present form of organisation, labour and management are seen as conflicting structures of power, when in fact their social reality stems from the fact that they are each an essential element of the business enterprise.

Proposed solutions which accept the existing structures of power will never find a solution for their conflict, for the decision maker, the person in authority, in each structure of power is the captive of its system of values and resulting social equilibrium. The proposed solution of governmental seizure compels labour to continue to work and to bargain collectively without the sanction of the strike to reinforce its bargaining strength. Compulsory arbitration is a most primitive legislative technique for the compromise of the group differences involved and also relies on the authority of government to make its decisions effective—an authority which is not always accepted. Fact finding and mediation are in general only interstitially effective.

Our social system must, therefore, reintegrate itself in new structures of co-ordination if we are to find any lasting solution for the problem of industrial conflict. The sharing in decision making in the lower supervisory levels of the plant has proved to be an effective means for increasing morale and production. The co-determination movement in Germany may possibly point a way to the reintegration of our management-labour structure into patterns of co-ordination. The representation of labour on the boards of directors and management committees of concerns in the steel and mining industries seems there to have led to a greater identification by the worker with the concern, and a corresponding lessening of the tensions of conflicting group membership in the concern and the union.[1] The transplanting of a solution which grew up in one culture is not necessarily likely to take root in its new soil; co-determination in some situations in the United States might lead to the supplanting of competition by unified industry regulation through the industrial union leaders selected for management bodies. Nevertheless, for the national enterprise a sharing by labour in the responsibility for management decisions, together with a carefully adjusted system for sharing in profits, may eventually be a road to industrial peace. For the international industry, a system of authority similar to that of the Schuman Plan, but one in which labour and consumer interests are more effectively represented and possess more effective power, may be the eventual answer.

The full potentialities of the organisation as a structure of social action will not be realised, however, until the relationship between the requirements of the organisational role and the personality of its occupant is seen. Each individual is each day constantly faced with the problem of adjusting his behaviour to the requirements of the several roles which he occupies, and in overcoming resistances produced by his own personality structure in fitting himself to these roles. To the extent that his participation in any one role is voluntary, when that resistance becomes too great he ceases to participate. In the corporate organisation, however, the price of withdrawal is too high to permit of ready withdrawal. The acceptance of authority in directing the role to be occupied by the individual member of the organisation is habitual and reinforced by the penalties of search for employment elsewhere. Hence the individual may accept without protest a role for which his personality is not inherently suited. Until management has adopted procedures for relating the individual to his organisational role so as to utilise his personality effectively in the performance of his corporate role, it will not tap the full

[1] See W. H. McPherson, 'Co-determination in Practice,' 8 *Industrial and Labour Relations Review* (1955), p. 499.

energy which is available within the individual and hence will not bring into being the power which the organisation might otherwise produce. Here is to be found the next great area for the expansion of techniques of corporate management.

Perspective

As we come to the close of our study of some of the many aspects of authority and power in modern society, it may be well to ponder for a few moments, not the problems of political and economic freedom which have heretofore occupied us, but the problem of intellectual freedom. If any one thing has made it possible for billions of persons to live and, in many cases, to find comfort and leisure in a world of limited resources, it is the principle of free scientific inquiry. It is this principle which brought into being all the systems of co-operative effort, political as well as economic, which support modern man.

It was the spirit of free inquiry, of factual orientation and analysis, which enabled the Roman *praetor* and jurist to mould the system of Roman law to fit the changing and expanding world of the Roman empire. It was this spirit which lifted the English judge from the ruts of feudalism and enabled him to mould the common law to fit an emerging industrial civilisation. The heritage of Roman and common law, however, is insufficient to meet the problems of western civilisation in the mid-twentieth century. The devotion of enormous human effort in the field of the physical sciences under the principle of free scientific inquiry has brought the possession of vast physical energy to the western world. The power and energy of that civilisation rests upon organisational unity and national interdependency. Yet man only dimly realises the existence of this new world. The social scientist can only point out its larger configurations because those who have laboured in this field are few, as against the natural scientists, and their findings insufficient to point the way to the solution of the problems which the world faces. Emotion rather than the intellect and knowledge thrusts each national society down the course of the years and shapes the world we live in.

In the last analysis, the scientific knowledge which we today possess is a product not only of the principle of free scientific inquiry but of faith, faith in the symmetry, order and self-consistency of facts. The scientist and the artist have a kinship in the blazing incandescence of their creative inspiration. The new and daring hypothesis has its own beauty of symmetry and order. Disorder and inconsistency clamour to be reshaped to consistency with the system of verified postulates. There is a faith continually tested and continually justified that eventually explanation and resulting order will be reached.

It is this principle of free scientific inquiry and this sustaining faith which must carry the social scientist forward in his work and be assured him in his findings. The inspiration of his work must draw many more to the tasks to be done than have been called forth in the past. Society must be prepared to support a much larger proportion of productive effort in this field than it has in the past. In return for that support, the social scientist must be prepared to meet much higher demands than have previously been required of him.

Western civilisation is today confronted with the question whether the extraordinary maturity of its technological development and of its corporate life of production, trade and intercourse will survive, because of the laggard growth of the social sciences and the disruptive forces of the system of national States. The State, which should be a shelter for the cultural uniqueness and freedom of its people, has become in some instances a source of oppression for its people and always a dam against the flowing tides of trade and communication in the world. As the power at the disposal of the national State has increased, so has the threat of the destructive force of that power in war increased, until we are now faced with the question whether the solution of controversy through war will not be found in the peace of the grave for national populations.

The necessary correlative for freedom is always responsibility. Each individual in his particular social role or area of freedom, each group or organisation in its particular sphere of activity or area of freedom, each State in its particular sovereign sphere or area of freedom, is always subject to responsibility in the exercise of its freedom to the end that social purpose shall be served. That responsibility is imposed through leadership and authority and through law. The responsibility in turn of the leaders and of the law-makers, the responsibility of the followers of leaders and the subjects of law, who bring authority and law into social reality, is today indeed heavy. Inexorably, a failure of leadership to solve the problems of a society, and of law to integrate and control its behaviour will result in the dissolution of that society. Will the failure of western man to couple the concept of freedom with that of responsibility bring to an end the magnificent history of western civilisation?

Finally, the content of freedom lies in participation, participation of the individual in the basic institutions of the society. The western democratic State has gone far toward extending to each individual within it equality of access to, and opportunity for, participation in its political and legal institutions. It is still, however, in the process of working out in practice another principle, that of equality of opportunity for participation by all its members in its basic social institutions.

The relationships of the individual with others from which groups, organisations and society emerge thus give content and meaning to the concept of the freedom of the individual. Freedom becomes a positive rather than a negative concept. The individual is not isolated and independent from others, but finds in his relations with others the source of his happiness. Similarly, groups and organisations cannot exist in society in isolation but are inevitably dependent upon their external relationships as well as the satisfactions they afford their members for their continued existence. Yet we still adhere to the myth of the independence of States. No State exists in isolation or independence. Each State is a vast pattern of groups and organisations accepting a common authority of political and judicial institutions and existing only by virtue of the linkages of its groups and organisations with those of others within other States. Until we discard the myth of the independence of the State, and in its place accept the social fact of its interdependence; until we see that the meaning of the freedom of the State lies in the purposeful direction of its activities to develop its relations with others and thereby constantly to raise the plane of satisfactions of its subjects; until we are driven by the menace of atomic war finally to understand that the will of no nation can be made the supreme power of the world, for no nation which is sufficiently industrially advanced to wage an atomic war can survive such a war; just so long will the enormous productive potentialities of the western world be diverted to the waste and destruction of war instead of social progress and the satisfaction of the needs of man.

BIBLIOGRAPHY

Books and Official Publications

B. Adams, *The Theory of Social Revolutions,* 1913.
T. W. Adorno and others, *The Authoritarian Personality,* 1950.
C. H. Alexandrowicz, *International Economic Organisations,* 1952.
C. K. Allen, *Law in the Making,* 1946.
American Law Institute, *Restatement of the Law of Conflict of Laws,* 1934.
Annual Report of the American Bar Association, Vol. 69, 1944.
P. Arminjon, *Précis de Droit International Privé,* 1925.
T. W. Arnold, *The Folklore of Capitalism,* 1937.
—— *The Symbols of Government,* 1935.
C. I. Barnard, *The Functions of the Executive,* 1948.
E. Bartin, *Principes de Droit International Privé,* 1930.
S. Basdevant, *Les Fonctionnaires Internationaux,* 1931.
J. H. Beale, *A Treatise on the Conflict of Laws,* 1935.
J. W. Bennett and M. M. Tumin, *Social Life, Structure and Function,* 1948.
A. F. Bentley, *The Process of Government,* 1908.
A. A. Berle, *The Twentieth Century Capitalist Revolution,* 1954.
A. A. Berle and G. C. Means, *The Modern Corporation and Private Property,* 1932.
H. J. Berman, *Justice in Russia,* 1950.
B. Bosanquet, *The Philosophical Theory of the State,* 1910.
K. E. Boulding, *The Organisational Revolution,* 1953.
M. Bourquin, *Dynamism and the Machinery of International Institutions,* (Geneva Studies, Geneva Research Centre, Vol. 11, No. 5), 1940.
R. A. Brady, *Business as a System of Power,* 1943.
H. G. Brainard, *International Economics and Public Policy,* 1954.
J. L. Brierly, *The Law of Nations,* 1955.
—— *The Outlook for International Law,* 1944.
J. F. Brown, *Psychology and the Social Order,* 1936.
W. A. Brown, *The United States and the Restoration of International Trade,* 1950.
W. W. Buckland, *A Text Book of Roman Law from Augustus to Justinian,* 1932.
A. S. de Bustamente y Sirven, *Derecho Internacional Privado,* 1931.
H. Cairns, *Law and the Social Sciences,* 1935.
Carnegie Endowment for International Peace, *Co-ordination of Economic and Social Activities,* United Nations Studies 2.
A. T. Carter, *A History of English Legal Institutions,* 1910.
D. Cartwright and A. Zander, *Group Dynamics: Research and Theory,* 1953.
E. Cassirer, *The Myth of the State,* 1946.
G. C. Cheshire, *Private International Law,* 1952.
K. von Clausewitz, *On War,* Modern Library Ed., 1943.
Commerce Clearing House, *Antitrust Law Symposium,* 1951, 1953.
—— *Trade Regulation Reporter,* 1952.
Commission on Foreign Economic Policy, *Report to the President and Congress,* January 23, 1954.
Commodity Research Bureau, Inc., *Commodity Year Book 1953,* 1953.
J. R. Commons, *The Legal Foundations of Modern Capitalism,* 1924.
Contracting Parties to the General Agreement on Tariffs and Trade, *International Trade,* 1954.
W. W. Cook, *The Logical and Legal Bases of the Conflict of Laws,* 1942.

P. E. CORBETT, *Law and Society in the Relations of States,* 1951.
—— *The Individual and World Society,* 1952.
W. COUTU, *Emergent Human Nature: A Symbolic Field Interpretation,* 1949.
F. R. COWELL, *Cicero and the Roman Republic,* 1948.
D. AND A. DALLOZ, *Recueil Dalloz de Doctrine de Jurisprudence et de Législation, Législation,* 1946.
R. DENNETT AND J. E. JOHNSON, *Negotiating with the Russians,* 1951.
A. DE RUSSET, *Strengthening the Framework of Peace,* 1950.
A. V. DICEY, *A Digest of the Law of England with Reference to the Conflict of Laws* (5th Ed. by A. B. Keith), 1932.
E. D. DICKINSON, *The Equality of States in International Law,* 1920.
P. F. DRUCKER, *The Concept of the Corporation,* 1946.
F. DUNN, *War and the Minds of Men,* 1950.
E. DURKHEIM, *Division of Labour in Society* (Trans. by G. Simpson), 1953.
C. D. EDWARDS, *Maintaining Competition; Requisites of a National Policy,* 1949.
F. EGGAN (Ed.), *Social Anthropology of North American Tribes,* 1937.
E. EHRLICH, *Fundamental Principles of the Sociology of Law* (Trans. by W. L. Moll), 1936.
P. EINZIG, *Bloodless Invasion,* 1939.
P. T. ELLSWORTH, *International Economics,* 1938.
S. ENKE AND V. SALERA, *International Economics,* 1951.
H. P. FAIRCHILD (Ed.), *Dictionary of Sociology,* 1944.
H. FAYOL, *General and Industrial Management* (Trans. by Constance Storrs), 1949.
F. W. FERNAU, *Moslems on the March,* 1954.
H. FINER, *The Theory and Practice of Modern Government,* 1934.
A. W. FORD, *The Anglo-Iranian Oil Dispute of 1951–1952,* 1954.
France, *Journal Officiel.*
W. FRIEDMANN, *Law and Social Change in Contemporary Britain,* 1951.
E. FROMM, *Escape from Freedom,* 1946.
—— *Man for Himself,* 1947.
J. K. GALBRAITH, *American Capitalism: The Concept of Countervailing Power,* 1952.
W. GALENSON (Ed.), *Comparative Labour Movements,* 1952.
O. GIERKE, *Das Deutsche Genossenschaftsrecht,* 1868–1881, Vol. 3.
—— *Political Theories of the Middle Age* (Trans. by F. W. Maitland), 1900.
M. R. GODINE, *The Labour Problem in the Public Service, A Study in Political Pluralism,* 1951.
J. GOEBEL, *Cases and Materials on the Development of Legal Institutions,* 1946.
R. A. GORDON, *Business Leadership in the Large Corporation,* 1945.
C. E. GRIFFIN, *An Economic Approach to Antitrust Problems,* 1951.
B. M. GROSS, *The Legislative Struggle,* 1953.
V. GSOVSKI, *Soviet Civil Law,* 1948–1949.
L. GULICK AND L. URWICK, *Papers on the Science of Administration,* 1937.
R. L. HALE, *Freedom Through Law,* 1952.
W. E. HALL, *A Treatise on International Law* (8th Ed.), 1924.
S. S. HARCAVE, *Russia, A History,* 1952.
E. S. HARTLAND, *Primitive Law,* 1924.
Harvard Research in International Law, 'Draft Convention on Jurisdiction with Respect to Crime,' 29 *American Journal of International Law,* Supplement, 1935.
Harvard University, Research in Entrepreneurial History, *Change and the Entrepreneur, Postulates and Patterns for Entrepreneurial History,* 1949.
H. C. HAWKINS, *Commercial Treaties and Agreements,* 1951.

T. M. Haynes, *Institutional Theories of Law: Hauriou and Jordan* (Doctoral thesis, Urbana), 1949.
J. N. Hazard, *Law and Social Change in the U.S.S.R.*, 1953.
M. A. Heilperin, *The Trade of Nations*, 1952.
L. J. Henderson, *Pareto's General Sociology; A Physiologist's Interpretation*, 1935.
E. T. Hiller, *Social Relations and Structures*, 1947.
L. T. Hobhouse, *Morals in Evolution* (5th Ed.), 1924 (?).
E. A. Hoebel, *The Law of Primitive Man*, 1954.
H. I. Hogbin, *Law and Order in Polynesia*, 1934.
W. H. Hohfeld, *Fundamental Legal Conceptions*, 1923.
W. S. Holdsworth, *A History of English Law* (3rd Ed.), 1922–1938.
G. C. Homans, *The Human Group*, 1950.
M. Huber, *Die Soziologischen Grundlagen des Volkerrechts, 2 Internationalrectliche Abhandlungen*, 1928.
M. O. Hudson, *International Legislation*, 1937, Vol. 6.
J. E. Hulett, Jr. and R. Stagner (Eds.), *Problems in Social Psychology*, 1952.
C. C. Hyde, *International Law Chiefly as Interpreted and Applied by the United States*, 1945.
International Chamber of Commerce, *Fair Treatment for Foreign Investments; International Code* (Brochure 129).
International Court of Justice, *Reports*, 1949, 1952, 1954.
E. Jackson, *Meeting of Minds*, 1952.
E. Jenks, *Law and Politics in the Middle Ages* (2d Ed.), 1929.
—— *A Short History of English Law*, 1912.
P. C. Jessup, *A Modern Law of Nations*, 1948.
H. F. Jolowicz, *Historical Introduction to the Study of Roman Law* (2d Ed.), 1952.
E. Jordan, *Forms of Individuality*, 1927.
—— *The Good Life*, 1949.
—— *Theory of Legislation*, 1952.
A. Kardiner and others, *The Psychological Frontiers of Society*, 1945.
G. W. Keeton and G. Schwarzenberger, *Making International Law Work* (2d Ed.), 1946.
H. Kelsen, *The Law of the United Nations*, 1950.
G. H. T. Kimble, *The Way of the World*, 1953.
C. P. Kindelberger, *International Economics*, 1953.
C. Kluckhohn, *Mirror for Man*, 1949.
C. Kluckhohn and H. A. Murray, *Personality in Nature, Society and Culture*, 1949.
O. Knauth, *Managerial Enterprise, Its Growth and Methods of Operation*, 1948.
R. T. La Piere and P. R. Farnsworth, *Social Psychology* (3d Ed.), 1949.
H. J. Laski, *Authority in the Modern State*, 1919.
—— *The State in Theory and Practice*, 1935.
H. D. Lasswell and A. Kaplan, *Power and Society*, 1950.
H. D. Lasswell, T. V. Smith and C. E. Merriam, *A Study of Power*, 1950.
E. Latham, *The Group Basis of Politics*, 1952.
H. Lauterpacht, *International Law and Human Rights*, 1950.
—— *The Function of Law in the International Community*, 1933.
League of Nations, *Official Journal* (Special Supplement No. 53), 1927.
—— *The Network of World Trade* (Publications, II, Economic and Financial 1942. II. A. 3).
—— Report of Committee of Experts for the Progressive Codification of International Law, *Criminal Competence of States in Respect of Offences Committed Outside their Territory*, January 29, 1926. Publications, V Legal 1926 V 7 C. 50 M. 27. 1926. V.

A. LEISERSON, *Administrative Regulation*, 1942.
M. J. LEVY, JR., *The Family Revolution in Modern China*, 1949.
—— *The Structure of Society*, 1952.
K. LEWIN, *Resolving Social Conflicts*, 1948.
R. LINTON, *The Cultural Background of Personality*, 1945.
—— *Most of the World*, 1949.
—— *The Science of Man in the World Crisis*, 1945.
W. LIPPMANN, *An Inquiry into the Principles of the Good Society*, 1937.
K. LLEWELLYN AND E. A. HOEBEL, *The Cheyenne Way: Conflict and Case Law in Primitive Jurisprudence*, 1941.
V. R. LORWIN, *The French Labour Movement*, 1954.
R. H. LOWIE, *Primitive Society*, 1947.
R. M. MACIVER, *The Web of Government*, 1947.
N. R. F. MAIER, *Principles of Human Relations*, 1952.
H. S. MAINE, *Ancient Law*, 1907.
F. W. MAITLAND, *The Constitutional History of England*, 1909.
—— *The Collected Papers of Frederic William Maitland*, 1911.
B. MALINOWSKI, *Crime and Custom in Savage Society*, 1926.
K. MANNHEIM, *Freedom, Power, and Democratic Planning*, 1950.
—— *Man and Society in an Age of Reconstruction*, 1940.
J. MATTERN, *Concepts of State, Sovereignty and International Law*, 1928.
E. MAYO, *The Human Problems of Industrial Civilisation*, 1933.
E. MAYO AND G. LOMBARD, *Teamwork and Labour Turnover in the Aircraft Industry of Southern California*, Graduate School of Business Administration Research Study No. 32, 1944.
D. MITRANY, *A Working Peace System*, 1943.
J. D. MOONEY, *The Principles of Organisation*, 1947.
J. B. MOORE, *Report on Extraterritorial Crime and the Cutting Case* (1887), 1887 *Papers Relating to the Foreign Relations of the United States*.
H. J. MORGENTHAU, *Politics among Nations*, 1948.
—— (Ed.), *Peace, Security and the United Nations*, 1946.
J. H. C. MORRIS (Ed.), *Dicey's Conflict of Laws*, 1949.
G. P. MURDOCK, *Social Structure*, 1949.
G. MURPHY, *Personality: A Bisocial Approach to Origin and Structure*, 1947.
National Planning Association, *The Next Step of American Foreign Policy*, 1951.
F. S. C. NORTHROP, *The Taming of the Nations*, 1952.
E. G. NOURSE, *Price Making in a Democracy*, 1944.
A. NUSSBAUM, *A Concise History of the Law of Nations*, 1954.
—— *Principles of Private International Law*, 1943.
L. OPPENHEIM, *International Law*, 8th Ed., 1955.
J. ORTEGA Y GASSET, *Mission of the University*, 1944.
Overseas Consultants, Inc., *Report on Seven Year Development Plan for the Plan Organization of the Imperial Government of Iran*, 1949.
B. PARES, *A History of Russia*, 1947.
V. PARETO, *The Mind and Society* (Trans. by A. Livingston), 1935.
Parliamentary Debates (*Hansard*), House of Commons.
T. PARSONS, *The Social System*, 1951.
—— *The Structure of Social Action*, 1937.
T. PARSONS AND E. A. SHILS, *Toward a General Theory of Action*, 1952.
A. H. PEKELIS, *Law and Social Action*, 1950.
T. F. T. PLUCKNETT, *A Concise History of the Common Law*, 1936.
F. POLLOCK AND F. W. MAITLAND, *The History of English Law*, 1899.
President's Materials Policy Commission, *Resources for Freedom*, 1952.
E. RABEL, *The Conflict of Laws: A Comparative Study*, 1947.
M. RADIN, *Handbook of Roman Law*, 1927.
E. F. RANSHOFEN-WERTHEIMER, *The International Secretariat*, 1945.
A. RAPAPORT, *Science and the Goals of Man*, 1950.
—— *Operational Philosophy*, 1950.

K. Renner, *The Institutions of Private Law and their Social Functions* (O. Kahn-Freund, Ed.), 1949.
W. H. Rivers, *Social Organisation* (W. J. Perry Ed.), 1924.
W. A. Robson, *Civilisation and the Growth of Law*, 1935.
F. J. Roethlisberger and W. J. Dickson, *Management and the Worker*, 1939.
J. H. Rohrer and M. Sherif (Eds.), *Social Psychology at the Crossroads*, 1951.
A. Rouast and P. Durand, *Précis de Législation Industrielle*, 1948.
B. Russell, *Power, a New Social Analysis*, 1938.
V. Sackville-West, *Passenger to Teheran*, 1927.
G. T. Sadler, *The Relation of Custom to Law*, 1919.
F. H. Sanford, *Authoritarianism and Leadership*, 1950.
S. S. Sargent and M. W. Smith (Eds.), *Culture and Personality*, 1949.
C. M. Schmitthoff, *A Textbook on the English Conflict of Laws*, 1945.
J. A. Schumpeter, *Capitalism, Socialism and Democracy*, 1942.
G. Schwarzenberger, *A Manual of International Law*, 1952.
W. Seagle, *The Quest for Law*, 1941.
W. Shiffer, *The Legal Community of Mankind*, 1954.
H. A. Simon, *Administrative Behaviour*, 1951.
H. A. Simon, D. W. Smithburg and V. A. Thompson, *Public Administration*, 1950.
S. S. Simpson, J. Stone and M. M. Schoch, *Cases and Readings on Law and Society*, 1948.
T. V. Smith, *The Legislative Way of Life*, 1940.
R. Sohm, *The Institutes* (3rd Ed.), 1907.
L. B. Sohn, *Cases and other Materials on World Law*, 1950.
Staff Papers Presented to the Commission on Foreign Economic Policy, February 1954 (Washington, D.C., 1954).
G. A. Steiner, *Government's Role in Economic Life*, 1953.
J. Stone, *Legal Controls of International Conflict*, 1954.
—— *The Province and Function of Law*, 1950.
F. Tannenbaum, *A Philosophy of Labour*, 1951.
H. Taylor, *Notes from Life. The Statesman.* 1878.
N. S. Timasheff, *An Introduction to the Sociology of Law*, 1939.
D. B. Truman, *The Governmental Process*, 1951.
United Nations, General Assembly, Fourth Session, Verbatim Record of the 255th Plenary Meeting (U.N. Doc. A/PV 255, 24 November 1949).
United Nations, General Assembly, Official Records: Seventh Session. Annexes, Vol. II. From 14 October 1952 to August 1953.
United Nations, General Assembly, Official Records: Sixth Session. Supp. No. 20 (A/2119).
United Nations, Official Records of the Security Council, Sixth Year, No. 559 (S/PV. 561).
United Nations, Economic Survey of Europe Since the War (U.N. Doc. No. E/ECE/157, February 1953).
United Nations, International Flow of Private Capital for the Economic Development of Under-Developed Countries (U.N. Doc. E/2546, 19 February 1953).
United Nations, The International Flow of Private Capital 1946–1952 (U.N. Doc. E/2531, ST/ECA/22, 1953).
United Nations, World Economic Report 1951–1952 (U.N. Doc. No. E/2353, Rev. 1, ST/ECA/19, April 1954).
United Nations, World Economic Report 1953–1954 (U.N. Doc. No. E/2729, ST/ECA/30, 15 April 1955).
United Nations, Opinion of Commission of Jurists, 29 November 1952 (U.N. Doc. A/INF/51 5 December 1952).
United Nations, Reports of the Secretary-General on Personnel Policy, 2 November 1953, General Assembly: Eighth Session, Agenda item 51 (U.N. Doc. A/2533).

United Nations, Permanent Staff Regulations (U.N. Doc. 2108, 1 February 1952).
United Nations, Report of the Ad Hoc Committee on Restrictive Business Practices to the Economic and Social Council (U.N. Doc. E/AC. 37/3, 30 March 1953), also Supp. No. 11A, E/2379 and E/2379/Add. 1, E/AC. 37/2 and E/AC. 37/2/Add. 1; Supp. No. 11B, E/2379/Add. 2, E/AC. 37/2/Add. 2.
United Nations, *Yearbook of the United Nations*, 1946–1947.
United States, Congressional Record, Vol. 21.
United States, Report of the Attorney General's National Committee to Study the Antitrust Laws, March 31, 1955 (Washington, D.C.).
United States, Statutes at Large.
United States, Treaties and other International Acts Series (Washington, D.C.).
United States, Treaties and other International Agreements (Washington, D.C.).
United States Department of Commerce, Statistical Abstract of the United States, 1952 (Washington, D.C.).
United States Senate, Subcommittee Print No. 5, 82nd Cong., 2d Sess., 1952, Foreign Legislation Concerning Monopoly and Cartel Practices, Report of the Department of State to the Subcommittee on Monopoly of the Select Committee on Small Business.
L. Urwick, *Notes on the Theory of Organisation*, 1952.
H. Vaihinger, *The Philosophy of 'As If'* (Trans. by C. K. Ogden, 1924).
R. W. Van Wagenen, *Research in the International Organisation Field* (Centre for Research on World Political Institutions, Pub. No. 1, Princeton), 1952.
A. Vyshinsky, *The Law of the Soviet State*, 1948.
M. Waline, *Traité Élémentaire de Droit Administratif* (5th Ed.), 1950.
W. L. Warner and J. O. Low, *The Social System of the Modern Factory*, 1947.
M. Weber, *The Theory of Social and Economic Organisation* (Trans. by A. M. Henderson and T. Parsons), 1947.
L. B. Wehle, *Hidden Threads of History: Wilson through Roosevelt*, 1953.
J. Westlake, *A Treatise on Private International Law* (7th Ed. by H. Bentwich), 1925.
T. N. Whitehead, *The Industrial Worker*, 1938.
C. R. Whittlesey, *National Interest and International Cartels*, 1946.
R. M. Williams, Jr., *American Society: A Sociological Interpretation*, 1951.
E. Wittmann, *History, A Guide to Peace*, 1948.
K. H. Wolff (Trans. and Ed.), *The Sociology of George Simmel*, 1950.
M. Wolff, *Private International Law*, 1950.
Q. Wright (Ed.), *The World Community*, 1948.

Articles

M. Adelman, 'Effective Competition and the Antitrust Laws,' 61 *Harvard Law Review* (1948), p. 1289.
—— 'Integration and Antitrust Policy,' 63 *Harvard Law Review* (1949), p. 27.
—— 'The A & P Case: A Study in Applied Economic Theory,' 43 *Quarterly Journal of Economics* (1949), p. 238.
H. Aufricht, 'Personality in International Law,' 37 *American Political Science Review* (1943), p. 217.
R. F. Bales, 'A Theoretical Framework for Interaction Process Analysis,' in J. H. Rohrer and M. Sherif (Eds.), *Social Psychology at the Crossroads*, 1951, p. 29.
J. H. Beale, 'The Jurisdiction of a Sovereign State,' 36 *Harvard Law Review* (1923), p. 241.

G. Bebr, 'The European Coal and Steel Community: A Political and Legal Innovation,' 63 *Yale Law Journal* (1953), p. 1.

W. E. Beckett, 'The Exercise of Criminal Jurisdiction over Foreigners,' 6 *British Yearbook of International Law* (1925), p. 44.

G. W. Berge, 'The Case of the S.S. "Lotus,"' 26 *Michigan Law Review* (1928), p. 361.

A. A. Berle, 'Constitutional Limitations on Corporate Activity—Protection of Personal Rights from Invasion through Economic Power,' 100 *University of Pennsylvania Law Review* (1952), p. 933.

—— 'The Developing Law of Corporate Concentration,' 19 *University of Chicago Law Review* (1952), p. 639.

W. S. Bowman, 'Toward Less Monopoly,' 101 *University of Pennsylvania Law Review* (1953), p. 577.

R. Bullard, 'Behind the Oil Dispute in Iran,' 31 *Foreign Affairs* (1953), p. 461.

K. S. Carlston, 'Arbitration: An Institutional Procedure,' 4 *Arbitration Journal* (New Series) (1948), p. 248.

—— 'Equality of Access to the Basic Social Institutions of Society as a Goal of the Democratic State,' 3 *Journal of Public Law* (1954), p. 71.

—— 'Theory of the Arbitration Process,' 17 *Law and Contemporary Problems* (1952), p. 631.

M. B. Carroll, 'Postwar International Organisation and the Work of the Section of International and Comparative Law of the American Bar Association,' 39 *American Journal of International Law* (1945), p. 20.

R. B. Cattell, 'The Principal Culture Patterns Discoverable in the Syntal Dimensions of Existing Nations,' 30 *Journal of Social Psychology* (1950), p. 1.

—— 'The Investigation of Cultural Dynamics: Concept and Methods,' in J. E. Hulett, Jr. and R. Stagner (Eds.), *Problems in Social Psychology*, 1952, p. 171.

D. F. Cavers, 'A Critique of the Choice-of-Law Problem,' 47 *Harvard Law Review* (1933), p. 173.

J. T. Chadwell and R. W. McLaren, 'The Current Status of the Anti-trust Laws,' *Illinois Law Forum* (1950), p. 491.

E. H. Chamberlain, 'Product Heterogeneity and Public Policy,' 40 *Proceedings of the American Economic Association* (1950), p. 85.

W. C. Chamberlain, 'Collective Bargaining and the Concept of Contract,' 48 *Columbia Law Review* (1948), p. 829.

E. E. Cheatham, 'American Theories of Conflict of Laws: Their Role and Utility,' 58 *Harvard Law Review* (1944), p. 361.

J. M. Clark, 'Toward a Concept of Workable Competition,' 30 *American Economic Review* (1941), p. 241.

M. Cohen, 'The United Nations Secretariat—Some Constitutional and Administrative Developments,' 49 *American Journal of International Law* (1955), p. 295.

Committee on Foreign Law and Committee on International Law, 'Protection Abroad of Private Investments,' 7 *Record of the Association of the Bar of the City of New York* (1952), p. 219.

W. W. Cook, 'The Application of the Criminal Law of a Country to Acts Committed by Foreigners Outside the Jurisdiction,' 40 *West Virginia Law Quarterly* (1934), p. 302.

P. E. Corbett, 'Power and Justice,' in H. J. Morgenthau (Ed.), *Peace, Security and the United Nations*, 1946, p. 11.

W. B. Cowles, 'Revision of the United Nations Charter and the Development of the Law,' 33 *Nebraska Law Review* (1953), p. 35.

G. H. Dession, 'The Trial of Economic and Technological Issues of Fact,' 58 *Yale Law Journal* (1949), pp. 1019, 1242.

W. Diebold, 'Imponderables of the Schuman Scheme,' 29 *Foreign Affairs* (1950), p. 114.

M. DOMKE, 'The United Nations Draft Convention on Restrictive Business Practices,' 4 *International and Comparative Law Quarterly* (1955), p. 129.

E. EHRLICH, 'Sociology of Law,' 37 *Harvard Law Review* (1922), p. 130.

J. FRED, 'The Relation of Ideal Norms to Actual Behaviour in Tarahumara Society,' 9 *Southwestern Journal of Anthropology* (1953), p. 286.

L. FILLER, 'Some Reflections on Legal and Economic Freedoms—A Review of Robert L. Hale's "Freedom Through Law,"' 54 *Columbia Law Review* (1954), p. 70.

F. GAZIER, 'Le syndicalisme dans la fonction public,' 11 *Droit Social* (1948), p. 274.

H. F. GOODRICH, 'Conflicts Niceties and Commercial Necessities,' *Wisconsin Law Review* (1952), p. 199.

L. GROSS, 'The Peace of Westphalia, 1648–1948,' 42 *American Journal of International Law* (1948), p. 20.

A. . HALLOWELL, 'Sociopsychological Aspects of Acculturation,' in R. Linton (Ed.), *The Science of Man in the World Crisis*, 1945, p. 171.

—— 'The Nature and Function of Property as a Social Institution,' 1 *Journal of Legal and Political Sociology* (1943), p. 115

J. N HAZARD, 'Socialism, Abuse of Power, and Soviet Law,' 50 *Columbia Law Review* (1950), p. 448.

—— 'Soviet Government Corporations,' 41 *Michigan Law Review* (1943), p. 850.

R. P HERNACKI, 'Mergerism and Section 7 of the Clayton Act,' 20 *George Washington Law Review* (1952), p. 659.

M. J HERSKOVITS, 'The Process of Cultural Change,' in R. Linton (Ed.), *The Science of Man in the World Crisis* (1945), p. 143.

E. H HOEBEL, 'The Political Organisation and Law-Ways of the Comanche Indians,' 42 *Memoirs of the American Anthropological Association*, Supplement No. 54, 1940.

O. V. HOLMES, JR., 'The Path of the Law,' 10 *Harvard Law Review* (1897), p. 457.

V. IDELSON, 'The Law of Nations and the Individual,' 30 *Transactions of the Grotius Society* (1944), p. 50.

L. L JAFFE, 'Law Making by Private Groups,' 51 *Harvard Law Review* (1937), p. 301.

E. F. JOHNSTON AND J. P. STEVENS, 'Monopoly or Monopolisation—A Reply to Professor Rostow,' 44 *Illinois Law Review* (1949), p. 269.

M. V. JONES, 'International Agreements other than "Inter-State Treaties,"' 21 *British Yearbook of International Law* (1944), p. 21.

H. KELSEN, 'Will the Judgement in the Nuremberg Trial Constitute a Precedent in International Law?,' 1 *International Law Quarterly* (1947), p. 153.

C. KLUCKHOHN AND W. H. KELLY, 'The Concept of Culture,' in R. Linton (Ed.), *The Science of Man in the World Crisis* (1945), p. 98.

C. KLUCKHOHN AND OTHERS, 'Values and Value-Orientations in the Theory of Action,' in T. Parsons and E. A. Shils, *Toward a General Theory of Action* (1952), p. 388.

S. K C. KOPPER, 'The International Regulation of Cartels—Current Proposals,' 40 *Virginia Law Review* (1954), p. 1005.

H. D. LASSWELL, 'World Loyalty,' in Q. Wright (Ed.), *The World Community*, 1948.

H. D. LASSWELL AND M. MCDOUGAL, 'Legal Education and Public Policy: Professional Training in the Public Interest,' 52 *Yale Law Journal* (1943), p. 203.

E. LATHAM, 'The Politics of Basing Point Legislation,' 15 *Law and Contemporary Problems* (1950), p. 273.

H. LAUTERPACHT, 'Codification and Development of International Law,' 49 *American Journal of International Law* (1955), p. 16.

H. Lauterpacht, 'The Subjects of the Law of Nations,' 63 *Law Quarterly Review* (1947), p. 438, 64 *Law Quarterly Review* (1948), p. 97.

O. Lee, 'Social Values and the Philosophy of Law,' 32 *Virginia Law Review* (1946), p. 802.

E. H. Levi, 'A Two Level Anti-Monopoly Law,' 47 *Northwestern University Law Review* (1952), p. 567.

E. C. Lindeman, 'Community,' 4 *Encyclopedia of the Social Sciences* (1931), p. 102.

E. J. Lindgren, 'An Example of Culture Contact without Conflict; the Reindeer Tungus and Rûssian Cossacks of Northwest Manchuria,' 40 *American Anthropologist* (1938), p. 305.

R. H. Lowie, 'Hidatsa Men's Societies,' 11 *Anthropological Papers of the American Museum of Natural History* (1916), p. 225.

—— 'Military Societies of the Crow Indians,' 11 *Anthropological Papers of the American Museum of Natural History* (1916), p. 147.

B. Malinowski, 'A New Instrument for the Interpretation of Law—Especially Primitive,' 51 *Yale Law Journal* (1942), p. 1236.

—— Introduction to H. I. Hogbin, *Law and Order in Polynesia*, 1934.

D. G. Mandelbaum, 'Cultural Changes among the Nilgiri Tribes,' 43 *American Anthropologist* (1941), p. 19.

F. A. Mann, 'The Law Governing State Contracts,' 21 *British Yearbook of International Law* (1944), p. 11.

—— 'The Proper Law of the Contract,' 3 *International Law Quarterly* (1950), p. 60.

G. Manner, 'The Object Theory of the Individual in International Law,' 46 *American Journal of International Law* (1952), p. 428.

E. S. Mason, 'The Current Status of the Monopoly Problem in the United States, 62 *Harvard Law Review* (1949), p. 1265.

B. McAllister, 'Stating the Issues,' Commerce Clearing House, *Antitrust Law Symposium* (1951), p. 13.

—— 'The Big Case: Procedural Problems in Antitrust Litigation,' 64 *Harvard Law Review* (1950), p. 27.

M. S. McDougal, 'International Law, Power and Policy: A Contemporary Conception,' 82 *Academie de Droit International, Recueil des Cours* (1953), Vol. 1, p. 137.

—— 'Law and Power,' 46 *American Journal of International Law* (1952), p. 102.

—— 'The Role of Law in World Politics,' 20 *Mississippi Law Journal* (1949), p. 253.

J. A. McKesson, 'The Schuman Plan,' 67 *Political Science Quarterly* (1952), p. 18.

W. H. McPherson, 'Co-determination: Germany's Move Toward a New Economy,' 5 *Industrial and Labour Relations Review* (1951), p. 20.

—— 'Co-determination in Practice,' 8 *Industrial and Labour Relations Review* (1955), p. 499.

—— 'Should Labour Arbitrators Play Follow-the-Leader?,' 4 *Arbitration Journal* (New Series) (1949), p. 163.

D. Mitrany, 'The Functional Approach to World Organisation,' 24 *International Affairs* (1948), p. 353.

G. P. Murdock, 'The Common Denominator of Cultures,' in R. Linton (Ed.), *The Science of Man in the World Crisis* (1945), p. 123.

H. A. Murray, 'Toward a Classification of Interactions,' in T. Parsons and E. A. Shils, *Toward a General Theory of Action* (1952), p. 434.

S. Nakasian, 'The Security of Foreign Petroleum Resources,' 68 *Political Science Quarterly* (1953), p. 181.

National Planning Association, *The Next Step of American Economic Foreign Policy* (December 4, 1951).

F. L. Neumann, 'The Concept of Political Freedom,' 53 *Columbia Law Review* (1953), p. 901.

Note, 'Case Law or Free Decision in Grievance Arbitration,' 62 *Harvard Law Review* (1948), p. 118.
Note, 'National Ideologies and the International Public Function,' 81 *Journal du Droit International* (1954), p. 277.
Note, 'Patent Abuses and Antitrust: The Per Se Rule,' 64 *Harvard Law Review* (1951), p. 626.
Note, 'Precedents in Labour Arbitrations,' *Washington University Law Quarterly* (1949), p. 71.
Note, 'Trouble Begins in the "New" Sherman Act: The Perplexing Story of the A & P Case,' 58 *Yale Law Journal* (1949), p. 969.
Note, 'Section 3 of the Clayton Act—Coexisting Standards of Legality?,' 49 *Columbia Law Review* (1949), p. 241.
Note, 'Vertical Integration in Aluminum: A Bar to 'Effective Competition,"' 60 *Yale Law Journal* (1951), p. 294.
R. de Nova, 'Solution du conflit de lois et règlement satisfaisant du rapport international,' 37 *Revue Critique de Droit International Privé* (1948), p. 179.
R. Pound, 'Law in the Service State: Freedom versus Equality,' 36 *American Bar Association Journal* (1950), p. 977.
E. B. Prettyman, 'Six Suggestions for Improvement,' Commerce Clearing House, *Antitrust Law Symposium* (1951), p. 34.
J. H. Provinse, 'The Underlying Sanctions of Plains Indians Culture,' in F. Eggan (Ed.), *Social Anthropology of North American Tribes* (1937), p. 341.
A. R. Radcliffe-Brown, 'Primitive Law,' 9 *Encyclopedia of the Social Sciences*, 1933.
J. A. Rahl, 'Conspiracy and the Anti-trust Laws,' 44 *Illinois Law Review* (1950), p. 743.
R. Redfield, 'Culture Contact without Conflict,' 41 *American Anthropologist* (1939), p. 514.
J. S. Reeves, 'La communauté internationale,' 3 *Academie de Droit International, Recueil des Cours* (1924), Vol. 2, p. 5.
M. Rheinstein, 'Conflict of Laws in the Uniform Commercial Code,' 16 *Law and Contemporary Problems* (1951), p. 114.
E. V. Rostow, 'Monopoly under the Sherman Act: Power or Purpose?,' 43 *Illinois Law Review* (1948), p. 745.
Th. Ruyssen, 'Les caractères de la communauté humaine,' 67 *Academie de Droit International, Recueil des Cours* (1939), Vol. 1, p. 125.
S. S. Sargent, 'Conceptions of Role and Ego in Contemporary Psychology,' in J. H. Rohrer and M. Sherif (Eds.), *Social Psychology at the Crossroads* (1951), p. 355.
C. Savouillan, 'Pour l'étude de l'arbitrage obligatoire,' 14 *Droit Social* (1951), p. 96.
D. Schindler, 'Contribution a l'étude des facteurs sociologiques et psychologiques du droit international,' 46 *Academie de Droit International, Recueil des Cours* (1933), Vol. 4, p. 233.
C. M. Schmitthoff, 'The International Corporation,' 30 *Transactions of the Grotius Society* (1944), p. 165.
G. Schwarzenberger, 'The Frontiers of International Law,' 6 *Year Book of World Affairs* (1952), p. 246.
—— 'The Inductive Approach to International Law,' 60 *Harvard Law Review* (1947), p. 539.
S. M. Schwebel, 'The International Character of the Secretariat of the United Nations,' 30 *British Yearbook of International Law* (1953), p. 71.
W. N. Seymour, 'The Big Subpoena: Proceedings to Quash or Limit: Compliance,' Commerce Clearing House, *Antitrust Law Symposium*, 1953, p. 32.
D. W. Smythe, 'Facing Facts About the Broadcast Business,' 20 *University of Chicago Law Review* (1952), p. 96.

R. M. Stogdill, 'Leadership, Membership and Organisation,' 47 *Psychological Bulletin* (1950), p. 1.

A. Sturmthal, 'Quelques réflexiones sur les relations industrielles en France et aux États-Unis,' 14 *Droit Social* (1951), p. 387.

C. W. Summers, 'The Right to Join a Union,' 47 *Columbia Law Review* (1947), p. 33.

—— 'Union Power and Workers' Rights,' 49 *Michigan Law Review* (1951), p. 805.

S. Timberg, 'Corporate Fictions: Logical, Social and International Implications,' 46 *Columbia Law Review* (1946), p. 533.

—— 'An International Trade Tribunal—A Step Forward Short of Surrender of Sovereignty,' 33 *Georgetown Law Journal* (1945), p. 373.

—— 'The Rights of Customer Selection,' Commerce Clearing House, *Antitrust Law Symposium* (1951), p. 151.

J. Trouvé, 'The French Civil Service Office,' 11 *Public Administration Review* (1951), p. 180.

J. G. Van Cise, 'Practical Planning,' Commerce Clearing House, *Antitrust Law Symposium* (1951), p. 103.

R. Vernon, 'The Schuman Plan,' 47 *American Journal of International Law* (1953), p. 183.

L. B. Wehle, 'International Administration of European Inland Waterways,' 40 *American Journal of International Law* (1946), p. 100.

K. Wilk, 'International Law and Global Ideological Conflict; Reflections on the Universality of International Law,' 45 *American Journal of International Law* (1951), p. 648.

G. Williams, 'International Law and the Controversy Concerning the Word Law,' 22 *British Yearbook of International Law* (1945), p. 146.

R. R. Wilson, 'Property Protection Provisions in United States Commercial Treaties,' 45 *American Journal of International Law* (1951), p. 83.

L. Wirth, 'World Community, World Society, and World Government: An Attempt at Clarification of Terms,' in Q. Wright (Ed.), *The World Community*, 1948.

C. Wissler, 'Societies and Ceremonial Associations in the Oglala Division of the Teton-Dakota,' 11 *Anthropological Papers of the American Museum of Natural History* (1916), p. 11.

M. Wolff, 'Some Observations on the Autonomy of the Parties in the Conflict of Laws,' 35 *Transactions of the Grotius Society* (1950), p. 143.

C. E. Wyzanski, Jr., 'Process and Pattern: The Search for Standards in the Law,' 30 *Indiana Law Journal* (1955), p. 133.

H. E. Yntema, 'Autonomy In Choice of Law,' 1 *American Journal of Comparative Law* (1952), p. 341.

INDEX

Bei Fragen zur Produktsicherheit wenden Sie sich bitte an:
If you have any questions regarding product safety,
please contact:

Walter de Gruyter GmbH
Genthiner Straße 13
10785 Berlin
productsafety@degruyterbrill.com